Timeless Rapture

The Tsadra Foundation Series

published by Snow Lion Publications

Tsadra Foundation is a U.S.-based non-profit organization that was founded in 2000 in order to support the activities of advanced Western students of Tibetan Buddhism, specifically those with significant contemplative experience. Taking its inspiration from the nineteenth century non-sectarian Tibetan scholar and meditation master Jamgön Kongtrül Lodrö Tayé, Tsadra Foundation is named after his hermitage in eastern Tibet, Tsadra Rinchen Drak. The Foundation's various program areas reflect his values of excellence in both scholarship and contemplative practice, and the recognition of their mutual complementarity.

This publication is part of Tsadra Foundation's Translation Program, which aims to make authentic and authoritative texts from the Tibetan traditions available in English. The Foundation is honored to present the work of its fellows and grantees, individuals of confirmed contemplative and intellectual integrity; however, their views do not necessarily reflect those of the Foundation

Tsadra Foundation is delighted to ally with Snow Lion Publications in making these important texts available in the English language.

TIMELESS RAPTURE

Inspired Verse of the Shangpa Masters

Compiled by Jamgon Kongtrul

Translated and introduced
by Ngawang Zangpo

SNOW LION PUBLICATIONS
Ithaca, New York
Boulder, Colorado

Snow Lion Publications
P.O. Box 6483
Ithaca, NY 14851 USA
(607) 273-8519
www.snowlionpub.com

Printed in Canada on acid-free recycled paper.

ISBN 1-55939-204-5

Library of Congress Cataloging-in-Publication Data:

Timeless rapture : inspired verse of the Shangpa masters / Translated,
introduced and edited by Ngawang Zangpo.
    p. cm.
 ISBN 1-55939-204-5 (alk. paper)
 1. Spiritual life—Śaṅs-pa (Sect) 2. Śaṅs-pa
(Sect)—Rituals—Texts. 3. Śaṅs-pa (Sect)—Biography.
4. Śaṅs-pa lamas—China—Tibet—Biography. I. Ngawang Zangpo, 1954–
BQ7680.6.T56 2003
294.3'4432--dc21

                                2003004314

Text designed and typeset in Adobe Garamond by Gopa & Ted2

To Bokar Rinpoché,
Golden vessel of the Shangpa Golden Doctrines

CONTENTS

List of Illustrations

FOREWORD BY BOKAR RINPOCHÉ

Two wisdom dakinis, Niguma and Sukasiddhi, received instruction directly from Buddha Vajra Bearer. They were the foremost among the 150 Indian scholars and meditation masters who granted an entire trove of Teachings to the learned and accomplished master Kyungpo Naljor, who was proficient in tantra's five ultimate practices.

Kyungpo Naljor established his residence in Tsang, western Tibet, at Zhang-zhong in Yéru Shang, and lived for 150 years, during which time he imparted an infinite number of instructions. Chief among them, the wisdom dakinis' oral transmission replete with three outstanding qualities includes the Five Golden Doctrines. The successive tradition of their experiential cultivation, which leads to states of accomplishment, has become known as the Illustrious Shangpa Kagyu Lineage.

Our lineage's past spiritual masters used songs to express their manifest experience and realization of the spiritual path's vital subjects, such as the trio of basis, path, and result; or view, meditation, and conduct; as well as to dispel hindrances and enrich meditative experience. For us, their followers, their songs have a special impact: they turn our attention to the Teachings and nurture our faith, renunciation, and compassion. The blessings of the lineage enter our heart, the very best technique to realize our mind's abiding nature, Great Seal.

I sincerely rejoice that the Illustrious Shangpa Kagyu Lineage's compendium of songs has been translated into English, and I pray that all who see, hear, or read this book be blessed.

Written by him who holds the title of Bokar Tulku,
January 13, 2003.

FOREWORD BY
LAMA DRUBGYU TENZIN

NOT SO MANY YEARS AGO a generation of curious young Western spiritual adventurers first encountered a generation of Tibetan Buddhist masters abruptly uprooted from their mountain solitude. Enthralled by the lamas' powerful presence and deeply touched by their authenticity, these spiritual adventurers were drawn to the masters and their exotic world. Yet very little in the way of translated and published literature informed this courtship. Among the few texts that did exist, however, one above all became a touchstone: *The Hundred Thousand Songs of Milarepa*. All Tibetans know and love this work that resonates deeply with their natural devotion. Those encountering the world of Vajrayana Buddhism for the first time found a text that was both informative and captivating.

The Hundred Thousand Songs owes its perennial success to both its form and its content. The book's content is recorded oral history: the story and advice of an awakened master, delivered in a direct and unapologetic manner. The life story of Milarepa reflected in the songs is an extraordinarily human tale describing the climb from the very depths of human desolation to the pinnacle of spiritual accomplishment in the course of a single lifetime. Conceivably, therefore, anyone with determined commitment could follow the path of Milarepa and achieve similar results within a comparable time frame. In his songs, Milarepa is clearly concerned only with truth and the spiritual well-being of his students, rather than with convention or politeness. This resonated well with a generation disillusioned by the artifice of social and political expediency, and thirsting for truth and authenticity. At the time of the book's Western publication, the hero's proximity to nature echoed our sensibilities and a soon-to-emerge ecological imperative. Most important for its universal appeal, however, is the book's form—inspired verse, poetry. Where philosophical treatises must be studied and practical manuals applied, poetry inspires! Song and verse use the concrete and immediate to catapult our imagination and awareness into states of exaltation and experience otherwise difficult to access.

The Hundred Thousand Songs offered the West its first experience of a genre of Tibetan spiritual literature that more than any other embodies the sacred world of Vajrayana experience. In this inspired verse songs of realization literature we find down-to-earth advice and instruction, heartfelt devotion and appreciation of the importance of transmission and lineage, and, above all, soaring expressions of mystical states of awareness and freedom. We discover all of this in a form—poetry—that combines insight, humor, and an esthetic appreciation for language. Exhortations to renunciation are interwoven with an evident delight in language and in images of this world. The apparent paradox of this is misleading, since in fact such delight is the true fruit of a freedom born of detachment. Dreams, visions, and states of "mystical" experience are referred to as common everyday events, the relative and the absolute dancing to the tune of the adepts' devotion. And we discover that while the spiritual path does require renunciation and discipline, commitment and application, the sacred and mystical we seek are inherent, immediate, present, the very nature of things as they are.

Since its first appearance in English, *The Hundred Thousand Songs of Milarepa* has been joined by translations of a number of other texts of this genre. *Timeless Rapture* now takes its honored place beside such books as *The Hundred Thousand Songs*, *Drinking the Mountain Stream*, and *The Rain of Wisdom: Vajra Songs of the Kagyu Gurus*. Each of these texts shares the quality of inspiration described here, yet each offers its own distinct perspective on the vajra world. *The Hundred Thousand Songs* and *Drinking the Mountain Stream* are the episodic heart advice of Milarepa, the renunciant yogi-poet. We remember him as a yogi, or spiritual adept, determined to live a life of simplicity in mountain solitude, nourished, as the story goes, mainly on wild nettles and the practice of Inner Heat to the point that his body turned green! Disciple of Marpa the Translator, and master to countless disciples, principal among whom were Gampopa and Réchungpa, Milarepa remains one of the most significant figures in the Kagyu lineage. *The Rain of Wisdom* is a collection of songs by various Kagyu masters including Tilopa, Marpa, Milarepa, Réchungpa, Gampopa, and a number of the Karmapas. This text allows the reader to develop an appreciation for the character of this illustrious "practice" lineage and to discover many of its masters in story and song. The reader finds that each master is unique and, as is often the case with realized masters, totally unconventional. *Timeless Rapture* compiles the songs of realization of another lineage's masters, those of the Shangpa Kagyu.

Before describing the Shangpa Kagyu, I would like to comment on the organic nature of lineage. In a Buddhist context, and particularly in Vajrayana (tantric) Buddhism, lineage signifies the integrity of transmission. From the time of Buddha Shakyamuni (or Buddha Vajra Bearer, his "pure" form aspect; see the discussion of Buddha Vajra Bearer in Part 2), each master in the lineage fully realizes a specific instruction, technique or insight, and then transmits it to a disciple. That disciple's responsibility is to apply, practice, and realize the teaching to the point of mastering it. This new "master" then passes on the transmission to his or her own student/disciple(s). The instructions thus maintain the vitality of direct experiential awareness from generation to generation. Lineage, then, reflects an organic process through which individuals preserve the teachings' integrity.

Formal transmission in the Vajrayana context implies three elements: empowerment, scriptural authority (conferred by the master reading the text aloud), and instructions. Over time, collections of transmissions became grouped and gradually developed into "traditions." Accomplished masters, in the interest of facilitating their activity, often established institutions—monasteries, colleges, retreat centers, and so on. "Traditions" subsequently became associated with these institutions, to the extant that today some individuals might unwittingly mistake the political structures and hierarchies of these institutions for the instruction lineage itself.

In fact, it is the transmission from master to disciple, and the disciple's subsequent application, that assures the continuity of lineage. As the disciples of a master we receive instructions and transmissions and then nurture these with intention, application, practice, and inspiration—inspiration such as that found in these inspired songs. We encourage our own awakening and at the same time in a very real sense, nurture the lineage itself, of which we have become a part.

The lamas and practices of the Shangpa Kagyu tradition are referred to in a number of existing English-language texts. Among these the following deserve mention: *Jamgon Kongtrul's Retreat Manual* and *Sacred Ground* both translated by Ngawang Zangpo; as well as Cyrus Stearns's *Buddha from Dolpo*; and E. Gene Smith's *Among Tibetan Texts*. The appearance of *Timeless Rapture*, however, marks the first publication of a translation of a significant text specific to this tradition. To adepts of the Shangpa this text offers the same wealth as *The Rain of Wisdom* does to adepts of the Kagyu tradition. It can be used in personal study to provide advice and inspiration. More specifically, however, it has a place of honor in the tradition's ritual life. During the liturgy honoring the masters of the Shangpa lineage with offering and praise, participants recite this text aloud along with a separate collection of biographical poems.

The Shangpa Kagyu lineage originated during the eleventh century with the learned and accomplished Kyungpo Naljor. This Tibetan master reportedly traveled to India seven times and received teachings from more than 150 different masters. Of these he considered four to be most significant, and of these four, two women, Niguma and Sukasiddi, provided his primary inspiration. The vital process of unbroken transmission has ensured that the quality of their awareness animates the lineage to this day.

Exceptionally, the Shangpa Kagyu lineage remained for seven generations a one-to-one transmission, each master transmitting these instructions to a single disciple. This "sealed" lineage's seven "jewels" were Vajra Bearer, Niguma, Kyungpo Naljor, Mokchok-pa Rinchen Tsöndru, Kyergang-pa Chökyi Sengé, Rigong-pa Sangyé Nyentön, and Sangyé Tönpa. The lineage later included such luminaries as Tangtong Gyalpo, Taranata, and Jamgon Kongtrul Lodrö Tayé. This lineage has managed to remain unobtrusive; most of the primary lineage holders have chosen to live as concealed yogis, to avoid institutional responsibilities, and to commit themselves to solitude and meditation. Nevertheless, this lineage of teachings has been so valued as to spread through virtually all Tibetan traditions. As such, many important masters of a variety of Tibetan religious traditions have played a significant role in the lineage's continuity. The biographical section in Part 2 develops in some detail the stories of the illustrious masters of this tradition and the character they imparted to it.

Those who have met living masters of Vajrayana Buddhism will know that each one is unique, exhibiting the qualities of awakened being in his or her own manner. In spite of Buddhism's language of detachment, renunciation, emptiness of the self and so on, the process of awakening does not imply abdication of individuality. Rather, awakening implies the discovery of freedom. This freedom is yet another quality of the wisdom of awakened awareness. Full enlightenment, then, can be understood to imply a total creative freedom, as the profound intelligence of wisdom and the selfless altruism of compassion, both natural to this awakened mind, respond spontaneously and appropriately in any situation.

This freedom in awakening is undistracted and uninhibited. "Detachment" from distraction leads to the ease of relaxed natural awareness. Perfectly focused in a state of utter ease and nondistraction, accomplished masters can be experienced by others as having a presence imbued with a vividness or intensity that is the natural expression of undissipated being. Moreover, free of self-preoccupation, and hence purely altruistic, their being is totally free of inhibition, authentically grounded in and fearlessly expressing the integrity of the true nature of being.

With profound gratitude and appreciation, awakened masters past and present integrate into their personal identity every one of the lineage's extraordinary individuals who preceded them. And they communicate awakening's qualities as the display and activity of the various deity configurations and techniques that characterize the vajra world of their tradition.

In the verses of *Timeless Rapture* we encounter references to many of these illustrious figures. We encounter as well a celebration of the meditations that form the body of the Shangpa tradition. It should be understood that an adept can approach the world of Vajrayana only after a solid basis has been established with the discipline and compassion of the earlier cycles of the Buddha's teachings. The Lesser Vehicle's discipline of nondistraction ripens as stable attention. The Great Vehicle's appreciation of emptiness ripens as selfless compassion. Application of these trainings leads to a contemplative experience of openness and clarity, the necessary ground for the world of Vajrayana's techniques. Vajrayana is based on the premise that being itself is pure—what we term buddha nature—and that ignorance of our pure nature results in the delusions that imprison us and cause our suffering. The vajra path uses a multitude of techniques to reveal this pure reality and to skillfully transform our deluded experience into a direct experience of awakened being.

Generally speaking, Vajrayana comprises meditations described as "creation phase" and "completion phase." In creation phase meditations, we transform identity and perspective through deity yoga; and in the completion phase meditations we further refine these through such techniques as Fierce Inner Heat, Illusory Body, Lucid Dream, and Clear Light. In the first case we harness the rich power of creative imagination in the panoramic display of the deity configurations; in the second we refine our focus and reveal an ever more subtle quality of experience as we meditate on the pathways, circulating energy, and vital essence drops. In the first we transfer our need for structures of identity to the clear yet insubstantial forms of the deities, and in the second we gradually transcend the need for any conventional support for identity at all. These meditative techniques reveal our buddha nature and the complete freedom of awakened being.

In these songs we encounter the deities and techniques of the Shangpa Kagyu as though they were cherished friends, as indeed they are for adepts. While many creation phase deity configurations are shared by different traditions, the specifics of the liturgy and the visualizations often remain unique to each. The Shangpa tradition's two principal deity configurations are Wheel of Supreme Bliss and the combined configuration of the Five Tantras' Deities. Yet another deity of this tradition is Horse Neck. The protector particular to the Shangpa Kagyu is the Six-Armed Awakened Protector. Completion phase teachings include both the Six Doctrines of Niguma and the Six Doctrines of Sukasiddhi. While the specific details of these two vary, both comprise teachings on Fierce Inner Heat, Illusory Body, Lucid Dream, Clear Light, Transference of Consciousness, and Intermediate State. Most particularly, however, we encounter in the Shangpa Kagyu what are known as Kyungpo Naljor's Five Golden Doctrines. These five are likened to the parts of a tree: the roots, Niguma's Six Doctrines; trunk, the Great Seal Amulet Box; branches, the Three Paths of Integration; flowers, White and Red Sky Dancers; and fruit, Immortal Body and Infallibile Mind. The songs' references to such teachings are inevitably inspiring; yet needless to say, if we wish to put them into practice, we must receive formal transmission and follow the careful guidance of a qualified teacher of the tradition.

The Shangpa Kagyu tradition made its way from Tibet and became accessible to the world in the person of a tall, thin, and ageless lama known as Kalu Rinpoché. Because of political tensions, he traveled from Kham (eastern Tibet) to Lhasa in the early 1950s to confer with the His Holiness the Sixteenth Gyalwa Karmapa. In 1956 he accepted the invitation of the queen mother of Bhutan to assume responsibility for a monastery in that country. During the 1960s he moved to a small monastery in Sonada, near Darjeeling, India. By the late 1960s Kalu Rinpoché's presence had attracted a number of Western students. By this time the Karmapa, who had taken up residence at his monastery in Rumtek, Sikkim, was also accepting many Western students. He asked Kalu Rinpoché, a highly respected yogi and meditation master of the Kagyu tradition, to travel to the West as his representative, to determine if others in Europe and North America had serious interest in Buddhist teachings.

Kalu Rinpoché and a small entourage left India in 1971. He stopped in the Holy Land to pay his respects to the source of the Judeo-Christian traditions and in Rome to meet the Pope, Paul VI. He proceeded to visit Paris and Scotland, then traveled across North America. Before returning to India he established his first Dharma Center in Vancouver, Canada in April 1972. During his second trip to Vancouver in 1974, Kalu Rinpoché hosted the first visit to Vancouver by the Sixteenth Gyalwa Karmapa, and at that time he met the great Sakya lama Dézhung Tulku, who was residing in Seattle, Washington. Since the fall of 1972 Dézhung Rinpoché had visited the Vancouver Dharma center a number of times to instruct and encourage Kalu Rinpoché's students and had expressed profound respect for Kalu Rinpoché's ability to inspire students to actually practice Buddhism. A few months later, at Dézhung Rinpoché's request, Kalu Rinpoché imparted to him the full transmission of the Shangpa Kagyu's empowerments and teachings, the first time such a transmission had taken place outside Asia. At that time he invited a handful of his senior Western students to participate. By the time Kalu Rinpoché made his third trip to the West in 1976, he had decided to establish the first-ever traditional three-year retreat center for Occidental Buddhists. The three-year retreat provides formal training of Drup-la (lama by virtue of contemplative training); Rinpoché's decision signified his honoring Western Buddhists with complete training in the Shangpa Kagyu lineage's teachings and meditations. He thereby took an important step to assure the continuity of the lineage. His example inspired other lineages' masters to provide similar opportunities to their senior Western students.

By the time Kalu Rinpoché left his body in 1989, he had established some sixty Buddhist centers worldwide and at least half a dozen three-year retreat complexes in Europe and North America. Throughout his life, he focused on meditation practice, when possible in retreat settings. He completed an initial three-year retreat at age nineteen. After some years engaged in study, this committed yogi pursued solitary practice for twelve years in caves and isolated mountain hermitages. He was then appointed retreat master of the three-year retreat center at Tsadra Rinchen Drak, where his own master Lama Norbu Döndrub had been retreat master and where Kalu Rinpoché had completed his own three-year retreat. In his teaching activity he was always engaging and tireless, transmitting his wisdom to his students in a way that was unprejudiced and unrestricted. Personal encounters with him were usually quite moving; individuals often left his presence after even a short meeting with the feeling that they had received instruction or been touched deeply in a way that would nurture their practice for the entirety of their lives. Kalu Rinpoché generously gave to any committed student—regardless of gender, race, age, or sexual orientation—every opportunity to deepen his or her understanding and experience. For those adequately committed and prepared, he opened the door to three-year retreats, during which he and his teaching assistants bestowed the Shangpa tradition's full depth and breadth. Well over two hundred Western individuals have completed the Shangpa Kagyu three-year retreat, have received the full transmission of this tradition's teachings, and now aid this vital lineage in taking firm root in the West.

Kalu Rinpoché's compassion and global activity required that he assume responsibility for monasteries and Buddhist meditation centers, yet all who met him would quickly discover that his principal, enduring interests were the contemplative path and its fruits. In fact, he spent much of his long life in solitary or group retreat. With his love of solitude and retreat, his emaciated ascetic body, his profound compassionate awareness, his total disregard for conventional sensitivities, his irrepressible sense of humor, his evident mastery of awareness and appearances, and above all his extraordinary personal presence, it is hard to imagine anyone who more resembled the Milarepa of our imagination. His students so considered him a second Milarepa that they once asked him to pose for photos wearing nothing but a white yogi cloak and meditation belt.

When Kalu Rinpoché passed away, the mantle of the Shangpa Kagyu tradition passed to his spiritual heir, Venerable Bokar Tulku Rinpoché. This exquisite lama, so gentle, open, and kind, is recognized today as the Kagyu tradition's preeminent meditation master. Although he is as different from Kalu Rinpoché as night from day, he continues this lineage's noble tradition in his discretion and his profound commitment to a life of simplicity and meditation. From his home base at his monastery in Mirik, near Darjeeling, he too has begun to put his own stamp on the continuing evolution of the Shangpa Kagyu tradition.

The Shangpa tradition also owes profound gratitude to the great masters of our time belonging to various traditions who have taken care to encourage and ensure the continuity of these precious teachings: the Sixteenth Karmapa Rangjung Rikpé Dorjé, Pawo Rinpoché, Jamgon Kongtrul Rinpoché, Dujom Rinpoché, Dilgo Kyentsé Rinpoché, Dézhung Rinpoché, and Nyoshul Khen Rinpoché, of recent memory, as well as the Seventeenth Karmapa Orgyen Trinlé Dorjé and Tai Situpa, to name but a few.

Those who have been fortunate enough to meet and sit at the feet of Kalu Rinpoché and Bokar Rinpoché realize that in encountering these masters, they have touched the wisdom of the entire Shangpa Kagyu lineage. While it is difficult to describe the qualities of true great masters, meeting them in person is always profoundly moving and leaves a lasting impression. Whether or not you have had the good fortune to meet such masters, I invite you to turn the pages of *Timeless Rapture*, and in reading these verses to find yourself seated at the feet of these extraordinary individuals, listening to their songs, and transported by their devotion, awakened wisdom, and blessing to the vajra world that has become their home.

Drubgyu Tenzin (Anthony Chapman)
Beaulieu, France
August 6, 2002

TRANSLATOR'S PREFACE

Y EARS AGO, I heard with some amusement a comment that fell
from an unnamed Tibetan lama's lips: "Buddha was the world's
biggest liar!" At the time, I thought the words funny but unfounded. Now,
after a little more study of Buddha's Sacred Word, I am forced to admit
that the lama may have a point. Our Refuge, our Guide, our Teacher, once
the Light of Asia and now the Light of the World, was a sly and slippery
salesman for enlightenment. He said whatever it took to lead his audience
to spiritual awakening, and he was astute enough to know that it wasn't
always the truth that set beings free or even set them on the path to freedom.

None of us is fortunate enough to have met the Buddha; we meet his
representatives, modern spiritual masters. And true to the Buddha's example, some of them are creative with the truth some of the time. I have in
mind two stories of my teacher, Kalu Rinpoché.

A Canadian woman, one of his first Western disciples, visited him a
few months before he passed away. He said, "Do you remember that first
time we met? I asked your age, then told you that you had reached the ideal
age and stage—neither too old, nor too young—to practice Buddhism."

The woman had been forty-something at the time. Now, more than
twenty years later, she replied, "Of course I remember! That meeting
changed my life." She had let her career slide and had eventually entered
retreat, first a three-year retreat, then a life devoted to contemplation and
retreat that continues to this day.

Rinpoché smiled a little impishly and said, "Well, right after you left,
the next person who came to see me was a young woman in her early
twenties, and I told her exactly the same thing!"

I suspect that at the end of his life the Buddha took the same glee in
recalling his own skillful means.

The second story, in a similar vein, is pertinent to this book.

In 1974 I had my first personal interview with Kalu Rinpoché. I had taken refuge in him a couple of years before and was interested in meditation. Not a lot of information on Tibetan Buddhism was available in those days, but I had read Gene Smith's introduction to a collection of the life stories of the Shangpa Kagyu masters.[1] He reported that the lineage originated with two women, Niguma and Sukasiddhi, and that Kalu Rinpoché was the present-day lineage holder of their teachings. I felt thrilled at the news, eager to find out more, and wondered if it was possible to practice that lineage's meditations.

To my dismay, Rinpoché told me that the lineage no longer existed. It had died out, disappeared.

Sigh. I remember walking home disappointed, wishing that I could someday meet anything like the defunct Shangpa lineage, should such a rare thing exist. But I didn't dwell on it—what was the point?—and I did not let what did not exist interfere with the incredible chance to meet a teacher like Kalu Rinpoché.

That, I believe, was precisely the point. For what Rinpoché told me that day in our first conversation was a complete fabrication, a lie. Yet, in telling me that lie, Kalu Rinpoché had chosen a way to help me focus on the most important among a number of competing truths: what matters first and foremost is the teacher, not the teaching nor the lineage. Indian tantric texts state these words, and the Tibetans have repeated them for centuries:

> The spiritual master is the Buddha.
> The spiritual master is the Sacred Teaching and the Spiritual
>   Community.
> The spiritual master creates everything.
> Spiritual master, to you I bow.

Tibet's Buddhists have long been warned against considering their relationship with the teachings to be like that of a hunter toward prey. Specifically, prospective students are counseled not to think of the teachings as musk, a rare and profitable commodity, the teacher as a musk deer, and themselves as a hunter. Had Rinpoché told me that the Shangpa lineage existed, I might have become such a hunter. Once I had received the teachings I sought, I could have gone my merry way to practice them to my heart's content. What is the matter with that? Outwardly, nothing at all, of course, but it is not the Buddhist way. Such behavior, no matter how good it looks, will not lead to enlightenment, even though it may lead to high levels of erudition or seeming proficiency in meditation.

The attitude we are advised to adopt is that of a patient who seeks the advice of a doctor. We approach a doctor cautiously, speak frankly, and follow the advice we receive. We continue to consult with the doctor until our health and well-being returns. The teacher is the doctor, we are the patient, and the teachings are medicines the doctor prescribes according to our needs. The state of health and well-being to which the doctor's treatments restore us is our innate, primordial enlightenment.

The primacy of the role of spiritual master in tantra is not an invitation to a personality cult. In fact, my experience with Kalu Rinpoché prepared me well for meeting many of the best spiritual masters of our day: like him, they never, ever talk about their meditative experience or realization. They are endlessly energetic and dedicated to the work of bringing awakening to the world but do so in a completely self-effacing manner. We could say that they accept the role of spiritual master, so central to tantric Buddhist practice, in an impersonal manner. Their degree of self-effacement is worth reflecting upon. To take an example we can all verify, the Dalai Lama, familiar to us all and universally loved and respected, does not speak of his meditative experience, his "pastlife experience," and so on. It is not as if we aren't interested or intrigued by his inner life, but he is far too concerned with us to waste our connection by creating a personality cult around himself. If we recall any of the great Tibetan masters of our time, they share his extreme self-effacement and dedication to Buddhism and others' needs, even while they serve as vajra master, the central focus of tantric practice.

Further, Kalu Rinpoché, like any other lama worthy of the title, did not see his role as that of a dispenser of information, a professor or scholar in monk's clothing. His only criterion for sharing information was whether it would help the person enter and continue on the path to enlightenment. In that way, he was probably no different from the Buddha, whose forays into the realm of half-truth (or less!) we call "provisional meaning"—just enough truth to lead to the next step and eventually to the final, definitive meaning. Buddhists are very comfortable with the Buddha's and his followers' dedication to enlightenment above all else. For example, my Canadian friend and I profited immensely from Kalu Rinpoché's concern for us, which was far more important to him than an empty notion of honesty at all costs.

I found another example of Rinpoché's handiwork recently, in a book optimistically entitled *Indestructible Truth*:

> Also considered a Kagyü subschool is the Shangpa Kagyü. Originally an independent lineage, the Shangpa was established by the accomplished yogin Khyungpo Naljor (or Naljorpa, 978–1079). This master studied in India with some of the great siddhas of his day and received transmission in a vision from Niguma, the tantric consort of Naropa. Subsequently, the lineage was brought into the Kagyü orbit and is now considered Kagyü. One of the most well-known representatives of the Shangpa Kagyü is the late Ven. Kalu Rinpoche, quoted frequently in this book, a master who spent much of his life in retreat and, at the request of the sixteenth Karmapa, taught meditation widely in the West. (p. 183)

By the end of this book, the reader will be in a position to recognize that much of the "information" contained in this paragraph reflects the willful misinformation that I have every reason to suspect was spread by my beloved spiritual master. (For example, it is not true that the Shangpa lineage is a Kagyu subschool, that it is no longer independent, or that it has been brought into another school's orbit.) The author, who commendably seems to have gone directly to Rinpoché for his information, is not to blame. We can imagine that Rinpoché, who spent much of his life in retreat, wanted to keep his Shangpa lineage in retreat too and out of the spotlight.

This book, a collection of the songs of realization of the Shangpa masters, constitutes a major source of the lineage's spiritual nourishment. Kalu Rinpoché told those of us in retreat under his guidance to read this collection if we wanted to read something apart from the texts of our program's meditations. During retreat or after, in Western meditation centers or in Asian monasteries, we sometimes gather to sing these songs in unison. They guide us, nourish us, remind us, and take on new meaning as the years go by. We return to them, as to trusted friends, for the support and encouragement we need to keep on giving our best to this precious life. We have always enjoyed them in Tibetan; they appear here in translation for the first time.

As the translator, I have some concerns to share. First and foremost, I felt it important to relate my own introduction to the lineage—"Sorry, it doesn't exist"—as this brings into focus the correct approach to these or any lineage's teachings.

Another concern is that this book might be construed as a way for the Shangpa lineage to gain some "market share" in the crowded modern spiritual bazaar. This has never been a concern of the Shangpa lineage throughout its history and is not the intent of Shangpa lineage holders today. Kalu Rinpoché did much to discourage public knowledge of the Shangpa lineage, leaving it practically invisible during the first wave of Tibetan Buddhist teaching in the West. He wasn't trying to be exclusive—this is the way it has always been. Bokar Rinpoché, Kalu Rinpoché's successor, has followed in the footsteps of past Shangpa masters, doing little to promote the lineage, apart from giving the transmission for those who want to do its meditations in three-year retreats. The late Jamgon Kongtrul the Third (1954—1992) is another example of a master who always presented himself as a Karma Kagyu lama, yet his still-functioning three-year retreat center in India is Shangpa Kagyu. During his lifetime and afterward, it has continued without the slightest fanfare or self-promotion.

To say that the Shangpa lineage does not talk about itself in public, does nothing to attract followers, and does not build public institutions is not to criticize lineages that do. There are eight separate lineages of meditation practice in Tibetan Buddhism. Each has its own distinctive style. The Shangpa style is homelessness, apart from a few retreat centers. It doesn't suit everyone, but a prospective meditator in tantric Buddhism who prefers a more substantial worldly presence or tangible support structure has an embarrassment of riches: seven other truly wonderful lineages to choose from. Moreover, those of us who have chosen Shangpa masters as our teachers can contribute to other lineages' projects if we want to get involved in public work, as we've done for centuries.

During one of my visits with probably the most wonderful woman alive, Khandro Tsering Chödron, I foolishly asked her, "Wasn't Jamyang Kyentsé Chökyi Lodrö (her late husband, famously nonsectarian) a lama of the Sakya tradition?" It was the only time I ever saw her taken aback, "Oh!" she said, startled, "He wasn't *that sort* of lama!" In the same way, I think Niguma and Sukasiddhi would tell us, if we had ears to hear, "Ours isn't *that sort* of lineage." You may thus read the songs reassured that you are welcome to take from them anything meaningful to you without having to "buy" this tradition.

On the other hand, if you want to find a Shangpa lama to further your connection with this lineage, you may find one where you least expect—in the person of your chosen spiritual master whom you know as a lama of another school. Many lamas from all traditions have received and practiced these meditations. In part, this is due to the work of Jamgon Kongtrul Lodrö Tayé (1813—1899), who compiled these songs. When he gathered the major meditations of Tibet's eight lineages of meditation into a collection called *The Treasury of Profound Instructions*, he included all the Shangpa empowerments and meditations, as well as the verses contained in this book. *The Treasury of Profound Instructions* is passed on regularly in the Himalayan region; thus lamas from all schools have received the Shangpa transmission.

For example, when I first received the Shangpa transmission, it was as a participant in a group led by Dézhung Rinpoché, a venerable Sakya lama, who had asked Kalu Rinpoché for the empowerments. Chadral Rinpoché, a pillar of the Nyingma lineage, received the transmission one-to-one from Kalu Rinpoché (during which time Rinpoché said that he had to hide his snuff box, to prevent Chadral Rinpoché, one of his closest friends, from stealing it to make him stop his bad habit). Dilgo Kyentsé Rinpoché, with whom you may be acquainted through the wonderful book *Journey to Enlightenment*, wrote this at the end of a prayer for the spread of the Shangpa teachings:

> Through the kindness of the perfect Buddha, Gyurmé Péma Namgyal, the great master of Zhéchen Monastery, I became a vessel for profound teachings that constitute the essence of the lineages of accomplishment's eight chariots. I have particularly strong faith in the glorious Shangpa lineage's Five Golden Doctrines.

Lamas of every tradition—Gélug, Sakya, Nyingma, and Kagyu—have received and practice the Shangpa tradition. The lineage is extremely discreet but not exclusive; it silently pervades the Himalayan region yet is centered nowhere. In this the Shangpa lineage resembles another lineage of tantric meditation begun by a woman: the Severance (*Chö*), established by Machik Lapdrön, a Tibetan reincarnation of one of the Shangpa lineage founders, Sukasiddhi. Her spiritual children as well have always preferred the freedom of homelessness, the exhilaration of total renunciation, and good-natured harmony with one and all. The Severance lineage often walked hand-in-hand with the Shangpa teachings through the walls of Tibet's religious institutions, whereas less ethereal traditions were often stopped at the gates. One Western scholar-translator, Matthew Kapstein, writes, "The Shangs-pa lineage like some vine that adorns a whole forest without being able to stand by itself may strike one who follows its twists and turns as being virtually an omnipresent element in Tibetan Buddhism."[2]

I have written here *about* the Shangpa lineage, but I hope you will read this book as *from* the lineage. I have translated this book not as a scholar but as a representative of the chief lama of the Shangpa tradition, Bokar Rinpoché. One of Bokar Rinpoché's main Western disciples, Lama Tcheuky Sengé of France, first asked me to translate this book, and Bokar Rinpoché himself was very generous with his time in answering hundreds of questions during the translation process. Lama Drubgyu Tenzin, the first Westerner whom Kalu Rinpoché chose to teach the three-year, three-month Shangpa Kagyu retreat, gave his full time and attention to this work as my adviser-in-chief for both form and terminology. A translation of such an intimate part of our lineage would have been inconceivable without each of their blessings and impossible without their active participation.

Tsadra Foundation was wholly responsible for funding my work on this translation, including repeated journeys to consult with Bokar Rinpoché, for which I am deeply grateful.

Christiane Buchet, a colleague in translation and a sister on the spiritual path, has translated these songs from my English translation to French. Her work, which was so often better than my version, has proved very helpful and inspiring. I am also very grateful to the best among us, Lama Chökyi Nyima (Richard Barron), for his permission to include his translation of one of Kalu Rinpoché's songs.

The Flavor of This Collection of Songs

Jamgon Kongtrul Lodrö Tayé compiled these songs in the nineteenth century, mainly from the autobiographies of the lineage's masters. What is clear from the first song is that this collection mainly gathers songs of spiritual teachings. Western readers have fallen in love, just as Tibetans do, with the songs of Milarepa and of Shabkar. Those realized masters were wandering yogis, who sometimes sang of profound teachings they'd received and practiced but often imparted down-to-earth advice to the good people they met. They would also sing of their surroundings, for these men often lived in the wilds, and their songs allow us to share their awe in the presence of enlightenment, reflected in the spiritual master who appears in symbolic form in nature, in all appearances. As Kalu Rinpoché sings:

> Thus the whole universe—visible, audible, and conceptual—
> Pointing out to myself and others the direct apprehension of the
>   underlying reality,
> Is nothing but the gesture of my lama.

Milarepa and Shabkar invite us to participate in that experience. Nevertheless, Kongtrul's choice of the Shangpa masters' songs reflects a different concern. He has mainly included songs of teaching. They do not transport us to the hills and valleys of Tibet but to terrain familiar to all Buddhists—the questions of how to live a meaningful life, how to confront death, and how to enter and remain within the sacred sanctuary of the mind's nature, enlightenment. I heartily recommend *The Hundred Thousand Songs of Milarepa* and *The Life of Shabkar* to one and all, in the hope that they become lifelong companions. However, readers should be forewarned concerning the very different style of the songs presented here, which do not situate the reader in the outer environment but in the inner landscape of meditation.

Songs of realization form a genre of Tibetan sacred literature. They usually blend two contrasting styles: On the one hand, they are usually extemporaneous and unpremeditated, and emerge as a response to an immediate situation—a student's request for guidance or a specific catalytic event. Songs arise fresh and alive, like sparks. Yet for all their spontaneity, they are highly formal in that they conform to the strict rules of Tibetan poetic structure. For example, the syllables of a seven-syllable line are always related as follows:

$$1\text{-}2/\ 3\text{-}4/\ 5\text{-}6\text{-}7$$

Every line follows that scheme. When the number of syllables increases, the line will inevitably hold an odd number of syllables, in the same pattern of pairs of syllables joined in juxtaposition or in unison, ending with a trio of syllables. Every song in this collection follows that rule, except one in six-syllable lines, and Kongtrul notes the single exception in his text.

Some songs in this collection might seem to have been written rather than sung, despite Kongtrul's claim that he compiled the Shangpa masters' songs, not written verse. I can venture two explanations for the impression of these as written works. First, many of our most enduring Western popular songs are of the June-moon-swoon variety, employing a common, fairly limited vocabulary to good, often surprising effect. By contrast, the singers and the first audience of these songs were most often persons steeped in the general vocabulary of tantric Buddhism and the specific technical terminology of the Shangpa tradition. If we cannot avoid the ugly fact of technical language on our spiritual path, Tibetan has the virtue of making it as terse as linguistically possible. Important words are often monosyllabic; two syllables designating opposites can be juxtaposed to indicate new meanings: we could think of the Chinese syllables *yin-yang*. Three- and four-syllable words (the maximum in Tibetan) are commonly abbreviated; the audience instantly recognizes the contractions: we could imagine an abbreviation of the Sanskrit word *bodhisattva* into *bosa* or even the term *buddha nature* into *budné*. This extraction of the first and third syllables from a multisyllable word is a routine operation in Tibetan. In translation into Western languages, the original's lightness and ease can quickly seem turgid, flat-footed, and bombastic.

In Nepal, I once translated for a Tibetan lama visited by both Westerners and Tibetans. As the private interviews were given at random, I stayed in the room while he spoke directly with Tibetans who came for his advice. On one occasion, an ordinary Tibetan woman in her forties or fifties asked a question, which I hadn't listened to and which the yogi began to answer in normal, conversational language. He then abruptly switched into song, continuing for a few minutes to sing his advice to her in verses that seemed to me both fluid and impromptu. It was stunning. There was a naked meeting of minds between them that produced the song. Yes, technically, there was a singer and a listener, two bodies and two faces, one of which had tears streaming down it. But there were less than two minds in that encounter, or even less than one mind: there was only nondual wisdom and the song that emerged from it. It was, in brief, the music of timeless rapture.

Such music is produced when empty appearances, sounds, or thoughts collide with nondual wisdom. A song in structured verse emerges, sometimes in the presence of a listener, who at best is also present in a nondual state. I felt that the Tibetan woman whose question and openness had triggered the song "listened" in that way. Yes, her body was crying, but I've witnessed that often enough to believe that for some people crying can be a physical, organic reaction to a sudden shift to nondual wisdom, and doesn't necessarily signal submersion in an emotional or ecstatic state.

An observer might also come to a variety of conclusions concerning the singer: that he or she must be in an ordinary state, or in a trance, or absent but "channeling," or singing spontaneously but watching a process in which he or she doesn't intervene, and so on. I'd guess that it is none of the above. The lama of this story and the spiritual masters of the Shangpa tradition were trained in tantric wisdom culture. From the outset the point of such training, clearly articulated by teachers and accepted by students, is to recognize nondual wisdom (also known as timeless awareness, awakened mind, buddha nature, the body of ultimate enlightenment, or simply awareness), to become familiar with and to stabilize that recognition, and to take that stable experience to its limits—the realization of awakening or enlightenment. This is the heart of Himalayan tantric Buddhist culture. Nondual wisdom is not a chance occurrence; Buddhist culture is consciously mobilized around it. Without such wisdom, tantric Buddhism would be just another collection of spiritual techniques.

Those who continue their training to its rapturous conclusion live within the state of primordial awakening. At that point, any gestures or words are meaningful, including songs. At the beginning of this collection, Jamgon Kongtrul introduces the Shangpa masters' songs as follows:

> The garland of jewels who appear in this Oral Instruction Lineage have reached the citadel of the mind's nature, the body of ultimate enlightenment. The radiant splendor of their meditative experience and realization overflows from their mouths, expressing their profound enlightenment as vajra songs. The laughter of these songs of realization reverberates throughout space to nourish adepts' faith and devotion; to strike with the ridingcrop of encouragement to turn away from attachment and to foster renunciation; to augment meditative experience; to instill firm confidence in realization's wisdom; to please the spiritual heroes and dakinis; to lead others to freedom along the narrow passage through obstacles and impediments; and to satisfy infinite numbers of human and nonhuman

beings with the unsurpassable gift of the Teachings.

How do we listen to songs of timeless, nondual rapture? Ideally, in a nondual state. I can only guess at the state of mind of the Tibetan woman whose question prompted the lama's song. I never saw her before nor after that encounter. Nevertheless, my impression was positive. She was probably illiterate, as are too many women of her generation, yet familiar, as are many of her fellow Himalayan Buddhists, with timeless wisdom. She heard a new song that day and it was unexpected, but she had obviously heard the underlying "music"—nondual wisdom—before and knew how to listen to it. Her listening (or ours) is not a passive act; I felt she rose to the occasion and met the lama halfway. A nondual state is not "learned," as we would commonly use that word to indicate that we add something to our survival or social skills. It's who we really are—it is innate, inherent, the nature of mind. As one teacher says, it's like peeling an orange: remove the peel of dualistic experience, and there it is. Much of the content of this collection concerns the recognition, care, and feeding of that nondual state.

Jamgon Kongtrul gives us some assistance in preparing for these songs by setting them within a traditional framework of a tantric ritual. He includes the Shangpa lineage's style of taking refuge and developing the mind of awakening, then makes this comment:

> Those who sing these songs must relinquish thoughts of themselves as ordinary persons and remain steadfast within contemplative practice.

He then proposes that we visualize ourselves as deities and our environment as a pure realm. Curiously enough, this contrivance can prepare us for nondual wisdom. In normal life, we wear different clothing for specific occasions, choices that have major effects on our mental state. Fun clothing for the beach; somber clothing for a funeral. Here, we step away from our ordinary sense of self-identity by putting on our tantric uniform, for our immersion in the self-image of a deity and the deity's world. In itself, this is not nondual wisdom; it's just the tantric dress code, as vital to tantra as refuge and the mind of awakening are to the Great Way. After dressing for the occasion, we invite the lineage's spiritual masters and deities and make offering and supplications to them. We human beings are sensitive to our surroundings. From our birth, we tend to identify ourselves with gender, race, language, parents, family, gods, and country. Even in adult life, many of us are strongly influenced by friends and their interests, which we catch like a bad cold that is going around. Here we invite a large crowd of those who epitomize nondual wisdom, in the expectation that our intentional association with them will infect us with awakening. A self-image as the deity along with faith and devotion weaken our resistance to enlightenment-germs.

Following prayers of supplication to the lineage masters, Kongtrul leads us through the songs, beginning with one sung by Buddha Vajra Bearer, heard and recorded by Niguma. The songs of this collection generally appear in chronological order, each with a short introduction by Jamgon Kongtrul. At Bokar Rinpoché's request, I have added songs by Kalu Rinpoché. These were given to me by an elderly lama, a devoted disciple of Kalu Rinpoché, who never left Palpung Monastery in eastern Tibet, where Kalu Rinpoché once lived and taught. It seems many of these songs stayed in Tibet with him, as Bokar Rinpoché had not seen most of them. I am delighted that Lama Tcheuky Sengé received Bokar Rinpoché's permission to include a number of Rinpoché's songs as well.

In the book's second half, I have included some details of the lives and times of each of the masters whose songs appear in the collection and some information concerning the Shangpa lineage in general. I have not commented upon or added notes to the songs. In the years that we have sung them, these songs have revealed many new dimensions of meaning, and I suspect they will continue to do so. I feel they can be enjoyed without our understanding every last word—that has been, and remains, true for me. Further, most of us read or sing these songs as meditation texts, useful in our training under the guidance of a qualified teacher, the most appropriate context for delving into the text's deeper meanings.

Finally, readers will soon discover in these pages the meaning of the phrase "something got lost in the translation." In this case, it is the music of the songs: they cannot be sung in English as they are in Tibetan. You may chant them if you wish, of course, but a translation that respects the form as well as the meaning of these precious songs still eludes us. I sincerely pray (and you should too) that translators someday become able to render these songs in a form that can fly far above simple chants, to the realm of music. For the moment, we must all content ourselves with the meaning alone.

Kongtrul named this collection *A Sea of Blessing*. I find that title amusing, for most Tibetans over the centuries, including Jamgon Kongtrul himself, never saw an ocean. Those who have left Tibet recently and have seen the sea have been amazed and sometimes intimidated by its size and power. All are taken by surprise when they taste the sea for the first time: salt water! It strikes me as ironic that Kongtrul used that word alongside "blessing," a word that we are familiar with in the same way Tibetans know the word "sea"—although we have a word for it, many of us have never seen, felt, or tasted "blessing." My hope is that this translation will allow you to experience this sea of blessing as Kongtrul and the Shangpa masters intended.

PART 1

A SEA OF BLESSING

*A Remarkable Collection of Vajra Verses and Melodious Songs
of Realization of the Glorious Shangpa Instruction Lineage
Compiled by Jamgon Kongtrul*

Illustrious Buddha Vajra Bearer's regents, lord bodhisattvas of awakening's tenth stage, appear in an uninterrupted line of indisputably accomplished masters, known throughout the three worlds as lord protectors of beings, the Shangpa Instruction Lineage, adorned with many particularly wonderful and exalted qualities—at your lotus feet I respectfully bow.

BUDDHA VAJRA BEARER, sixth lord of all families of enlightenment, bestowed deep, secret vajra tantras, verses of profound meditation instruction, in the innate sound of his indestructible, melodious voice. From that time forth, the garland of jewels who appear in this Oral Instruction Lineage have reached the citadel of the mind's nature, the body of ultimate enlightenment. The radiant splendor of their meditative experience and realization overflows from their mouths, expressing their profound enlightenment as vajra songs. The laughter of these songs of realization reverberates throughout space to nourish adepts' faith and devotion; to strike with the ridingcrop of encouragement to turn away from attachment and to foster renunciation; to augment meditative experience; to instill firm confidence in realization's wisdom; to please the spiritual heroes and dakinis; to lead others to freedom along the narrow passage through obstacles and impediments; and to satisfy infinite numbers of human and nonhuman beings with the unsurpassable gift of the Teachings.

Now, with a respectful attitude, let us make a few of these songs resound, beginning with the stages of the preliminary spiritual practices and with visualized meditations.

After that encouragement [given by the leader of the ritual], recite the following prayer of refuge three times:

All sentient beings, my mothers, whose numbers fill the expanse of
space, take refuge in the union of all refuges, my precious spiritual
master.

Then recite this development of the mind of awakening three times:

For the benefit of all sentient beings, I will attain great Buddha Vajra
Bearer's state of integral union; for this reason, I now recite the
vajra songs of realization.

*Those who sing these songs must relinquish thoughts of themselves as ordinary
persons and remain steadfast within contemplative practice. To bring this
clearly to mind, recite the following:*

This environment and the beings within it are pure, a celestial realm.
This place is a palace of perfect freedom, decorated within and without by ornaments and offerings in infinite designs. Each person here
among us personifies the circle of the five héruka deities [in the sacred
circle of Supreme Bliss].

From each of our hearts, tremendous light shines forth and illuminates all buddhas' realms. This light invites spiritual masters, buddhas
and their spiritual heirs, the bodhisattvas, in the form of wisdom
deities' sacred circles. They arrive here and fill the sky before us.

Vajra Sama Ja

Spiritual master, conquerors and your heirs,
Deities, spiritual heroes, and yoginis—
In your display as ultimate enlightenment that pervades space,
Signs of movement, of coming and going, have no hold over you.

You are magical manifestations of wisdom who guide beings
    according to their needs.
In the open expanse of our minds' devotion, you are vividly present.
Until you complete your work for others' sake, remain,
And bless the circle of this vajra gathering.

Padma Kamala-ya Tram

Offer The Mandala of the Sealed Instruction:

Sublime mandala, exquisitely disposed—
At the center, the sovereign mountain, four continents, and adjacent lands,
Beautiful with the resplendent sun and moon circling round,
Adorned with iron mountains beyond and dancing seas between.

Jewels, wish-fulfilling trees, and bountiful cattle;
Seven royal articles, with the precious treasure vase the eighth;
Effortless harvests, water of eight qualities,
Inconceivable clouds of outer, inner, and secret offerings—

This adept, who wishes to achieve the two goals,
Offers with enthusiasm
This delightful and appealing mandala
To you, ocean of masters, deities, and victors.

This adept, descendant of all buddhas,
Offers you this fine and pleasing mandala:
May my mass of faults, errors, and impurities be cleared away,
And may you grant me common and sublime accomplishment.

Recite the common confession, as follows:

I take refuge in the Three Jewels.
I acknowledge each of my negative, unvirtuous acts.
I rejoice in beings' virtue.
I have confidence in Buddha's awakening.
Until awakening, I take refuge
In Buddha, his Teaching, and the sublime Community.
I engender the mind of awakening
To perfectly accomplish my own and others' welfare.
Having developed this sublime mind of awakening,
I will serve all sentient beings.
May I exemplify the inspiring supreme conduct conducive to awakening
And attain enlightenment for the benefit of all beings.

It is the precious Kagyu masters' tradition to begin the songs' recitation
with prayers of devotion, to perform the main service while maintaining
firm confidence within meditative experience and realization, and to con-
clude with joyful, auspicious declarations. Therefore, we prepare by considering our principal spiritual master, the lineage's masters, and the
conquerors and their spiritual heirs, with intense, undivided faith. Such
faith can capture and overpower ordinary appearances, forcefully change
our outlook, and enhance the wisdom of our realization. With such faith,
please recite the following prayer as a preliminary to the songs:

Namo Guru!

Vajra Bearer, lord of all families of enlightenment,
Father, kind spiritual master, to you I pray.

Supreme Bliss, Binder of the Net,
Glorious Héruka, to you I pray.

Wisdom Dakini Niguma,
In the expanse of uncontaminated bliss and emptiness, to you I pray.

Lady Sukasiddhi,
In your abode, perfect rapture's celestial realm, to you I pray.

One hundred fifty scholars and accomplished masters,
In your abode, the palace of manifest enlightenment that appears
    according to others' needs, to you I pray.

Son of the dakinis, learned and accomplished Kyungpo Naljor
Endowed with the tantras' five ultimate teachings, to you I pray.

Noble Mokchok-pa, bodhisattva in your final life,
Holder of the single-disciple lineage, to you I pray.

Noble Kyergang-pa, Bodhisattva Powerful All-Seeing One
In the body of a pure meditator, to you I pray.

Noble, great Nyentön,
Hidden form of the six families' lord, to you I pray.

Noble Sangyé Tönpa, exemplar of the seven-jewel lineage
And their lives of freedom, to you I pray.

The three noble, learned, and accomplished masters,
The ground on which the river of our lineage flows, to you I pray.

Lineage from the illustrious masters Jakchen Gyaltsen Büm and
    Samding Zhonnu Drub,
Endowed with wondrous lives of freedom and enlightened activity,
    to you I pray.

Noble Tsultrim Gön, Ritrö-pa,
And Shangkar Rinchen Gyaltsen, to you I pray.

Noble Kuklung-pa, Namgyal-wa,
And Gyagom Lekpa Gyaltsen, to you I pray.

Noble Tangtong Gyalpo, who accomplished immortality
And was accepted by the dakini, to you I pray.

Glorious Kunga Drolchok,
Whose conduct of tantric discipline guided beings, to you I pray.

Noble Draktong-pa,
Who actualized the true experience of ultimate enlightenment, to you
    I pray.

Noble Taranata, Héruka,
Illustrious Lord of Secrets, to you I pray.

Masters who preserved the glorious Shangpa Instruction Lineage,
A series of sublime individuals, to you I pray.

The Five Tantras' Deities
In your abode at my body's five indestructible energy centers, to you I
　pray.

Male and female wisdom dakinis,
In drops of the body's vital essence, circles of five-colored light, to you
　I pray.

Swift Awakened Protector,
In your abode, the charnel ground of compassion's display, to you I
　pray.

Outwardly, may appearances of conceptual deluded thoughts
　collapse;
Inwardly, may I realize the relative and ultimate to be inseparable;
Between, may my intrinsic face, ultimate enlightenment, manifest,
And may I then empty the depths of the three realms' wheel of life!

BUDDHA VAJRA BEARER

THE SIXTH CONQUEROR, great Buddha Vajra Bearer, lord who pervades all families of enlightenment, sang this song of vajra verses[3] of the abiding nature to his own appearance, the wisdom dakini [Niguma]. In the innate sound of the unborn nature, he introduces cyclic life and transcendence as the nature of Great Seal:

Great bliss, spontaneously present and uncompounded—
Great Buddha Vajra Bearer, enlightenment's perfect rapture,
Sang this unborn, innate melody I heard:

Ordinary mind: how amazing!

The preliminary practice is threefold natural repose.
The main practice frees the four faults in their own ground.
At the point of culmination, enlightenment's four bodies arise of
    themselves.

The preliminary vow is the secret vajra.
Compassion and prayer enrich meditative experience.
Whatever appears merges with the path.

Manifest realization is nonmeditation without distraction.
Blend this in a state without thought to integrate it on the path.
Clear light and gazes enrich the experience.

After waking, merge clarity with absence of thought.
Regard the luminosity of day, night, and the intermediate state
As enlightenment's self-arising, inseparable three bodies.

No one knows this, the tantras' concealed, ultimate meaning,
Disclosed in a single instruction:
Nonmeditation and nondistraction.
With familiarity and stability in this,
You can now traverse awakening's paths and stages.
Without mental activity, the two obscurations are purified in their
    own ground.
The three bodies arise of themselves;
The result is spontaneously present.

All discourses and tantras teach this, but it is naturally concealed:
You must learn it from the mouth of a blessed spiritual master.

From thoughts' clouds that billow within the space of ultimate
    enlightenment,
The five poisons' lightning flashes—see it as timeless great wisdom!
Without mental activity, free from hope and fear—
Ordinary mind, to you I bow!

When he requested these vajra verses [from Niguma], the learned and
accomplished Kyungpo Naljor offered five hundred measures of gold to
the wisdom dakini. He placed this text like a heart in an amulet box he
always wore at his neck.

NIGUMA

THE WISDOM DAKINI known as Nigupta, illustrious Narotapa's sister, was a self-manifest yogini, a powerful lord bodhisattva on awakening's tenth stage, who received direct instruction from Conqueror Vajra Bearer. She sang these vajra verses of self-liberating Great Seal:

Nature of mind,
Wish-fulfilling jewel, to you I bow.

Wishing to attain perfect enlightenment,
Visualize your body clearly as the deity
To purify ordinary thoughts.
Develop a noble intention to help others
And pure devotion to your spiritual master.

Don't dwell on your spiritual master or the deity.
Don't bring anything to mind,
Be it real or imagined.
Rest uncontrived in the innate state.

Your own mind, uncontrived, is the body of ultimate enlightenment.
To remain undistracted within this is meditation's essential point.
Realize the great, boundless, expansive state.

Myriad thoughts of anger and desire
Propel you within the seas of existence.
Take the sharp sword of the unborn state
And cut through them to their lack of intrinsic nature.
When you cut a tree's root,
Its branches won't grow.

On a bright ocean,
Bubbles emerge then dissolve back into the water.
Likewise, thoughts are nothing but the nature of reality:
Don't regard them as faults. Relax.

When you have no clinging to what appears, what arises,
It frees itself within its own ground.

Appearances, sound, and phenomena are your own mind.
There are no phenomena apart from mind.
Mind is free from birth, cessation,
And formulation.

Those who know mind's nature
Enjoy the five senses' pleasures
But do not stray from the nature of reality.
On an island of gold,
You search in vain for earth and stones.

In the equanimity of the great absolute expanse,
There is no acceptance or rejection,
No states of meditation or postmeditation.

When you actualize that state,
It is spontaneously present,
Fulfilling beings' hopes
Like a wish-fulfilling jewel.

Persons of the highest, middle, and common levels of capability
Should learn this in stages suitable to their understanding.

SUKASIDDHI

THE WISDOM DAKINI known as Sukasiddhi received full empow-
erment into a sacred circle emanated by the illustrious master
Virupa and in one night reached awakening's eighth stage. She then met
Buddha Vajra Bearer and became inseparable from the Honored Buddha
Selfless One. She sang this song to bestow the essential instructions on
her fortunate disciples:

Disengaged from the six senses' domains,
Not thinking is the path of transcendence.
The absolute expanse has no concepts.
Freedom from mental activity is Great Seal.

Don't meditate! Don't meditate! Don't meditate with the mind!
The mind's meditation amounts to deluded thoughts.
Thoughts bind you to cyclic existence.
With release from the mind, there is no meditation.

In space, emptiness without awareness,
Tame the root of the mind endowed with awareness.
Tame its root and relax.

MÉTRIPA

T HE ILLUSTRIOUS, accomplished master Shavari accepted as his
direct disciple Métripa, who received a prediction that he would
reach Great Seal's supreme accomplishment during the intermediate state
after death. Conqueror Métripa, also known as Advayavajra, was chief of
infinite numbers of spiritual heroes and dakinis and lord of the profound
teachings of dwelling without mental activity in the essential, ultimate
nature of mind.

While he lived as a hidden [tantric practitioner] in Vikramashila
Monastery, he drank alcohol and enjoyed sexual relations with a woman.
When other members of the monastic community discovered this, they
expelled him from their grounds. At the banks of the Ganges, Métripa
spread a mat made of antelope's skin [on the water], used his staff as an oar,
and sailed away, singing this song:

> To approach the noble master brings happiness.
> To drink his profound teachings' ambrosia brings happiness.[4]
>
> To gain experience in them brings happiness.
> To gain no experience at all brings happiness.
>
> To have a view without hope or fear brings happiness.
> If it is spontaneously present, this brings even more happiness.
>
> To meditate without dualistic clinging brings happiness.
> To have no reference points brings even more happiness.
>
> To engage in choiceless conduct brings happiness.
> To have no hesitation brings even more happiness.

To use the mind to watch the mind brings happiness.
To cut off the mistaken path of hope and fear brings happiness.

To stay in retreat in the mountains brings happiness.
To have a view without hope or fear brings happiness.

To set aside homeland, friends, and relatives brings happiness.
To live on begged food brings happiness.

To eat the food of great bliss brings happiness.
To wear the clothes of luminosity brings happiness.

To practice the path of the messenger brings happiness.
To keep one's focus at the tip of the nose brings happiness.[5]

Having sung this, he sailed unhindered across the surface of the water. Everyone realized that he was an accomplished master and in regret [for their thoughts and actions] bowed to him from the shore.

This great lord and spiritual master touched the dust on the feet of the noble Shavari at the Glorious Mountain in south [India]. When Shavari gave him the empowerment of Great Seal, Métripa sang this song to define the nature of reality:

Hung! Hung!

The wheel of life and transcendence are inseparable,
Like waves and water.

Buddhas and sentient beings are nondual—
The difference between them is like poison [before and] after mantras
    neutralize it.

The mind's single nature appears in manifold ways,
Like crystal that changes color in different surroundings.

Myriad substances arise but are your own mind,
Like all rivers that have the same salty taste in the sea.

After you abandon everything real or imagined, original mind
    remains,
Like a bird's trace in the sky.

A single small lamp
Dispels one thousand years' dense darkness.
Likewise, an instant of realization of your own mind
Disperses anger and desire's dense fog in the wheel of life.

Contemplative practice that unites means and knowledge
Stills the waves of thought from existence's sufferings.

A bright jewel placed in mud
Does not gleam, is formless, and neither comes nor goes.
As soon as realization of Great Seal arises,
The mind dilates to become as vast as the sky.

Clarity without thought is like space.
Appearances, without intrinsic nature, are like the moon on water.
Clarity without clinging is like a rainbow.
Like a young person's pleasure, it is indescribable.

This is not localized and exceeds all bounds.

Unbiased, it is not stained by anything,
Like a crystal ball that mud cannot taint.

Mind without hope or fear is like a lion.
Mind's great bliss flows uninterruptedly like a river.
Like the light of the sun and moon, it is impartial.

How amazing!
This self-manifest mind is wonderful!

Settle in this innate state, o adept,
And within it, do nothing whatsoever to change it.
The uncontrived state is ultimate enlightenment itself.
The fault of contrivance prevents sight of the exalted path—
Let the mind's elephant go free.

Knowing this heart of contemplative practice,
Without practice, you will attain enlightenment.
Without having done anything, you will complete all difficult tasks.
Without effort, you will gain accomplishment within yourself.
Without meditation, you will gain the ultimate result.

The three existences are all primordially liberated—
You don't need to affirm or deny anything here!

This is the vajra song to define the view.

É Ma Ho!
How wonderful!

If you want to meditate on the innate abiding nature,
You don't need to consult astrology
For [auspicious] dates, planets, or stars.
When you recall the King of Time [death], the time is right!

Don't search for isolation in a mountain retreat;
The mountain of your body is the best sanctuary.

Don't renounce your distractions;
When you know them to be your multifaceted mind,
They arise as an aid, like grass in a forest fire.

Don't go into retreat; don't post a list [of those who can enter].
To stop talking is the best retreat.

Relax, like a tuft of cotton wool.
Give up doing; don't focus your mind.
Don't restrain your consciousness—let it go.

If you become dull or agitated, look directly at it.

Gradually give up acts that harm your mind.
If anger or desire arises, know it to be demons.

Mind left uncontrived is the Buddha.
At all times—walking, lying down, or sitting—relax.

The root of all discursive thought is the mind.
When there is no mind, there is no thought.

As soon as a support for spontaneous presence arises,
No anger or desire can possibly arise in the meditator.
Therefore, a realized meditator's mind is very happy.

As soon as the path without reference points is found,
No partiality can possibly arise in the meditator.
The experience of impartial consciousness is very joyful.

As soon as the uncontrived stream is born,
No judgment can possibly arise in the meditator.
Not to affirm or deny, accept or reject, is exhilarating.

As soon as the mind of awakening of equanimity is born,
No self or other can possibly arise in the meditator.
When self and others are equal, this is true equanimity.

Settle within the three existences' primordial liberation.

This is the vajra song to define meditation.
Iti. [6]

É Ma Ho!
How wonderful!

To be careful is the best conduct.
Don't be careless; be vigilant and mindful.
Whatever you do, don't set limits.

Do anything at all, like a child.
Be uncontrived, like an infant.
Be fearless, like a lion.
Have no hesitation, like an elephant entering water.
Have no concern with cleanliness—play like dogs or pigs.
Consider all places to have the same flavor, like a fly.
Don't impede what naturally arises, like a madman.
Be without reference points, like a flesh-eating spirit.
Go everywhere, like the wind.
Such movement without attachment is best.

Seal whatever you experience with the mark of the unborn state.

This is the vajra song to define conduct.

Without hope or fear, remain in the nature of mind's innate state—
Without mental activity, you will attain an unforgettable[7] meditative
    state.
Without coming into being, you will attain the changeless view.
Without clinging, you will attain impartial conduct.
Without added causes, you will attain a result that exceeds your
    limited expectations.
Without having done anything, you will complete all difficult tasks.
Without accumulation, you will collect an inexhaustible treasure.

Without meeting, you will encounter an inseparable companion.

Like an excellent vase or a wish-fulfilling jewel,
This self-manifest result is truly amazing.

This is the vajra song to define the result.

RAHULA

RAHULA WAS BORN in southern India; the special four deities, including Vajra Yogini, manifestly nurtured and blessed him. He attained an immortal vajra body, traveled to Tibet through miraculous power, and then returned to India, where he still lives and benefits beings in a mountain forest on what is called Black Mountain. Rahula-gupta-vajra, a powerful master of contemplative practice who gained realization, gave these oral instructions for meditation on the inconceivable:

To all spiritual masters I bow.

Their realization in a concise practice for experiential cultivation is
     this:
Meditation on the four immeasurables,
Inconceivable teachings I will now explain.

In the nature empty of cause and effect,
Form is insubstantial, sound nondual,
And the imperceptible result arises effortlessly,
Like rain without thunder.

Therefore, enter the discipline
Of the selfless nature, fortunate meditator!

Existence's myriad appearances
Are insubstantial, empty, and selfless.
Their essence is pure.

Within such compassion,
Buddhas and sentient beings are nondual.

Natural luminosity without meditation, without thought,
Beyond center or limits, is the meaning of the Middle Way.
Meditate on the mind's nature like that.

Toward beings who do not realize this,
Meditate with compassion toward their sickness and demons.
Whichever being is before you,
Settle in evenness and meditate on equality.
Meditating thus in all circumstances,
You will accomplish the nondual meaning.

Here are the oral lineage's meditation instructions:
Meditate on the union of all buddhas' bodies
And all beings' nature of mind
As a white syllable *Hung*
At your and others' hearts on the seat of a sun.
Imagine it as a drop of vital essence.
Think that this itself tames beings
And purifies all obscuring emotions.

This is the nondual meaning—
Deities have no intrinsic nature [apart from this].

After having meditated thus on compassion,
In inconceivable love,
Think this for beings' benefit:

At your heart, you the meditator
Imagine an eight-petaled lotus the size of a pea.
Then, between white and red clear lights
Stands the Fire God, a white syllable *Om*.
There is no material practice.
Do not think of anything at all.

Whoever meditates on this contemplation
Will accomplish nondual wisdom—
Ultimate enlightenment, clarity without [clinging to] awareness.

This subtle contemplative practice produces clairvoyance.
You will realize the nondual state.
The nature of joy will arise,
And you will attain the result, equanimity.

Some dwell in meditation on the four deities;
Some rely on verbal recitations.
They do not know nondual meditation.

These oral teachings given for others' benefit
Come from a lineage passed from face to face
And have been taught here by Rahula.

Rahula-gupta, who accomplished immortality, followed the predictions of his accomplished spiritual masters and left the sublime land of India at dawn. He traveled to Tibet by means of his miraculous powers and arrived at daybreak at Penyul Jokpo, the retreat place of the learned and accomplished Kyungpo Naljor. Rahula displayed some miracles and stayed for eleven months, during which he gave various instructions, both common and extraordinary. At the time of Rahula's return to India, Lama Shangpa accompanied him as far as Mangyul, where Rahula gave his disciple these oral instructions in six-syllable vajra verses:

The root of suffering
Is clinging to a self.

Renounce biased anger and desire;
Settle in the meaning of equanimity.

Life is impermanent
But doesn't end at death: you'll be reborn.
Be vigilant in relation to acts and their consequences
And diligent in keeping your tantric vows.

The abiding nature is interpenetration [of appearance and emptiness].
Always remember this:
Your rainbowlike body appears
Yet has no intrinsic nature.

The Buddha-like spiritual master
Provides what you need and desire in this life
And leads you on the path for the next—
Always remember him.

Until you reach stability,
Hectic distractions run wild;
Like a wounded deer,[8]
Meditate alone.

Sentient beings in this age of conflict
Harbor intense pride and jealousy;
Like a lamp in a vase,
Hide your qualities in your mind.

Having sung this, he flew up, circling in the sky, and instantly traveled
to the Vajra Seat [at Bodhgaya, India], where he led a vajra feast.

KYUNGPO NALJOR

Namo Guru!

THE RENOWN of the great learned and accomplished master Kyungpo Naljor, Tsultrim Gönpo, pervades every buddha's pure land. The three worlds' beings, including the gods, bow to touch their crowns to his toes' jewel mirrors. In the Himalayan region, he ranks beyond compare. Here is the essence of his life story in brief, in verses that he himself composed:

To spiritual masters, deities, dakinis, and protectors
I, Kyungpo Naljor, respectfully bow.

To help lineage holders of future generations,
I will relate a portion of my life story. Listen respectfully.

This humble monk was born in Gangkar Da, at Nyémo,
In the Kyungpo family, a clan of nobles.
My father's name was Kyungyal Takyé;
My mother, Goza Tashi Kyi.
When I entered her womb,
My parents and the people of my homeland became happy.

I left my mother's womb in the Tiger year.
At that time, the accomplished Indian master Amogha foretold:

This child, a reincarnate master, will travel to India.
He will collect the heart-essence of all scholars and accomplished
    masters
And lead beings to spiritual maturity and liberation.

He will guide his disciples with many emanations.
He will proclaim the Great Way's essence beyond extremes
And sound to the ten directions the lion's roar
Of the ultimate tantric teachings of indivisible bliss and
emptiness.

His body is that of Wheel of Supreme Bliss;
His speech, Mahamaya personified;
His mind, glorious Vajra Creator of Delight;
His sublime place of emanation, Matrix of Mystery;
And his secret place that holds bliss, Slayer of Lord of Death.
He will not only embody these deities' sacred circles
But will actually manifest them to his disciples.
Moreover, he will transform himself into various other deities
And guide countless numbers of difficult beings.

He will live for one hundred fifty years.
At the end of his life, as his final deed,
He will demonstrate many signs and miraculous displays
And depart to Blissful Pure Land.
He will attain enlightenment in that land praised by all buddhas
And turn the wheel of the Great Way Teachings.
All disciples of future generations who have faith in him
Will travel to that buddha's pure land: have no doubt of this!

This said, the accomplished master left for India,
Flying like a bird through the sky.

When I turned five, my parents related this prophecy to me.
By the age of ten, I was proficient in writing and calculation.
At twelve, following my family's tradition,
I learned Bön mind teachings.
[Later] I learned Great Completion and Great Seal.

Then, without material needs, I carried gems and gold powder
And underwent hardships without concern for my precious life
To travel seven times to Nepal and India.
I approached one hundred fifty Indian scholars,

Among whom fifty were particularly learned and accomplished.
Four were my especially exalted root spiritual masters;
Two were wisdom dakinis who received teachings
Directly from enlightenment's perfect rapture, the sixth Buddha Vajra
    Bearer.
I pleased them, received their ultimate teachings,
Resolved my misunderstandings, meditated single-mindedly,
And attained two forms of accomplishment—common and supreme.

This has been a short account of my life: listen respectfully!

Thus, as he said in his own words, the learned and accomplished master Shangpa Dugu-pa first became proficient in Bön and gained accomplishment. He then received instruction in Great Completion's three classes of teaching from Jungné Sengé and in Great Seal's Indian source tantras from Kor Nirupa. Although he became outstandingly proficient in all these traditions, his previous karmic connections awakened, and at the age of fifty he journeyed to India. There, from such masters as 150 learned and accomplished masters, four root masters, and two wisdom dakinis, he received and mastered an inconceivable number of instructions, both common and extraordinary, from the Lesser and Great Ways. He thereby attained every common and supreme accomplishment.

First, Kyungpo Naljor sang this song to relate his meeting with one of his four especially exalted spiritual masters, Dorjé Denpa, Punyakara-gupta:[9]

I, Kyungpo Naljor,
Feel deep and intense fear
Toward life's unbearable sufferings.
Such an endless wheel of life
Entails immeasurable suffering in life and death
And inconceivable anguish in the miserable realms.
I'm not afraid of death; I'm afraid of rebirth!

Karma pursues us in our rebirth—
We helplessly wander through the wheel of life.
For me or for all sentient beings,
There's no solution but to recognize death.
In the face of death that can come at any moment,
I dedicated my life to the Teachings,
And, without concern for my body or well-being,
I not only thought of going to Nepal
But went directly to the source of one thousand buddhas,
Vajra Seat,
Where our Teacher attained manifest enlightenment.
There, I met the one Conqueror Great Sage foretold
To be the second Buddha—
The illustrious master Dorjé Denpa.

Upon meeting him,
I offered five hundred measures of rare gold from Gulang.
Thinking that I had encountered Buddha himself,
My hair stood on end, tears streamed down my face,
And I felt deep, great devotion.
I joined my palms in prayer and made this request:

> I ask you to be the source for the doctrine—
> Preceptor for my full monastic ordination—
> And then to teach me its discipline.
> After I develop the mind of supreme awakening,
> I request teaching in the Great Way.
> After you bestow tantric empowerments that bring maturity,
> I request teachings that lead to liberation—creation
>   and completion.

After I had made this request,
The illustrious master Dorjé Denpa
Smiled and replied:

> In the hinterland of red-faced cannibal demons [Tibet],
> People's minds are troubled by wrong views and filled with
>   doubt.
> They search for many teachings but are unable to practice them.
> Without first gaining spiritual maturity, they try to help others.
> They criticize one another and harbor jealousy.
> They are but common persons who know Buddhist tales.
> You've come from a country such as that,
> A man endowed with faith, fearful of birth and death,
> And full of courage.
> Unmistaken, you've searched for sacred Teachings.
> You've traveled to India in hardship,
> Without regard for your well-being.

> Fortunate one, Kyungpo Naljor,
> In a past life in the northern Himalayas,
> You were a Listener known as Great Magician
> With unlimited miraculous powers.
> You tamed those with wrong views,
> Non-Buddhists, gods, nagas, noxious spirits,
> Ghouls, and groups of human beings.
> Surrounded by your circle of Listener-followers,
> You soared like a bird in the sky
> And passed unhindered over rivers and through mountains.
> You had various manifestations,
> Such as one or multiple appearances.
> You were a great foe-destroyer [arhat]
> And, as such, I and other Indian scholars
> Cannot be your preceptor.

> In the northern, snowy region
> Lives Langri Öden, of golden color,
> An emanation of Buddha Limitless Light.
> Go to see him

And ask him to be your preceptor for full monastic
   ordination.

Here in the central region of the supreme sacred place,
Maghada's Vajra Seat,
And in other places,
I will give as you have requested,
Any instruction that you wish in monastic discipline,
The transcendent perfections, and tantra.

Having said this, Dorjé Denpa acted as preceptor for Kyungpo Naljor's novice monk ordination. After he gave [him the monastic] name Tsultrim Gönpo, Lama Dorjé Denpa's nose bled, [a sign that] Kyungpo Naljor could not change his name. At that time, the master exclaimed, "Kyungpo Yogi Maha Pala Pala!" ["Kyungpo Naljor, you have gained the great result!"]

Dorjé Denpa first gave him the transmission of the Collection on Monastic Discipline [*vinaya*] and [Gunaprabha's] treatise of *The Main Discourse on Discipline*. He followed this with a gradual transmission of the discourses and tantras' major texts and instructions. His teaching that was outstanding compared to all others was based on the root explanatory tantra *Ocean of Jewels*—the empowerment and teachings for meditation on the Five Tantras' Deities in a single sacred circle. Here is [Kyungpo Naljor's song that relates] how he studied these instructions:

The special features of the five great deities'
Empowerments, tantras, means of accomplishment,
And supreme teachings are these:
The liberation tantra of Supreme Bliss
Teaches the cause, path, and result.
To accomplish great bliss,
The vajra of awakening
Is the practice of bliss.

These five ultimate teachers—

Glorious Matrix of Mystery;
The essence, Mahamaya;
The inner essence, Vajra Creator of Delight;
He who consumes great ecstasy,
Great magical manifestation,
Glorious Binder of the Wheel;
And wrathful Fearsome Vajra—

Represent the integration
Of tantras of means and knowledge.
Therefore, even the empowerment's initial path of maturation
Has outer, inner, and secret levels.

The path itself has two phases—
Creation and completion.
Creation is appearances; completion is emptiness.
They are inseparable, merged like the moon and water.
The completion phase includes your own body, the other's body,
And their merging in inseparable bliss and emptiness.

The result is common and supreme accomplishment.
Common accomplishments are eight activities and eight great feats.
Supreme accomplishments, enlightenment's four bodies and
    their acts,
Arise of themselves, spontaneously guiding others according
    to their needs.

Anyone with a pure karmic connection [to this teaching],
Who energetically practices it single-mindedly, without distraction,
And who keeps the vows, will definitely attain [these results].

Your own body constitutes the path of means;
The other's body, the seal of activity.
This sublime, vital instruction for integrating pleasure on the path
Comes through a sublime lineage:

The exalted master Nagarjuna,
Foretold by Buddha;
The one known as Kampala,
Who attained accomplishment by relying on luminosity;
Great Kukuripa,
Who manifested his consorts in the form of dogs;
The one known as Luyipa,
Who gained accomplishment by eating fish entrails;
And the one blessed by the high deities,
Illustrious Harikéla.

Dombipa, Kusulu,
And Mahavajra
Gathered the successive lineages through these masters.

The lineage came to me
Through these masters: the one known as Shri Jnana,
Vairochana Raksheeta,
The adept known as Sumati,
Tathagata Raksheeta,
Amoghani-vajra,
And illustrious Dorjé Denpa.

Then, from the noble masters Shri Jnana, Vairochana Raksheeta, and
Dakini Kanakashri, Kyungpo Naljor received an uncountable number of
teachings on the discourses, the path of characteristics, as well as on the
outer and inner tantras' meditations and profound instructions. At the
time of his departure for Tibet, Kyungpo Naljor visited his master Dorjé

Denpa at the summit of Mount Malaya and offered him thirteen measures of gold. While they performed offerings on the tenth lunar day, signs appeared and a prophecy was given, as this song relates:

Flowers fell like rain from the sky.
Gods and dakinis filled the horizon.
Sounds, lights, and rainbows stirred
As we made offerings to the deities.
Dorjé Denpa sang this:

Son of enlightenment's family, return to Tibet.
Liberate many sentient beings,
Your disciples in the snowy region.
One of your lineage holders, a yogi,
Will spread these teachings in the future.
He will receive the transmission of these teachings
And maintain an altruistic attitude.
Regardless of what happens,
He will teach the unerring path of the bodhisattvas.
He will reach the stage of nonstatic transcendence
[And lead] many to gradual realization of the meaning.

The four major philosophical systems[10]
Delineate the difference
Between the Way of Characteristics and the Vajra Way,
The path of the cause and the path of the result.

The stages of [valid cognition], direct perception, and inference
Produce the four great proofs,
Which establish the three characteristics.
That is the graded path of debate.

The Way of the Transcendent Perfections and the Vajra Way
Have the thirty-seven aspects of awakening in common
And differences in the five paths.

To apply the pith instructions' concise meaning
Is known as the stages of meditative practice,

The second graded path.
It actualizes what is known as the path of seeing—
Timeless manifest wisdom
Untouched by wrong views.

Texts that present the meaning free from extremes
As integral union
Enter the great Middle Way.
They teach the path of training
On which tranquillity, insight, and meditative states increase.
This is known as the sublime path of mind.[11]

Your realization will equal mine;
My life was foretold by Buddha.
You will go from here
To the Buddha's Blissful Pure Land.

Don't be discouraged by the age of conflict's beings,
Who are difficult to guide.
Meditate on the mind of awakening.
At the place of a self-manifest configuration of Supreme Bliss,
Ten of thousands of your disciples will appear.

Kyungpo Naljor then returned to Tibet and helped others for a while. He found a vein of gold that had overflowed in Gulang and was able to take a lot for himself. He brought the gold with him on his return to Nepal and India. From many learned and accomplished masters, such as Dorjé Denpa, Conqueror Métripa, Dha Bodhisattva, the noble woman Ratnadévi, Sumati-kirti, and the great Nepalese master Pamting-pa, he received an infinite number of instructions, such as profound teachings and the cycle of the Swift Awakened Protector.

These teachings did not satisfy him, and he carried five hundred measures of gold while traveling east, west, south, and north, throughout India.
"Which accomplished master has met the Buddha directly?" he asked. The
scholars and accomplished masters he met replied with the same answer:
"Pandit Naro's sister, the wisdom dakini known as Niguma, has reached
awakening's three pure stages and can receive instruction directly from
Buddha Vajra Bearer." "Where does she live?" he asked. They replied, "If
your vision is pure, you can see her face anywhere. If your vision is impure,
you will never find her no matter where you look, since she has reached
awakening's pure stages and has attained a rainbow body. Nevertheless,
sometimes she appears in the great charnel ground of Sosa Park forest, to
lead a group of dakinis in vajra feasts."

On his merely hearing the dakini's name, devotion welled up in
Kyungpo Naljor; he was moved to tears and his hair stood on end. He left
straightaway for the charnel ground at Sosa Park forest, reciting the *Namo
Buddha* prayer as he walked. There, a dark-brown dakini hovered in space,
at a distance of seven palm trees' height. She wore bone ornaments and carried a trident and a skull cup in her hands. She displayed various forms,
such as single and multiple, as she danced. Seeing her, Kyungpo Naljor
thought, "This must be Dakini Niguma!" and he offered prostrations, circled her a few times, and requested true profound instruction.

"I'm a cannibal dakini! When my group arrives, they'll devour you.
You'd better flee quickly!"

Again he offered her prostrations and circumambulations. "Please give
me teaching in the tantras!" he begged.

"To ask for Great Way tantric teaching, you need gold," she replied. "If you have some, give it to me." He offered her five hundred measures of gold, but she threw it into the forest.

He thought, "Is she really a cannibal dakini?! She's thrown all my gold away; I have no more!"

The dakini then glanced up into space and her entourage of countless dakinis appeared from the sky. Some erected a three-tiered celestial palace in an instant; some constructed a sand mandala; and some gathered the articles for a vajra feast offering. On that full moon night, Niguma bestowed the empowerments of Illusory Body and Lucid Dream.

At the end of the empowerment, she said, "Humble Tibetan monk, come up here!" Through the dakini's miraculous power, they instantly rose to a height of three fathoms. He saw [below them] a small mountain of gold, above which circled a group of dancing dakinis. From each of the mountain's four sides, golden rivers flowed. "Is this gold mountain in India?" he asked, "Is it an emanation of the dakinis?" She replied with this song:

When you realize that your many thoughts of anger and desire,
Which churn the sea of existence,
Have no intrinsic nature,
Everything becomes a land of gold, my child.

When you meditate that magiclike phenomena
Are like a magical illusion,
You will attain magiclike manifest enlightenment;
This through the force of devotion!

She gave him the empowerment for the Five Tantras' Deities and infinite numbers of their meditations and teachings. In particular, she gave him guidance in the Six Doctrines once during his dreams and three times in waking life. She sealed the lineage as a single-disciple transmission for seven generations [from Buddha Vajra Bearer] and promised that she would bless and give prophecy to each successive lineage holder.

Following this, Kyungpo Naljor again carried five hundred measures of gold to western India and asked, "What spiritual master has actually seen the Buddha?" Thirteen accomplished masters, including Pandit Lalitavajra, Aryadéva, and Dakini Sumati told him, "We'll first give you empowerment and profound instruction, then we'll give you our prophecy." Kyungpo Naljor offered them five hundred measures of gold and received many empowerments and teachings. Then they said, "The wisdom dakini known as Sukasiddhi is the root master of ten of us. In particular, she taught Aryadéva the inner practice of Buddha Selfless One: in seven months, he reached the realization of awakening's eighth stage. She received instruction directly from Buddha Vajra Bearer and Buddha Selfless One. She will bless you and teach you her profound instructions," they predicted.

"Where is she?" he asked.

"If your vision is pure, you can see that dakini anywhere. If your vision is impure, you'll never see her wherever you look. Sometimes you might find her at the place that brings happiness, known as Medicinal Sandalwood Grove. On the tenth day of the lunar month, she teaches by leading dakinis' vajra feasts, and sometimes she teaches through words. Go there and pray to her. She'll give you the full four empowerments as well as all her profound instructions and subsequent guidance."

Kyungpo Naljor carried five hundred measures of gold and traveled to the forest that brings happiness, while reciting the *Namo Buddha-ya* prayer. A white dakini with hair flowing down her back hovered in space above the sandalwood forest. Her two hands made a gesture to symbolize the unborn nature. A group of dakinis surrounded her; she sat in the center of rainbow light. When he saw her, Kyungpo Naljor's hair stood on end and his eyes filled with tears. Joy like that of awakening's first stage arose within him, and he had an experience of uncontaminated bliss.

He threw many flowers to her, such as blue lotuses, lotuses, and water lilies; he offered her many hundreds and thousands of prostrations and circumambulations, and asked for her teachings. The dakini replied with this song:

> Virupa, Buddha Selfless One,
> And Buddha Vajra Bearer gave me direct instruction
> In tantra's manifest path—
> The four empowerments that bring maturity
> And creation and completion's phases that liberate.
>
> This you ask me to teach, offering rare gems and gold powder,
> Joining your palms in respect, extending your body in prostration,
> And placing my lowly foot on the crown of your head.
> Now I will free you.
> What you'll receive today is the very best.
>
> Child of enlightenment, you're amazing!
> Child of enlightenment, you're amazing!
> Child of enlightenment, you're amazing!
> I will manifestly bless your disciples,
> Their disciples,
> And all your lineage holders of future generations.
> They will go to the pure celestial realms.

She first gave him the full four empowerments in an emanated sacred circle, then taught the secret practice of the circle of emanation at the navel, its creation and completion phase meditations, along with every vital instruction.

Kyungpo Naljor comments, "This was wisdom dakini Sukasiddhi's first great kindness: she granted me the full four empowerments in an emanated sacred circle. Her later great kindness was to become inseparable from a goddess and to be my secret consort. Her final great kindness was to give me all her profound instructions, to foretell that I would attain awakening's fourteenth stage in Blissful Pure Land; to nurture my disciples, their disciples, and all who hold my lineage; and to foretell that they would go to the pure celestial realms of bliss and emptiness. Therefore, the holders of my lineage will be particularly outstanding and will all be of the very highest level of cultivation [of merit and wisdom]."

Then Kyungpo Naljor received tantras and teachings from countless numbers of masters, including powerful dakinis, such as Samantabhadri; and powerful learned and accomplished yogis, such as Sukavajra, Lalitavajra, and Atayavajra. He resolved his doubts and pleased them with offerings of flowers of gold. When he made copious festival offerings at Vajra Seat, prodigious, amazing signs appeared. Everyone, high and low, in Land of the Exalted joined in a chorus of praises to him.

Upon his return to Tibet, he received full monastic ordination from the spiritual guide Langri Tangpa, an emanation of Buddha Limitless Light.

While he was in retreat in Penyul Jokpo, Rahula-gupta, who accomplished immortality, arrived by means of miraculous powers and gave Kyungpo Naljor unlimited teaching. During a later vajra feast, [Rahula] sang this song to give eight aspects of counsel for minor necessities:

These dualistic thoughts are really out of control!
For them, I have teachings on the three dissolutions.
They'll turn back dualism's attack.
Now, dualistic experience, do as you please!

This great god Pékar is really out of control!
For him, I have teachings of the three ropes.
They'll turn back the great gods' attack.
Now, great gods, do as you please!

These evil naga spirits are really out of control!
For them, I have teachings on the joined skulls.
They'll turn back the naga spirits' attack.
Now, naga spirits, do as you please!

These night ghouls are really out of control!
For them, I have teachings on the nectar vital essence.

They'll turn back the demons' attack.
Now, ghouls, do as you please!

This evil curse is really out of control!
For it, I have teachings of the flat, black stone.
They'll turn back the curse's attack.
Now, evil curse, do as you please!

This evil Lord of Death is really out of control!
For him, I have teachings on the skeleton's liberation.
They'll turn back Lord of Death's attack.
Now, Lord of Death, do as you please!

These evil planetary spirits are really out of control!
For them, I have teachings in the circle of the tortoise.
They'll turn back the planetary spirits' attack.
Now, Vishnu's forms, do as you please!

Previously, you didn't bless your voice,
Thus your recitation of mantras did not produce any power.
For this, I have teachings in the glorious A-li Ka-li.
Now have no fear that you won't accomplish the mantra.

Then Kyungpo Naljor went with three thousand disciples to Shang, where beginning at Zhang-Zhong, they constructed 108 monastic centers in the course of three years. When Kyungpo Naljor turned the Teachings' great wheel, fifty thousand monks assembled from central, western, and eastern Tibet. During this time, the majority became distracted; they disregarded study and meditation. Kyungpo Naljor took them sightseeing; he emanated many entertaining and enticing gods and goddesses of the Heaven of the Thirty-Three. The monks were delighted and became attached to them. Then he emanated many death demons whose work was to kill and to chop up [bodies], causing the monks to become terrified, panic, and faint. Kyungpo Naljor then sang this song to introduce the nature of reality:

Objects of attachment and aversion
All emerge from your own mind.
A meditator knows his experience
Of death demons' forms, such as cannibal spirits,
Who carry many weapons aloft
And will end his life right now,
To be a magical illusion, and is released.

Many enticing goddesses bedecked in jewelry,
Singing, and playing beautiful music
Might surround you,
Yet if you are convinced that your own experience is a magical illusion,
They cannot bind you.

He gave this and other teachings as well as instruction in the intermediate state between death and rebirth. All the monks applied themselves to study and meditation.

Once Rongpo Géshé Könchok Gyal made many offerings to Kyungpo Naljor and said, "You've gone to India three times and relied upon 150 learned and accomplished masters, including your four root teachers. It is said that you've become an accomplished master yourself and you've realized that appearances have no intrinsic nature. I ask you, go back and forth through that cliff; then sit in space."

Kyungpo Naljor passed uninhibited through the rock, sat in space, and displayed some miraculous powers, such as assuming single and multiple forms. Rongpo Géshé and the monks were moved to extreme faith. "What teachings can we meditate upon to attain such qualities?" they asked, to which Kyungpo Naljor replied,

When you cultivate the experience that magiclike phenomena
Are like a magical illusion,
You will attain magiclike manifest enlightenment.

Phenomena appear but are unreal.
Immature persons hold them to be real and are deluded.
Although they do not exist, phenomena appear: how amazing!

He gave them this and other teachings. As a result, after eleven months, Rongpo Géshé saw the deity's face and realized appearances' lack of reality.

Kyungpo Naljor became aware that his attendant Rinchen Dorjé had slipped into slight wrong views, thinking that his master was an ordinary, self-centered individual. Kyungpo Naljor had him meditate for seven days on [Vajrasattva's] hundred-syllable mantra and on the Purifying Ah of Inner Space. When Rinchen Dorjé returned to his master's room, he saw Kyungpo Naljor's body as the thirteen-deity configuration of weapon-bearing Vajra Creator of Delight, with circles of the Five Tantras' Deities at his body's five energy centers. When Rinchen Dorjé left the room, he saw forms of Kyungpo Naljor teaching on 108 thrones. At this sight he sang,

> Your body of enlightenment is the nine deities.
> The Five Tantras' Deities stand at your body's five centers.
> On each of one hundred eight thrones
> Sits one of your bodies, each perfectly captivating.
> You make the Great Way beyond extremes resound
> And demonstrate many manifesations in the ten directions.
> Emanation from the hearts of a sea of conquerors,
> Spiritual master, Buddha incarnate, you I praise.
> Please keep sentient beings, who are deluded in ignorance,
> On the true path.

Following this, Rinchen Dorjé never had even a moment's wrong view and served as an attendant who would do whatever Kyungpo Naljor asked.

Once, when Kyungpo Naljor taught *The Five Texts by Bodhisattva Loving-Kindness* and *The Secret General Tantra*, monks from central, western, and eastern regions of Tibet fell into discord over who would serve their master food. As the situation worsened, nearing a breach of the tantric commitments, the gods of the Four Classes of Great Kings appeared and sang this:

Rebirth in a land without freedom
And separation from places of freedom
Arise from disharmony,
While [the effects of broken] tantric vows are even more serious.

Those capable of the hardship of living in harmony
Can easily attain enlightenment in one lifetime.
Therefore, the gods assembled here
Will serve you during your teaching.

Come sit at seven palm trees' height, or at one!
Make the Teachings rain from the sky!
Sound the great conch of the Teachings!
Raise the Teachings' banner!

Kyungpo Naljor vowed not to eat human food for seven months and sat at one palm-tree height in space. For seven months, he gave the complete teaching of *The Five Texts by Bodhisattva Loving-Kindness* and *The Secret General Tantra*. Many gained understanding of the Middle Way's view. In a chorus, the gods proclaimed three times, "You have fulfilled the intentions of your master, Dorjé Denpa! You have satisfied the gods! You have liberated human beings! You have done great things for the Buddha's doctrine! Ah la la!" A great rain of flowers fell and the gods disappeared.

Once, Buddha Boundless Light showed Kyungpo Naljor the configuration of Blissful Pure Land and sang this:

This is your last rebirth.
In Blissful Pure Land,
You will vanquish demons and their hordes,
Gain manifest awakening, and turn the wheel of the Teachings.

Whoever trains in your footsteps
Or merely hears the name of Buddha Boundless Light
Will be reborn in Blissful Pure Land
Through great miraculous power.

The next three holders of your lineage
Will travel from pure land to pure land—
Blissful and Joyous—
And there attain manifest awakening.

The Buddha gave him this prophecy and many others.

Kyungpo Naljor heard these instructions from light that radiated from Bodhisattva Great Compassion and the two deities beside him:

If compassion does not arise unhindered
From phenomena's unborn nature,
You will be unable to bring the six realms' sentient beings,
Your venerable mothers, to maturity and liberation.

Therefore, whether walking, lying down, or sitting,
Hold fast with the hook of undistracted mindfulness
To thoughts of your mothers' kindness and sufferings.
Develop great, immeasurable compassion.

Cool streams of compassion
From the great snow mountain of love
Quench the fires of obscuring emotions.
I embody great compassion.

The bodhisattva gave this and other teachings on the meditation of universal compassion.

Kyungpo Naljor went to Oddiyana and there received empowerment into the five exalted female deities' sacred circle. Further, Lion-Faced Dakini, surrounded by dakinis of the four classes, sang this vajra song:

Vajra Dakini protects you from obstacles.
Jewel Dakini increases human and material wealth.
Lotus Dakini gathers consorts.
Activity Dakini accomplishes all acts.

Once under the sway of craving,
You fall under the self-dakinis' control
And any unwanted external event can occur:
Know the dakinis to be your own mind!

Knowledge of the mind's essence
And its nonconceptual nature is the vajra;
Vajra Dakini protects you from obstacles.

Contentment with no needs is a precious treasure;
Jewel Dakini provides all you need and desire.

Freedom from desire and discursive thought is the lotus;
Lotus Dakini attracts the seal [of activity].

Acts neither come into being nor cease;
Activity Dakini accomplishes all your acts.

Adepts who do not know this
Can practice [the dakinis] for an eon yet not accomplish them.
Therefore, to know the dakinis as your own mind
Is the supreme vital instruction.

The dakinis also gave him the profound instructions of the three rains and the three gatherings.[12]

Finally, as predicted by spiritual masters, deities, and dakinis, Kyungpo Naljor taught for some years to the ultimate assembly—eighty thousand persons; he gave every teaching to his six ultimate disciples; and he reached the ultimate in longevity—150 years. At that time, he considered departing for the ultimate pure land, Blissful, but infinite numbers of gods, nagas, and nonhuman spirits, including the Four Great Kings, the king of nagas Unheated, and the king of celestial musicians Five Topknots, gathered, presented Kyungpo Naljor with inconceivable clouds of offerings, and begged him to not transcend suffering. To this he replied,

> As my masters and deities foretold,
> The three ultimate events have arrived.
> Now I will go to the ultimate pure land,
> The realm of Blissful,
> Where there is unlimited pure enjoyment—
> I have no need for worldly gold or silver!
>
> If you have faith in me,
> Pray to be reborn in Blissful.
> You will be reborn there: have no doubt!
>
> There, on a single atom, all realms appear,
> Inconceivable and complete.
> The realm is pure;
> The Teacher, the entourage, and the teaching are infinite.
> This is the realm of Buddha Boundless Light,
> Blissful Pure Land.
>
> Therefore, have no doubt;
> Pray to be reborn in that realm.

With this and other teachings, he satisfied them.

Kyungpo Naljor attended a vajra feast on the fourteenth day [of the ninth lunar month]. There he displayed many forms in space and said,

> Alas! Composite phenomena are impermanent!
> Like clouds in the sky, they meet and part.
> To hold unreal, illusory phenomena to be real
> Is to deceive yourself.
>
> My body is the Conqueror's body:
> Do not see it as subject to birth or death.

My voice is the Conqueror's speech:
It is inexpressible, unborn, self-manifest sound.

My mind is the Conqueror's mind:
It is endowed with nonconceptual, timeless wisdom.

The sky filled with rainbows and music, and a great rain of flowers fell.

RINCHEN TSÖNDRU

T HE LEARNED and accomplished master Kyungpo Naljor had six great spiritual heart sons upon whom he bestowed the entire body of his profound instruction.[13] Among them, one alone was the designated inheritor of the lineage, the last of the six, known as Mokchok-pa Rinchen Tsöndru. Immediately after his life, he attained manifest, complete enlightenment in the eastern pure land, Radiant. This great bodhisattva in his final life saw that explanations in intellectual terminology were pointless. Therefore, he practiced the extensive profound teachings he received from such meditation masters as Khampa Aseng and Burgom Nakpo, but he failed to reach perfection in his meditation. The learned and accomplished master Kyungpo Naljor accepted him as a disciple and gave him the entire transmission.

First, he meditated for two years at Dingma, where he reached perfect realization in the practices of Illusory Body, Lucid Dream, and Clear Light. Following this, since the Shangpa master [Kyungpo Naljor] had passed away, he went to the spiritual master Doctor from Dakpo [Gampopa] to resolve doubts in his virtuous practice. Gampopa said that they had been teacher and disciple during many lifetimes. He was very pleased with Rinchen Tsöndru and gave him many profound teachings, which helped Rinchen Tsöndru resolve his misunderstandings of Great Seal's view. His experience and realization's energy increased in every respect. During a dream, as he emanated and transformed appearances, he sang this vajra song:

Appearances flow unceasing from the unborn expanse.
Merely thought, they rise unhindered.
Not distorted by anything,
The illusory body arises from the expanse of my awareness.
My concerns related to this life are forgotten and vanish.

My body of ripened karma is the Conqueror's body:
Precious noble master, you introduced me to this!

My mental body is the body of ultimate enlightenment:
Precious noble master, you introduced me to this!

My body of habitual patterns is the Conqueror's body:
Precious noble master, you introduced me to this!

Rinchen Tsöndru said from that time forth he never again experienced the arising of concerns related to this life.

Then, as his masters had advised, he remained in the mountains, thinking that he should set his sights either on death or on enlightenment. While he stayed at Mokchok Cliff for twelve years [in retreat] with little food, Sukasiddhi arrived and sang this:

Until you reach the nature of reality,
Human nourishment obscures your experience.
Cut your bonds to food and clothing;
Eat the food of nonconceptual meditation.

She repeated this three times; he cut his attachment to food and clothing. Inconceivable meditative states arose.

During that time, he sang many vajra songs, such as this one, which relates how the seven possessions of a universal monarch are complete within the meditator:

I tried to defeat my foes and to protect my friends,
Yet there was no time I finally overcame my enemies
And no time I finally satisfied my friends.
Now my principal activity is to live without friends or foes.

I tried to propitiate gods and to dispel demons,
Yet there was no time I finally satisfied the gods

And no time the demons finally left.
Now my principal activity is to live without gods and demons.

I pursued emptiness,
Yet I couldn't see the limit of its view.
Now my principal activity is to cut the single root of mind.

In one who is the lowest in human society,
The best in spiritual qualities has arisen.

If we don't attend to the correct meaning,
We lose ourselves striving for illusory wealth in business.

If we don't search for what helps our mind,
We lose ourselves pursuing intellectual knowledge.

If we don't maintain a humble life,
We busy ourselves with the haughtiness of the outwardly pure or
    mighty.

If we don't wander, begging aimlessly,
We'll mistakenly destroy anthills [while building a home] in an
    empty valley.

If we don't live alone in meditation practice,
We busy ourselves with acting as the leader of many.

This useful free and fully endowed human body
Can be wasted in meaningless acts.

This precious jewel of the mind
Can be lost when sunk in the mire of existence.

This nectar of the master's instructions
Can be lost under the sway of distraction.

This radiant flame of nonduality
Can die in thoughts' windy breezes.

This great bliss in the conduct of impartial taste
Can be smothered by the demons of the eight worldly concerns.

This pure land of the conquerors, your own body,
Can be lost when given ordinary work.

In the meditator's happy state,
The six senses' appearances arise as an aid.

Since I have no fear of either existence or transcendence,
I consider my own mind to be a monarch.
This sovereign who has realized his own mind
Owns the ornaments of the seven precious possessions.

I didn't pursue intellectual knowledge;
I felt devotion toward the profound meaning.
Certainty rose from the depths of my mind—
That's the precious minister's best advice.

The holy spiritual master himself
Spoke the profound teachings.
"Resolve your misunderstandings of the tantras and transmissions
In the lineage of noble Naropa's children," he said.
I gathered all the major pith instructions
And cut the root of existence and transcendence.
Ignorance vanished into the unborn state;
The precious supreme horse carried the five poisons to the absolute
    expanse.

Since all busyness where many gather
Amounts to distraction, I remain in retreat.
Making a basis of both creation and completion,
I train in my own mind's display.
Like a young garuda who soars in space,
Wherever I go is the precious wheel.

The six senses' appearances have suddenly vanished,
And in this I am content.

With no joy in many possessions,
I feel no pleasure or sorrow toward praise or blame.
Even in the face of Lord of Death's miraculous displays,
I have no fear, since I know them as appearances of my own mind.
The mind's nature is free from both permanence and transience;
Neither birth nor death frightens me.
Isn't that the precious general who conquers misleading thoughts?

For the meditator who realizes this,
Appearances arise as a teacher
In the mind's primordial purity.
This is like the precious elephant that moves armies.

Anger and desire vanish into the state without mental activity;
A bird flying in space has no support.
The six senses that arise are fleeting.
When I don't cling to them, they become an aid,
A grand, unimpeded sight,
Beautiful ornaments worn by the precious queen.

For the meditator who has realized this,
The mind's home has no boundaries
And is all-pervasive, like space.
In what cannot be identified, like the horizon,
The door to luminosity has no limits.
Since the absolute expanse and wisdom are inseparable,
The continuity of enlightenment's three bodies has no bounds,
Like the effortless sun
Whose rays shine in every direction.
That is the precious jewel that fulfills needs, hopes, and desires.

These seven precious possessions' supreme wealth
Are the meditator's great ornaments.
We can be separated from our bodies, but not from them.
I consider them our sacred wealth.
I have no need to aspire to the wealth of kings,
Nor do I take pleasure in scholars' technical terms.
This is no joke: I stake my life on it!

The song of the experience of six attitudes:

At first, I resolved my misunderstanding,
Yet doubt has now arisen.
The view seems to have deceived the meditator.
Now, may I remain forever without formulations.

At first, I realized the unborn state,
Yet fear has now arisen.
Meditation seems to have deceived the meditator.
Now, may I remain forever undistracted.

At first, I acted without grasping,
Yet attachment has now arisen.
Conduct seems to have deceived the meditator.
Now, may I remain forever without grasping.

At first, I rested one-pointedly,
Yet hope and fear have now arisen.
The result seems to have deceived the meditator.
Now, may I remain forever in spontaneous presence.

At first, I made rapid progress,
Yet hesitation has now arisen.
The eight worldly concerns seem to have deceived the meditator.
Now, may I remain forever irrational.

At first, I renounced friends and family,
Yet concern for my image has now arisen.[14]
Now, may I not care about my position.

At first, faith welled up in me,
Yet complacency has now arisen.
Laziness seems to have deceived the meditator.
Now, may I remain forever diligent and constant in contemplative
    practice.

May I not be weary or discouraged in faith and respect
Toward the only spiritual gods, the Three Jewels.
May I feel continual respect and devotion
Toward my sole father, the holy spiritual master.

May I not add any polluting words
To the vital essence of his heart's counsel.
Meditation is more precious than scholarship;
May I live alone and cultivate meditative experience.

To feel dissatisfaction with the faults of existence
And to feel interest in the teachings of transcendence is difficult.
To believe in the teachings on acts and their consequence
And to have unflagging faith is difficult.
To reject concern with sickness or pain
And to put this human life to service is difficult.
To find a compassionate teacher
Imbued with the scriptures, logic, and pith instructions is difficult.
To find a student who renounces all busyness and distraction
To cultivate meditative experience is difficult.
To renounce all anger and desire
And to have compassion serving others is difficult.
To be free from dualistic thought
In one-pointed meditation is difficult.

This counsel of eight difficult points
Is precious for any spiritual person.

Few in a hundred have them all.
That's why attaining awakening is difficult!

When misunderstanding is resolved,
This is called the view beyond extremes, is it not?
To it scripture and logic add a great ornament.

When discursive thought arises as the body of ultimate
    enlightenment,
This is called self-manifest meditation, is it not?
To it experience adds a great vital point.

When the six senses are released in their own ground,
This is called conduct free from attachment, is it not?
To it timely [conduct] adds a great ornament.

Connection to the experience of emptiness
Is called the oral lineage's profound instruction, is it not?
To it empowerment adds a great ornament.

When clear appearances arise in emptiness,
This is called progress on the paths and stages, is it not?
To it the paths' signs add a great ornament.

Taking mind to the point of exhaustion
Is called enlightenment in a single lifetime, is it not?
To it enlightenment's four bodies add a great ornament.

Individuals endowed with three characteristics[15]
Are called lineage-bearing spiritual masters, are they not?
To them profound instructions add a great ornament.

Individuals imbued with faith and great understanding
Are called worthy disciples, are they not?
To them respect and devotion add a great ornament.

On the jewel mountain of the spiritual master,
Springs of sacred Teachings flow.

Those who drink from them with unflagging faith
Will surely free themselves from every fault.

Within the vase of this composite body,
A coemergent lamp shines.
Those content to gain it in meditation
Will surely see clearly ultimate enlightenment within and without.

On the mountain of this illusory body,
The lion cub of consciousness plays.
Those who know training in nonattachment to the six senses
Will surely overpower existence and transcendence.

In the nest of ignorance,
The young garuda of consciousness dwells.
Those who can use the wings of means and knowledge
Will surely soar in the six realms' skies.

Look, look with the mind at the outer world.
Having looked at the outer world,
You'll see that like a mirror's reflections
Appearances have no intrinsic nature.

Look, look with the mind at the inner mind.
Having looked at the inner mind,
You'll see that like a candle untroubled by the breeze
Mind is clarity without discursive thoughts.

Look, look with the mind between outside and in.
Having looked between outside and in,
You'll see that like the sun rising in the sky
Marks [of dualistic experience] unravel in their own ground.

Meditate, meditate with the mind on the profound path of means:
Having meditated on the profound path of means,
You'll see that as if led by an excellent guide
Mind reaches the place it desires.

Meditate, meditate with the mind on Great Seal:
Having meditated on Great Seal,
You see that like a spreading forest fire
Whatever appears helps you.

Turn, turn the mind to begging aimlessly:
Having begged aimlessly,
You'll see that like snow falling on a lake
Your thoughts dissolve straightaway.

Thirteen disciples of [the Doctor from] Dakpo came to this noble master and asked for instruction in Great Seal to prevent harm from discursive thoughts. He replied with these words:

In the nature of reality that neither comes into being nor ceases,
What can be called a thought?
States with and without thought should be viewed
Like water and water bubbles.

With this and other instructions, they realized thought to be without a source or a root.

One géshé from Lo-wo asked for a technique to see the face of whatever deity he practiced. Rinchen Tsöndru replied with these words:

Banish worldly activity from your mind.
Without doubt or divided attention,
Meditate on the deity's form,
Clarity without discursive thought.
Don't engage in endless conversations;
Recite mantras—sound and emptiness.
If you do this, you will quickly see the deity's form.
Have no doubt!

This advice inspired strong certainty in the géshé; after three months of meditation, he saw Tara's face.

The following account is taken from this master's autobiography:

> One summer, a great famine beset us. The starving local people decided among themselves, "We must ask the lama's advice." [However,] when [other starving villagers] stole the offerings sent and overpowered the monks, [the monastery's] protector yak turned [in anger] toward the village. The monks prepared to do battle [with the villagers], so one day I called them together. First I put on my cloak, hoisted a sack of texts on my back, and sang this:

If you ask advice from the guide, the noble spiritual master,
You'll become skillful at treading the path.

If you turn your attention to the sacred Teachings,
You'll have taken good advice.

If you resolve your misunderstandings within,
You'll develop certainty.

If every act is related to the sacred Teachings,
Your virtuous activity will increase.

If you allow others to win,
You'll train your mind.

If you don't control others' minds but tame your own,
You'll have little concern for your public image.

If you always consider yourself a guest wherever you live,
You'll have little attachment.

If you accept the poorest in both food and clothing,
You'll be relaxed in body and mind.

After I sang this song, I left for a hermitage, the monks gave up their battle plans, and the protector yak turned away [from the village]. Bodhisattva Great Compassion remarked,

You've doused a great pyre of anger
With the cool waters of love:
Well done, o yogi!
Anger and desire lie at the root
Of existence and transcendence:
Spurn attachment, o yogi!

I then entered retreat during the Horse month and did not eat human food nor give empowerments. As a result, the appearances of luminosity increased and I was able to know all the monks' acts and the qualities or faults of the first and latter parts of their lives. In compassion and affection toward them, I gave each appropriate advice. Most developed certainty in my counsel and reached perfection in their virtuous practice. Nevertheless, many, such as Ngomshö Lachö, did not listen. He decided to return home to a lay person's life. As this would prevent my seeing him at death, I asked him not to leave. In sadness that he did not heed my request, I took his hand and sang this song:

Buddha is sentient beings' ancestor;
The sacred Teachings are sentient beings' common wealth.
Once a faithful person receives his spiritual inheritance,
To decline such wealth is pointless.

The source of the buddhas of the three times
Is surely the lineage-holding spiritual master.
To have no respect and devotion for him who produces
What we need and desire in this life and the next is pointless.

.
To not apply ourselves in undistracted diligence
During what time remains in our lives,
But to waste life meaninglessly
Trying to help others who can't be satisfied is pointless.

The small sparrow of awareness
Will receive a reminder from Lord of Death.
Since we ride the acts we've cultivated in the past,
To act negatively is pointless.

Our impure aggregates are suffering's vessel,
The place where birth, aging, sickness, and death dwell.
Since we'll one day throw this body away like a broken clay pot,
To always harbor hope for it is pointless.

To not use for our own and others' benefit
Food and wealth that have an illusory nature,
But to remain trapped by past habits of greed
And to not make gifts or offerings is pointless.

When the demons of discursive thought arrive,
To not see them as an invitation [to realize] the nature of reality,
But to become anxious in fear
Of the body and mind separating [at death] is pointless.

During the four daily sessions, to not meditate undistracted
On tantric practices that accomplish all activity,
But to pass the time
Indulging in endless conversations is pointless.

To not meditate on the mind's nature, this wish-fulfilling jewel,
As never separate from enlightenment's three bodies,
But to pursue terminology,
Like a wild animal chasing a mirage, is pointless.

To not reach the nature of reality's firm land,
But to continually maintain self-clinging,

Grasping the illusory city of life's six realms
And to wander there endlessly is pointless.

Rinchen Tsöndru's vajra song of the view, meditation, and conduct:

Once you've realized the meaning beyond birth or cessation,
Your view can be higher than others or not; it doesn't matter.
Settle the mind in a state without a focal point.
To be without dualistic clinging is the view.

Once you've realized that enlightenment's three bodies never separate
    from you,
Your tranquillity can be stable or not; it doesn't matter.
Settle in a state without effort.
Clarity without distraction is meditation.

If you are undistracted whether walking, lying down, or sitting,
Your conduct can be coarse or not; it doesn't matter.
Settle in a state without fear.
To live without attachment is conduct.

Once you realize clarity without substantiality,
Your experience can blaze or not; it doesn't matter.
Settle in the inexpressible.
To have certainty is meditative experience.

Once you've realized the meaning beyond hope or fear,
You can attain ultimate enlightenment or not; it doesn't matter.
Settle in a state without anger or desire.
That which exists primordially is the result.

The vajra song of immortal mind:

The discourses, tantras, pith instructions, and experience
Teach the vital instruction of immortality, enlightenment without
    meditation.

By means of these teachings, this body of ripened karma
Automatically arises as the body of wisdom.

In the place of this body of ripened karma,
Meditate on the deity's body,
Vivid, without grasping.
This is inseparable from your mind.

Since the mind's essence is not existent,
What is there in it that can die?
What is called "death" is a concept.

Collections of thoughts
And the phenomena of existence and transcendence
Have no intrinsic existence.
What leaves [at death] and what ejects it
Are liberated in their own ground.
Consciousness is not ejected anywhere.

This is the supreme result, boundless immortality.
This teaching that bestows manifest enlightenment merely through
    recollection
Is the dakinis' vital heart: guard it as you do your life!

This concludes the song of the self-liberation of immortal mind, by Ratna
Virya [Rinchen Tsöndru]. I offered fifty measures of gold to Lama Shangpa
to receive the instruction, then gained this experience. *Iti.*

When Mokchok-pa Rinchen Tsöndru was about to transcend suffering,
he sang this advice to Drongbu Tsengö:

My son, if you've resolved your misconceptions concerning terms,
You'll have no need for intellectual teachings.
They're difficult to learn but easily forgotten.
The Teachings' eighty-four thousand gates
All lead to the mind's nature.
When reflecting on any instruction,

Settle in the abiding nature and the uncontrived innate state.
Know appearances to be mind.
The mind's nature is unborn;
If you realize the unborn, it is clear light.
Always give your attention to this.
Since the relation between act, cause, and interdependent arising
    is certain,
Practice this only, my child.

CHÖKYI SENGÉ

IN ALL HIS PAST LIVES, Kyergang-pa Chökyi Sengé was spiritually nourished by Bodhisattva Great Compassion, and in this life, his intense diligence in meditation led him to the supreme accomplishment of inseparability with that exalted bodhisattva. Chökyi Sengé gained effortless mastery, like the stream of a river, of the mind of awakening's two aspects. From the noble master Mokchok-pa, he received the exclusive transmission of the dakinis' lineage. Bodhisattva in his final lifetime before enlightenment, he attained enlightenment in the eastern pure land Lapis Light, as Transcendent Buddha Glory of Immaculate Space.

To this master, Öntön Kyergang-pa Chökyi Sengé, buddhas and their spiritual heirs bestowed infinite numbers of teachings, including the following:

Noble Tara sang:

> The vital point of Illusory Body is lack of intrinsic reality:
> Destroy your firm belief in the solidity of things.
> The vital point of Lucid Dream is directed intent:
> Integrate this with your daily life.
> The vital point of Clear Light is devotion:
> Pray.
> The vital point of benefiting others is compassion:
> Renounce self-centered bias.

and [on another occasion, she sang]:

> If you give up dualistic clinging,
> Your desire will be calmed within itself.
> If you recognize beings as your parents,

Your anger will unravel in its own ground.
If you maintain clarity without discursive thought,
Your stupidity will dissolve into the absolute expanse.
If you bind the unceasing three poisons in their own ground,
Without grasping them, they will surely be released there.
Watch the emotions self-liberate as they arise.

Bodhisattva Great Compassion sang:

Distractions of busyness are demons' impediments.
Until the myriad forms of desire and anger help your meditation,
Always remain in seclusion, far from harmful conditions.
It's wise to consider that life is short and to reflect on death.

The Five Tantras' Deities sang:

If the four empowerments are incomplete,
How can empowerment bring spiritual maturity?
If you don't meditate on the phase of creation inseparable [from the
    phase of completion],
It's impossible to gain liberation.
Since wishing for attainment does not yield results,
Regard self-liberation on arising as inseparable from enlightenment's
    three bodies.

When the spiritual master Mokchok-pa departed for the state of quiescence, the noble [Vajra Yogini] sang:

Like space that does not come into being nor die,
How can the master be subject to birth and death?
Your devotion will make him inseparable from you.
Don't be sad; continually pray.

The vajra song that introduces one's own mind as the spiritual master:

Guru Bodhichitta Nama-mi

Incomparable spiritual masters who introduce the nature of mind,
Who have reached the bounds of benefit for themselves and who
    serve others,
Whose impartial, omniscient compassion embraces all beings equally,
And who are imbued with kindness, to you I bow.
Spiritual masters who symbolize the nature of reality,
You dwell within the spiritual master of the dawning of the mind's
    nature.

The characteristics of the spiritual master of my own mind are these:
Not produced from causes, his nature is spontaneously present.
As he is not destroyed by conditions, antidotes have no effect on him.
He neither comes nor goes; he does not change in the past, present,
    or future.
He transcends expression's extremes, such as "real" or "imagined."
He has no substance that the five sense faculties can perceive.
Nonexistent, he is the source for the appearance of myriad forms.

You might try to see him, but you can't identify anything at all.
You might give up searching for him, but his nature appears
    anywhere.
He doesn't fall into categories of virtue or nonvirtue.

Exalted above all, he is attached to nothing.
Separate from everything, he is the basis of all.
Free from the intellect, he appears clearly beyond the intellect's
     bounds.
In his impartiality, an impartial multiplicity appears;
Yet even though it appears, its location is uncertain.
Therefore, it's not possible to affirm "This is he!" alone.
That's the nature of my spiritual master.

If I were to relate his life story, it would be like this:

This master is not subject to distance;
There is no sentient being he does not pervade.

Because his aspirations are pure,
There is no one who does not belong to his family.

Because his compassion is vast,
There is no one he has not placed in enlightenment's primordial state.

Because this master's acts are powerful,
He enters both existence and transcendence with complete mastery.

Because this master is not subject to change,
You might have wrong views about him, but he remains the same.

You've never been separated from this master for an instant.
Such a longtime companion, but so difficult to see!

Because this master is not subject to death,
He keeps constant vigil: how amazing!

As for such a spiritual master of your own mind,
Look at his face and recognize your own nature.
Pray to him without doubt or hesitation.
Develop devotion to him by placing your mind on its own
     uncontrived ground.
Serve him by dwelling continually within it.

Feed him the food of clarity and emptiness without grasping.
Offer him the drink of the realization of inseparable mindfulness and
    distraction.
Clothe him in the robe of knowledge of appearance and sound as
    magical illusion.
Place below him the carpet of uncontaminated bliss.
Have him wear the hat of unsought primordial presence.
Offer him the gifts of no clinging to whatever arises.

In his residence of omniscience, without clinging to a self,
Surrounded by his entourage of cyclic existence and transcendence,
To whom he is never joined nor separated,
He dwells continually throughout the three times
And continually manifests his self-appearing, relaxed, profound
    teachings.

How wonderful, this spiritual master of my own mind!
That you continue to nurture me reveals your extreme kindness.
Master, adept who trained in past lives, who has a strong karmic
    propensity,
How wonderful that your compassion still has not relinquished me!

Once you've relied on the master in this way,
His blessings will arise like this:

Even though you haven't fled the mire of existence, you're freed
    from it.
Even though you haven't turned toward enlightenment, you reach it.
You understand that existence and transcendence are neither bad
    nor good.

The difference between buddhas and sentient beings is realization and
    lack of realization.
To realize the mind's characteristics without error
And to have that conviction become manifest is called enlightenment.
Its qualities surpass the bounds of expression.

To rely on something else as your spiritual master will result in this:

You won't realize the mind's nature as it is,
But you'll mistakenly cling to that which it isn't.
In its wake, you'll commit acts that lead to suffering.
That's what's called a sentient being.

Now you can take care of yourself.
You don't have to retrace the wheel of life's past nor anticipate its
    future.
You can undertake the great effort of not accomplishing
    transcendence.
Claim the natural ground of the mind's nature and dwell there as
    you will.
You can't identify the mind's nature as "this" or "that,"
But if you haven't yet understood, you will, through training in this.

You can now gain satisfaction in that understanding.
Based on that satisfaction, this will happen:
You won't need to search for ultimate enlightenment's body, intrinsic
    emptiness.
You won't need to block what arises of itself, enlightenment's form
    bodies.
You won't need to create enlightenment's three bodies, the nature
    of mind's own movement.
You won't need to reject existence; it is cut at the root.
You won't need hope; your own mind is Buddha.
You won't need to meditate; it's that way primordially.

To those who say, "To do this is wrong!"
Or to adepts who watch the mind without distraction,
I say, "Why not free yourself from the intellect that watches
    the mind?"

To meditators who never separate themselves from continual
    meditation,
I say, "Why not free yourself from the meditator?"

To practitioners who always cultivate the mind of awakening,
I say, "Why not understand spontaneous nonmeditation?"

To adepts who watch without contrivance,
I say, "Why not come to some conclusion about your own mind?"

I relied on many qualified masters,
Yet each had his own piece of advice,
All of which led to the root, the mind.
Therefore, with that spiritual master, my own mind,
I gazed at his face, listened to his teaching, and received many
 instructions.
I prayed in the presence of this master,
Offered him praise, and asked for his blessing.
Thereby the realization that my own mind is the spiritual master
Arose within me, and I express my understanding now in words.
If you see mistakes or delusion in this,
Don't look at my words, look at their meaning.

This is nonsense spoken by a madman.
I don't apologize for any of it:
I have nothing to offer in apology!

My Own Mind as Spiritual Master, by Kyergang-pa Rinpoché. *Iti.*

The vajra song that introduces the mind as immortal:

Namo Guru!

During the day, appearance and emptiness are the deity's body—
I realize that sickness and death do not exist.
At death, even if only the deity's eyes appear clearly,
The pain of death will be naturally purified and the body of rapture
    attained.
Even if clarity does not arise,
Previous training's impact will continue unabated,
Like a limpid pool hit by a stone.
The bliss of the body of rapture will arise of itself;
Until existence is emptied,
Boundless benefit for others will spontaneously arise.

This song of the self-liberation of one's own immortal mind was composed by noble Dharma Singha [Chökyi Sengé]. To my incomparable master Rinchen [Tsöndru, Mokchok-pa], I offered one hundred measures of gold, thirty female yaks, and a sheepskin coat, then gained this experience.

SANGYÉ NYENTÖN

GREAT ÖNTÖN KYERGANG-PA entrusted Sangyé Nyentön with the secret treasury of the lineage passed from one master to a single disciple. Sangyé Nyentön perfected the manifest realization of erudition and accomplishment, and he fully achieved the qualities of awakening's paths and stages. During his lifetime, he gained control of the citadel of great integration and was then reborn in the eastern pure land, Strewn Flowers, as the Conqueror known as Buddha Glorious Lotus. This bodhisattva at the stage of culmination, great Rigong Sangyé Nyentön, Chökyi Shérab, sang this vajra song during a tenth-lunar-day vajra feast, in response to his disciples' request:

> In the space of the absolute expanse, Niguma bestows bliss
> And gives birth to the conquerors' heirs.
>
> Noble Ratna Virya,
> Matured by the four empowerments
> And endowed with the three trainings,
> Approached the supreme master and realized the nature of reality.
>
> Incomparable Kyergang-pa,
> Essence of enlightenment's three bodies, Lord of the Teachings,
> Knew appearances and sound to be magical illusion
> And helped beings in a divine form, free from attachment.
>
> Never joined with nor separated from you,
> To you all I pray with unflagging faith.
>
> I urge all faithful persons gathered here
> To listen a moment to my song:

The holy master endowed with the lineage
Is definitely the Buddha of the three times.

To know the master to be the body of ultimate enlightenment
Is to not remain ignorant of the discourses' and tantras' meaning.

Realize the nature of the three ordinary bodies like this:
Mind creates your present body
Of ripened karma.
Habitual patterns are based upon it.
The wheel of life appears as its happiness and suffering.
It is said that this body is the result of the past
And the cause of the future.

Fertilized by daytime's patterns,
You dream of various faults and qualities.
This [dream-time body] is termed "body of habitual patterns."

The intermediate state's mental body is unhindered
And has every sense faculty.
It looks like your former body
And follows your karma.
If you realize its nature, it is the body of great bliss;
If you don't, you reenter the wheel of life.

Until now, existence's bloody seas
Have tossed with waves of anger and desire.
It is senseless to remain there, faint with suffering,
As an individual attached to objective reality.

The body of ripened karma is a collection of the four elements.
There are many ways to assume this body.
Without realization, you take rebirth within the six realms' circle,
Whereas I have assumed a pure, illusory body like this:

My body of ripened karma is the Conqueror's body.
It accomplishes all goals by thought alone.

I am a wanderer in this empty, illusory body.
That is what the spiritual master of my own mind has said.

My mental body is the Conqueror's body.
It accomplishes all goals by thought alone.
I am a wanderer in this empty, illusory body.
That is what the spiritual master of my own mind has said.

My body of habitual patterns is the Conqueror's body.
It accomplishes all goals by thought alone.
I am a wanderer in this empty, illusory body.
That is what the spiritual master of my own mind has said.

From cultivating that experience,
Enlightenment's three bodies arise like this:

Ultimate enlightenment's body, the meaning of the innate state,
Is free from formulation.
Its essence cannot be identified.
Its characteristics surpass the intellect's bounds.
That is the essence of ultimate enlightenment.

From this enlightenment, pure like space,
Two form bodies appear,
Like wish-fulfilling trees or jewels.
Until existence empties,
They continually work for others' benefit.
To bodhisattvas on awakening's tenth stage,
Enlightenment's body of rapture appears,
Adorned with the marks and signs of physical perfection.
To such beings as ordinary individuals
And impure disciples, such as Listeners,
Appearances of the manifest body arise.
The inseparable integration of these three bodies
Is called the body of enlightenment's great bliss.

I possess Illusory Body's instructions
That lead to maturity and liberation.

They originate with the wisdom dakini Niguma.
Since I don't need to wait three incalculable eons [until
  enlightenment], my mind is at ease.

I possess the doctrines of the deities' forms,
Such as Vajra Creator of Delight and Supreme Bliss,
And every vital point of their instructions.
Since I have no doubt in them, my mind is at ease.

I use the secret practice of the circle of emanation at the navel
And the four kinds of generosity to help other beings.
Since I don't need to resort to wrong livelihood, my mind is at ease.

I possess instructions for vase breathing,
The chariot that binds and liberates at the energy centers.
Each instant of meditation on them
Brings uninterrupted heat and bliss.
Since I have bliss and emptiness, my mind is at ease.

I possess instructions for Transference of Consciousness
Called Wisdom Star-Gate.
Since even evil persons merely recalling them at death
Go to the celestial realms, my mind is at ease.

I have a protector of the doctrine, Awakened Protector,
And an activity protector, Kshétrapala.
Since they guard Buddha's teaching
And obey me like servants, my mind is at ease.

Here on this special occasion, the waxing moon's tenth day,
During a vajra feast where dakinis gather,
In response to the request
Of my disciple-children,
Who are as dear to me as my own heart,
I have sung this open song of attaining bliss.
It comes with the dakinis' blessings:
May those who hear it
Realize the spiritual master as the body of ultimate enlightenment

And gain effortless realization
Of the deities' forms and of Great Seal.

I dedicate the merit I've cultivated in the three times
To all beings' great awakening.

Accompanying Yöngom a short distance on his trading journey, Sangyé
Nyentön responded to his request for teaching with this song:

Precious treasure of victors' enlightenment,
Radiant lamp that dissipates the darkness of ignorance,
Lord of the Teachings, who spontaneously accomplishes pure goals
    for yourself and others,
May your enlightened mind make everything auspicious.

Know that the mind that joins luminosity and the deity's form
To the body of ripened karma
Has no cause for sickness or death.

When breathing stops at death,
The pain at life's end is naturally purified.
Luminosity and the deity's form merge;
The object of meditation and the meditator are released in their
    own ground.

In unborn, luminous space,
The self-arising two form bodies
Spontaneously and continuously accomplish others' benefit
Until the seas of existence run dry.

That is my advice for a happy death!

I have given my command
To Six-Armed Awakened Protector, who heeds me like a servant—
He will accompany you, my son, on your journey to Tsang.
Be diligent in your cultivation of the four immeasurable thoughts and
    the mind of awakening,
And go wherever you please.
Please visit my spiritual father soon
And present him the auspicious offering of this song.

At the end of the explicit autobiography Sangyé Nyentön recounted in
response to the request of the monk Zhonnu Sengé, he sang this song of
vajra advice in conclusion:

My disciples, disciples of my disciples,
And all those who have a connection with me
Must give up all wrong conceptions of me
And develop devotion so we are never separate.

My body and that of the Victor
Are not separate, o yogi!
My voice and that of the Victor
Are not different, o yogi!
My mind and that of the Victor
Should be realized as one, nondual.
The result, the deity's self-arising form,
Inseparable from enlightenment's three bodies, is great bliss.

However, if you don't give rise to immeasurable devotion,
You won't see the spiritual master's qualities.
If you give rise to ultimate devotion,

The spiritual master,
Epitome of the buddhas' inexhaustible ornaments
Of body, speech, and mind,
Will bring you to spiritual maturity and liberation.
Realize this as the master's magnificent enlightened activity.

Toward the holy master's
Life of freedom,
Have only pure vision
And not an instant of wrong thoughts.

Until you realize the spiritual master as the body of ultimate
    enlightenment,
Apply yourself to sublime accomplishment.
The master's qualities will thereby fully arise.
The ultimate life of freedom arises from devotion.
Spiritual heirs, my disciples, develop pure vision!

The vajra speech that reveals the immortal mind:

Self-liberated, noncomposite great bliss—
Dharma Singha, at your feet I bow.

Realize that the mind that joins luminosity and the deity's form
To the body of ripened karma
Has no cause for sickness, nor for death.

Rejection of existence and acceptance of transcendence are
    self-liberated.

If you know this even for an instant
When breathing stops at death,
The pain at life's end
Is naturally purified
And luminosity will merge with the deity's form.

There is neither birth nor death,
Neither cessation nor existence.
Free from realization and realizer,
Meditation and the meditator are self-liberated.

Enlightenment's two form bodies
Spontaneously accomplish others' benefit.
They appear unceasingly
Until the seas of existence run dry.

By the kindness of spiritual master Kyergang-pa,
I realized exactly these instructions that lead to enlightenment
In a matter of months or years.
If you practice them having given up this life's concerns,
You can reach liberation after a week's practice.

This concludes *Natural Liberation of Your Own Immortal Mind*, by noble Dharma Prajna [Chökyi Shérab]. To receive this instruction, I offered the illustrious master Kyergang-pa ten *sho* of gold and one sheep-skin coat, then gained this experience.

The three preceding masters' songs of profound instructions, *Natural Liberation of Your Own Immortal Mind*, are completely *Iti*.

SANGYÉ TÖNPA

PROTECTOR OF BEINGS, Sangyé Tönpa, Tsöndru Sengé, received the single-disciple lineage of seven jewels that began with Buddha Vajra Bearer. The wisdom dakini foretold him to be the master who would untie the transmission's vajra knot. His enlightened activity completely pervaded the universe, including worlds of the gods. Here he encourages himself to be diligent:

Spiritual master, Buddha,
Epitome of blessing and compassion, at your feet I bow.

My body and mind are feeble in diligence and strong in doubts—
To them I give this advice:

I see that you've become distracted
In this short life's endless affairs.
Great meditator, I advise you to distract yourself
With the business of eternity, meditation practice.

If you don't use devotion to draw the master's compassion
From the clouds of his blessings,
Experience and realization's rains will never fall:
Great meditator, I advise you to pray.

If you don't use familiarization and accomplishment to draw the
    deities' compassion
From the clouds of their accomplishment,
Common and supreme accomplishment's rains will never fall:
Great meditator, I advise you to meditate and to recite mantras.

If you don't use torma and feast offerings to draw the protectors'
   compassion
From the clouds of their activity,
Enlightened activity's rains will never fall:
Great meditator, I advise you to amass torma and feast offerings.

When praying or performing creation and completion meditations,
Don't fall under the sway of discursive thoughts.
Give up hoping for desired attainments.
Great meditator, I advise you to meditate without distraction.

The root of helping others is compassion.
Don't think of your own happiness but of others'.
Don't mentally abandon other sentient beings.
Great meditator, I advise you to develop an altruistic mind.

To his faithful spiritual children Sangyé Tönpa sang this vajra song of
instruction in the twelve necessities:

Noble spiritual masters, to you I bow.
Kind [spiritual master], the one I need, to you I pray.
Masters who preceded him, to you I offer praise.

I ask you to listen to me for a moment:

Faithful persons afraid of birth and death
Need a spiritual master who has a lineage.

Toward profound instructions that are beyond doubt,
You need unswerving diligence.

For this short life in which you can't remain,
You need unconfused priorities.

To remain in isolated retreat,
You need continually increasing tolerance of hardship.

To integrate whatever arises with meditation,
You need profound instructions in alchemy.

For uncontrived, self-manifest conduct,
You need to release the eight worldly concerns in their own ground.

For the result to arise of itself, spontaneously present,
You need to free hope and fear in their own ground.

To achieve enlightenment in one lifetime,
You need unceasing respect and devotion.

To see the spiritual master as the body of ultimate enlightenment,
You need to free wrong views in their own ground.

To help beings by taming their minds,
You need immeasurable great compassion.

This short song of the twelve necessities
Provides favorable conditions for accomplishment.

When the protector of beings, Sangyé Tönpa, considered demonstrating departure for the eastern pure land, Strewn Flowers, he sang his disciples this song, which captures the essence of his oral counsel:

Spiritual masters, deities, dakinis, and protectors:
May you protect me as your child with immeasurable compassion!

Faithful and respectful ordained persons of central, western, and
    eastern Tibet,
Cultivate experience in this way:

Banish from your mind endless worldly activity
And discard your affection for those you are attached to but can
    never satisfy.

Spend your time in virtue and spurn your endless conversations.
Renounce hope and fear related to retracing the past or anticipating
    the future.

Life has no spare time; technical terms are pointless.
Animals aren't satisfied by water in a mirage: drink nectar.

If you haven't reached your goal, you can't help others:
First single-mindedly accomplish your own goal.

Immeasurable compassion spontaneously helps others in this and
    future lives;
Develop it toward all beings.

Don't be bound by your own wishes even for an instant;
Develop the attitude that whatever you do is to help sentient beings.

Reflect continually on death and impermanence;
You will feel you need nothing and you'll forget this life.

Never separate yourself from meditation on your body as the deity's,
Appearance and emptiness, free from attachment.
This accomplishes the two goals in months or years.

Never be separate from intense, heartfelt prayer to the spiritual
    master.
They cause experience and realization to arise effortlessly.

Approach the dakinis and protectors.
They will protect you from obstacles in this life,

At death, during the intermediate state, and in the next life.

Apart from your own mind, there is no Buddha, nor sentient being;
Know what seems external, whatever appears, to be mind.

This mind is appearance and emptiness, a magic display.
Freedom from grasping to magical illusion is luminous Great Seal.

Beyond concepts of affirmation or denial, birth or death, existence or
    nothingness,
Without meditation or mental activity, you are free from existence
    and transcendence.

Karma and ripened karma are released in their own ground.
Free from dualistic clinging, gaze into the great union.

How amazing! Everyone has this uncontrived, ordinary awareness
But is unaware of it.
I have realized it through the kindness [of my master].

Now, don't ask questions; develop determined certainty.
Actualize the indivisible three facets of spontaneous presence.[16]

The oral instructions of immortal mind:

Victorious buddhas of the three times' immortal wisdom,
    To you I bow.

After you finish prayers infused with the mind of awakening
And union with the spiritual master's mind,
Think of your own body as the deity, appearance and emptiness.

The mind's essence inseparable from the deity's form,
Emptiness,
Was not seen, is not seen, and will never be seen by any buddha.

In this, there is no sickness, no death,
No existence or transcendence, no affirmation or denial.

Even if the transition [from life to death] goes badly
And your presence of mind declines,
Suffering at life's end will be naturally purified
When you realize this for an instant,
Or recollect, hear, or are aware of it.

In the first stage of the intermediate state,
Clear light and the body of enlightenment's perfect rapture,
Inseparable as the manifest body of enlightenment,
Will spontaneously accomplish others' benefit unceasingly.

I have presented this, the buddhas' immortal realization,
For the benefit of my most mature disciples.

By the virtue of this teaching,
May sentient beings whose numbers fill space
Realize the meaning of the wisdom of immortality.

This concludes the composition for my true heirs, my most mature disciples, of *Natural Liberation of Your Own Immortal Mind*, by the noble Virya Singha [Tsöndru Sengé]. I offered [to Sangyé Nyentön] five hundred bags of barley, seven measures of gold, one *dzo*, and a bolt of fine cloth from the southern Himalayan region to receive these teachings, and then I cultivated their experience.

TSANGMA SHANGTÖN

T HE NAME OF the erudite and accomplished master Tsangma Shangtön was renowned throughout the three worlds. He reached the glorious stage of a master who brings complete liberation by sight, hearing, recollection, or touch. He sang this song as an oral instruction for [his disciple,] the learned and noble Jakchen Gyaltsen Büm:

Untouched by faults, endowed with wisdom,
You relieve suffering by sight, hearing, or recollection.
You introduced me to my mind as the body of ultimate enlightenment—
Lord spiritual master, to you I bow.

To accomplish sentient beings' every need
And with the wish to attain enlightenment,
You must cultivate the accumulation of virtue—
Develop the mind of supreme awakening.

To undo perceptions that arise from clinging to phenomena as
    permanent,
To diligently engage in virtue,
And to free yourself from anger and desire,
Meditate repeatedly on death and impermanence.

Reflect on the wheel of life's unbearable sufferings.
The causes that produce happiness and suffering
Are virtue and negative acts: adopt the first and reject the latter.
Their results will surely arise.

The means to undo attachment to your ordinary body
Is meditation on the deity, clarity without discursive thought,

Appearance without intrinsic nature—
The victors' body of perfect rapture will arise of itself.

The glorious one who bestows all accomplishment
Is the Protector who gives refuge from all fears.
Toward the glorious Protector and the authentic master,
Maintain respect and devotion that keep you inseparable from them.
Pray to them continually.

Meditate that whatever appears is a dream or a magical illusion.
Integrate this in your daily life through faith and directed intent.
Desire and anger will be released in their own ground.
[The experience of appearances as] a magical illusion without
    attachment will arise of itself.

To free yourself from clinging to the magical display,
Rest the mind in its uncontrived innate state.
Dualistic thoughts will unravel in their own ground.
Clarity and emptiness without clinging will naturally arise.

Phenomena's basic nature
Has neither faults nor qualities.
Therefore, the meditator who has realized it
Maintains conduct free from acceptance or rejection.

Appearances, this interdependent origination,
Are complete within the unborn Great Mother [of transcendent
    knowledge].
They arise as bliss, clarity, and emptiness without clinging.
The result is the spontaneous presence of enlightenment's four bodies.

I dedicate the virtue of this song
To the great, unlimited awakening
Of all beings together.
This is the Great Way's special quality.

This concludes the song for the teacher Gyaltsen Büm, sung by the spiritual master Shangtön Rinpoché.

TANGTONG GYALPO

T HE INCOMPARABLY GREAT accomplished master Tangtong Gyalpo
was taught directly by the wisdom dakini Niguma and received
from her the transmission of the Shangpa teachings' recent lineage. Once,
while he engaged in secret conduct at Gyédé Tang in western Tibet, five
wisdom dakinis promised to perform any enlightened activity he wished
and sang this song to give names that corresponded to him:

To this amazing person
Living in Gyédé Tang
We five women gathered here
Will each give a name.

On the great plain of the pervasive nature,
The yogi who realizes emptiness
Lives as a fearless king.
I name him King of the Plain of Emptiness [Tangtong Gyalpo].

In the valley of equanimity without formulation,
He with the view of inseparable appearance and emptiness
Is a madman who doesn't accept or reject.
I name him Madman of the Valley of Emptiness.

From whatever is served—food and drink of a hundred tastes
Or filthy, rotten vomit—
He extracts the essence that neither helps nor harms.
I name him Extractor of the Essence of Food.

He realizes whatever conditions arise
To be like dreams or echoes

And overpowers the eight worldly concerns into a single, even taste.
I name him Conditions in an Even Taste.

All phenomena of existence and transcendence appear
But resemble the moon on water.
He knows them thoroughly without reference points—
I name him Phenomena without Reference Points.

Incomparable yogi,
To enhance your immeasurable enlightened activity,
The time has come to lead all beings
To the plain of happiness!

Tangtong Gyalpo sang this vajra song to the learned and noble master
Déleg-pal as oral instruction in Great Seal's self-liberation:

Listen, child, learned, noble Déleg-pal:
Once, veiled in the darkness of ignorance,
You mixed your plans for spiritual life
With the eight worldly concerns.

To achieve what you intend for future lives,
I pray you to consider doing this:

Spurn entirely your wishes for this life.
Discard attachment to the eight worldly concerns.
Free yourself at once from concern with face saving.
Decisively cut your ties to those near and far.

Extract the worldly dagger of self-attachment.
Relax your thoughts of hope and fear.
Cut your bonds to food and clothing.
Don't wish for high rank; be humble.

Accept disillusionment and suffering.
Fling far away your desire, anger, and competitive spirit.
Banish deception and bad intentions.
Let go of false airs assumed in hopes of food.

Keep honestly your three vows and tantric commitments.
Reject pride, conceit, and anger.
Meditate on patience, even if all despise you.
Let common wild enemies do with you what they will.

Tame the anger in your own mind.
Renounce greedy plans to store goods.
Rely upon loving-kindness and compassion.
Whether in spiritual life or in human affairs,
Make your own mind your witness.

If you don't practice now as you intend,
You might harbor hope for the future,
But such hopes are in vain.

Relax in the innate state.
Cut the deepest root of delusion.
Look at your own mind without distraction.
Hold tightly to mindfulness without neglect.
If you don't recognize your own essence,
You can force yourself till it hurts,
But you'll only feel frustration.

If you don't grasp clear light when you sleep,
You might have been introduced to the mind's nature,
But it wasn't very useful.
If you don't grasp clear light in the intermediate state,
You'll tremble in suffering at life's end.

If you don't control your own mind,
You can meditate for ages, but you'll just become exhausted.

After the last thought has ceased
And before the next arises, there's a gap.
In its clarity without thought,
Without support, free from a root or foundation,
That fresh, present awareness
Is the body of ultimate enlightenment,
Your own mind, free from formulation.
Everything that appears is your own mind.
Mind itself is unformulated, ultimate enlightenment.

Therefore, thoughts are the body of ultimate enlightenment's display.
Without hindering appearances, emptiness is accomplished.
Be mindful of that, whatever arises, whatever appears.
Always remain relaxed.
If you recognize your mind's nature, repeatedly prolong the
   experience.
Don't contrive, don't wander, rest the mind in itself,
Free from coming or going; birth, cessation, or resting place.
That's Great Seal.

It's important to maintain nondistraction in your life.
It's important to keep it effortless and relaxed.
Cultivate experience like that.

I travel around the country without a destination.
A yogi without attachment
And the sun that circles the four continents
Both move slowly but never linger.

The vajra song of immortal mind's self-liberation:

> Noble spiritual master, Buddha incarnate,
> To you I respectfully bow with body, voice, and mind.
>
> The semblance of death, this thought,
> Has no intrinsic nature within the innate state's flow.
> The body and mind designated as mortal
> Are deathless in Great Seal's natural freedom.
>
> The inert body of fully ripened karma doesn't die;
> How can the body of habitual patterns or the body of dreams die?
> The nature of mind's intrinsic radiance is the deity's body—
> Clarity and emptiness without grasping, like the moon on water.
>
> In the empty, abiding character free of formulations,
> There is neither sickness nor death,
> No transcendence nor wheel of life.
> Everything is your deluded mind's display.
>
> This display's appearances are unceasing.
> This unceasing display dissolves into the sphere of the unborn.
> Free from birth, cessation, or abiding,
> The wisdom of immortality is amazing.
>
> Place experience of it in a settled state free from grasping.
> Meditate, merging it with every activity.

Whoever becomes deeply familiar with this
Will dissolve at death into the expanse of ultimate enlightenment,
Accomplish the body of rapture in the intermediate state,
And guide sentient beings with manifestations.

Cultivate this, fortunate ones!

This concludes the great accomplished master's vajra words on the immortal mind's self-liberation. *Iti.*

KUNGA DROLCHOK

GENTLE PROTECTOR, illustrious master and spiritual warrior of
accomplishment, Kunga Drolchok, [also known as] Losal
Gyatso-dé, was spiritually nurtured directly by the wisdom dakini Niguma
and thus became the main inheritor of the very recent lineage. Among the
garland of songs he sang to provide support for [the practice of] Niguma's
teachings, this is the vajra song that relates the source of the teachings:

Shri Vajradhara Sadhu-pada-pranamayam

In the highest point of the noble Oral Instruction Lineage's sky,
Our ancestors, accomplished spiritual masters, are as numerous as the
   stars.
Among them, the resplendent sun and moon that move unhindered
   through space
Are Naropa and Niguma, are they not?

The rivers of these siblings' lineages of meditation practice
Flow to the present day, bringing medicinal water
To satisfy the minds of thirsty, fortunate disciples.
Those rivers are the doctrines of Naropa and Niguma, are they not?

Both traditions are preserved by a spiritual lord,
An illustrious, incomparable body of manifest enlightenment,
The single crown of our many realized masters—
The two Kagyu lineages, Dakpo and Shangpa.

In the past, what Tilo and Naro began
Marpa and Mila preserved.
The profound vital instructions of Naropa's Six Doctrines

Produced incalculable accomplished meditators who showed
   manifest signs of realization.

These days, like milk sold in the market,
The words [of Naro's Doctrines] are of uncertain value, like a
   madman's prattle.
Since ordinary intellects created conflicting meanings,
My mind felt somewhat dissatisfied with them.

The inner essence of the sister dakini's secrets,
Words uncontrived, is sealed with a vajra knot.
Its meaning, reality's basic character, fell into my heart
And renewed this beggar's blissful path to liberation.

If you think you want to follow me,
Don't consider your painful tension to be meditation,
And don't exaggerate the practice you have done.
Sing this relaxed song of my heart's advice.

They say the spiritual master is the root of accomplishment;
They say the spiritual master is Buddha incarnate;
They say what he does should be seen as good—
They talk beautifully, but it's all just words.

If I attain accomplishment, that's fine; if I don't, that's fine.
Whether my spiritual master is a buddha or an ordinary being,
   that's fine.
Whether his behavior is good or bad, that's fine.
I harbor not the slightest iota of egotistical doubt.

It's said that in the Highest Pure Land's palace above
Dwells ultimate enlightenment's body, great Buddha Vajra Bearer,
Blue in color, radiating light.
These are deceptive words to guide those of limited capacity—
   how pitiful!

Below at Shang-pu, Mokchok's palace,
Stands a renunciant's hut.

There, the human form blazing with the radiance of melting and bliss
Is that of great Buddha Vajra Bearer, Gyagom Lekpa Gyaltsen.

Master, you are inseparable from the primordial basis,
But you momentarily appear clothed in the veil of concealed tantric
    discipline.
Fortunate persons see you directly as you are, do they not?
You appear like a lamp hidden in a vase.

In the past, my karmic affinity was not insignificant.
From a young age, I fully [realized phenomena to be] illusion's
    display.
Although I saw the mother dakini's lovely face,
My mind wasn't satisfied; it was just illusion's guise.

When I first saw the vase of my spiritual father Lekpa Gyaltsen's face,
All my hesitations were freed by themselves.
At that time a single certainty without any doubt was born,
And it remains unchanged.

In meditation, my attachment to postmeditative attainment
    dissolved.
I forgot the distinction between meditation sessions and intervals.
My affirmations and denials—"This is" and "This isn't"—collapsed.
I lost my bias toward those near or far, self or other.

As soon as all-pervasive great luminosity of clarity and emptiness
Arose in the mirror of my innate awareness,
I gained confidence that the terms used for analysis and commentary
Would be there when I needed them.

Lord, if you aren't one endowed with wisdom,
How is it that you made a fool like me wise?
If you aren't one imbued with blessing,
How has my realization and liberation appeared?

Now, even if the buddhas of the three times arrived,
I would have nothing more to ask them.

My mind's natural movement in space
Leaves not a trace, like a bird's path.

My meditation was merely my spiritual father's natural presence.
I who continually engage in contemplative practice
Should place my mind in vivid clarity.
If I ascend or descend, I pray you'll watch over me.

This song of prayer may be pleasant to hear,
But when listened to with doubt or hesitation,
It is nothing more than a prostitute's tune,
Sung to hook the hearts of fools.

Foolish laments others wail
Make the hearts of formless gods and demons tremble.
When I proudly recall you, spiritual father, and call you from afar,
Your compassion moves from the absolute expanse, does it not?

I, the father, and those who have become my heirs—
Spiritual companions of a single mind—
Have no other place to put our hopes and no one else to turn to.
Lord, please extend the length of your life!

This song gives a supportive teaching related to the practice of union
with the mind of the spiritual master, in which the single recollection of
devotion and respect completes the spiritual path. *Iti.*

Gyagom, sanctuary I do not search for elsewhere,
In you I take refuge with undivided attention.
Father, unerring spiritual master,
Make the mind of this, your only child, turn to the Teachings.

By engaging in worldly thoughts and deeds,
My body seems venerable, but my mind is shameful.
I am a pretentious person who has a spiritual title.
Look to me with compassion; be my guide!

Although I seem to have understood the wheel of life's natural faults,
My mind is always distracted in useless, ordinary activity.
Doubts run away with my mind, while my body stays behind in
    retreat.
It would be best for me to rid my mind of doubts, wouldn't it?
Please watch over me with your wisdom!

In my condition as a person with a truly coarse character,
I don't turn away from inconsequential activity.
I only cheat and deceive myself.
My father, doesn't this move you to tears?

In the artifice of teachings intellectually understood
And in knowledge of arts and sciences,
I take an idiot's delight.
I can't turn toward that which concerns meditation.
Father, don't you think about this?

My ordinary intellect, gate for the arising of karma, is not exhausted.
I have not rid myself of my character, a swamp of cyclic life.
I do not attend to my present consciousness.
This is a long song of negativity.

To concern myself with examining the study and training
Of this false effigy of a monk is a mistake.
To entertain positive or negative thoughts of attachment
Toward the ephemeral appearance of purity's pleasing qualities is a
    low concern.

The mind that considers delicious
The wells of cyclic life's evil vomit destroys itself at its touch.
To venture out on the precipice of affirmation or negation
Of the mind's infinite, uncertain appearances amounts to insanity.

Instead of maintaining a single vigilance within wisdom,[17]
I have become numb witnessing my own non-spiritual acts.
Whatever I have done, in the mirror of magical illusion,
Must be judged to be lies and distraction.

What I have done has scorched and destroyed
The crops of liberation
With the drought of concepts.

Now I will not merely be aware of my condition;
I won't let meditation become an empty word even for an instant.
Now it's good if I die but all right if I live.
I have understood that my intention should be to perfect my
    virtuous practice.

This song [calling the spiritual master] from afar spontaneously arose as a
whip to encourage me to vigilance. *Iti.*

Within ultimate enlightenment's expanse,
Permanent as the enduring cross of stability,
Unrestricted inner radiance manifests in the form of syllables.
The invincible, single innate sound, mind's movement-emptiness,
Arises as the essence of the syllable *Ah*.

On the lion throne of *É*, source of phenomena,
In the palace of the five syllables, the meaning of great emptiness,
Stands *Vam*, great bliss, non-composite luminosity,
The six syllables' inner vital essence, the assembled deities.

One name this is known by is "buddha nature,"
Lord who completely pervades all sentient beings,
Sacred glory that delights this meditator.

From this ever-unchanging configuration,
A streaming rain of pure nectar
Cleans the latent patterns of conceptual mind,
Obscuring emotions, and mental products.

The mind becomes brilliant, innately radiant natural awareness.
Look outward to see only the body of ultimate enlightenment;
Plumb inward to see the interruption of mind's movement.
Mind becomes wide open, spacious, and vivid.

Now mental patterns dissolve and disappear.
This body's flesh and blood become a pure, rainbowlike body of
    enlightenment.
Expressions of speech and thought are surpassed, like a mute.
The mind, like a bird's path in the sky,
Not leaving a trace behind, rests in space.
This is the ultimate appearance, original wisdom.

The small hut of dark ignorance collapses on the basis.
Impure latent patterns of karma and obscuring emotions are expelled.
The domain of the term "ordinary individual" is surpassed.
We reach a path well beyond the mind of meditation.

The divine Buddha Shakyamuni
Stated that his eighty-four thousand teachings are complete in *Ah*.
Without understanding this meaning that gathers all vital
    instructions,
You can repeat words, but they just amount to a senseless recitation.

This song was sung for meditation on the Purifying Ah of Inner Space.

The unveiled state's intrinsic form arises as the deity—
The yogini, glorious chief of dakinis,
A young woman drunk with bliss and emptiness,
Entwining the lap of the lord of mind.

Outwardly, appearances are a celestial sacred palace;
Inwardly, your body is a fine and brilliant tent of red silk.
To the sides, four drops blaze with fire.
The vital instruction is the navel's energy center, like a circle of flame.

Tongues of flame emitted by the syllable *Ram* at the triple junction
Flash within the central channel's pathway
And pass, like shooting stars—white and clear—racing through the
 sky,
Through the opening at the crown of your head.

Nectar flows from the spiritual master's body,
Enters through the path of Brahma's gate,
And creates connections with the path's four empowerments;
The spiritual master's mind and your own become indistinguishable.

This song was sung for the practice of Fierce Inner Heat. *Iti*.

All that appears to the mind and all that arises are the experience
of illusion.
Immediate, uncontrived mindfulness is the path of awakening.
The spiritual master's speech hammers the nails of the vital
instructions.
Remember them without failure.

To maintain mindfulness with grasping is beginners' meditation.
The path of analytic meditation is a temporarily useful teaching.
To remain relaxed and without activity in the nature of reality
Is to know the one that liberates everything: how perfectly amazing!

This song was sung for meditation on Illusory Body. *Iti.*

Find the gate for the arising of dreams at the edge of meditative
experience.
Join directed intent with the profound instructions.
The vital essences' four movements create the vital point of
interdependent arising.
These are the mother wisdom dakini's secret words.

Since the vagrant mind has no fixed reference point,
To travel upward to Joyful Heaven is not far.
Anything can appear to this mind that illumines everything.
To easily transform what appears into what is immediately needed is
the meditator's experience.

Accept what experience arises without affirmation or denial.
Steer your practice with constant vigilance.

This song was sung for the practice of Lucid Dream. *Iti.*

Clear light of the basis is enlightenment's changeless, eternal body.
Clear light of the path is unhindered bliss.
The final result is manifest, complete enlightenment.
This joins the vital instructions of basis, path, and result.

In the path of Transference of Consciousness, enlightenment without
   meditation,
The mind focuses on *Ah*
And shoots the arrow of its vigilance far through Brahma's gate.
The mind does not wander but settles, still, within the body of
   ultimate enlightenment.

All karmic appearances of this present moment
Do not fundamentally exist, like the moon on water.
If you gain certainty in this,
You will later accomplish the body of rapture in the intermediate
   state.

This song was sung for the [practices of Clear Light, Transference of Consciousness, and] Intermediate State.

KYENTSÉ WANGCHUK

THE FOLLOWING SONG, *My Heart's Nectar*, by Nésar-pa Jamyang Kyentsé Wangchuk, Tenpé Gyaltsen Palzangpo, is a prayer that gathers the essential points of the graded path of the glorious Shangpa Golden Doctrines:

Namo Guru Vé

Lord Buddha Vajra Bearer, all conquerors' manifest form,
Supreme crown ornament of the entire lineage of meditation
    teachings,
Spiritual father, [Lama] Kartsi-wa, with whom any connection is
    meaningful,
Bless me, your child, that I become equal to my father.

This fresh, ordinary knowing
Does not fall under the four faults' sway
And sees its own naked essence.
Bless me with realization of the basis, Great Seal.

At the navel, the blazing short *Ah*,
Churned by life-giving circulating energy,
Burns the firewood of dualistic experience.
Bless me with training on the path of Fierce Inner Heat.

All dualistic experience, apparent existence of the wheel of life and
    transcendence,
Does not exist but appears in myriad ways.
To realize the innate fault of these intrinsically empty appearances,
Bless me with training on the path of Illusory Body.

Habitual patterns' powerful supplementary confusion[18]
Can be recognized the moment it arises.
With intense skill in its lack of reality,
Bless me with training on the path of Lucid Dream.

When ignorance, habitual patterns, and firm belief in things' solidity
Collapse into the sphere of emptiness,
Brilliantly luminous, empty forms arise unhindered.
Bless me with training on the path of Clear Light.

The three bodies of delusion's appearances are the Conqueror's
      bodies of enlightenment
That primordially abide. This recognition
Liberates terrifying dualistic appearances in their own ground.
Bless me with training on the path of Intermediate State.

Not bound by attachment to this life,
Nor agonized in fear of death,
I travel unhindered in the space of the absolute expanse.
Bless me with training on the path of Transference of Consciousness.

In appearing existence, the spiritual master's display,
There is no need to accept or reject, to complicate or to simplify.
With intense devotion that knows no separation from the master,
Bless me with traveling the path with the spiritual master.

Not bound by considering the conquerors' sacred circle—
The wheel of life and transcendence—as ordinary,
Wisdom sees whatever object arises as the deity's form.
Bless me with traveling the path with the deity.

Not bound by concepts of things as solid,
I see whatever appears as an unreal illusion
Without constraint of attachment to the experience of illusion.
Bless me with traveling the path with illusion.

This, my own mind, is the empty yogini,
Whose intrinsic display is Vajra Sow's magic dance. [19]

I have pleased her with the substances of tantric feasts.
Bless me with the accomplishment of the basic nature's celestial
realms.

The practice of gathering the five supreme branches[20]
Has purified the impure gate to birth.
In emptiness, I playfully take pleasure in the vagina.
Bless me with realization of the path of integral union.

Karmic energy, the horse on which consciousness rides,
Is steered by means of physical exercises.
With control of the ultimate channels, circulating energy, and vital
essence,
Bless me with accomplishment of the immortal body.

Enlightenment's magical body, the uncontrived mind,
Dwells within the great bliss of sexual union's playful dance.
With undistracted preservation of the intrinsic essence,
Bless me with the accomplishment of infallible mind.

I rely on the glorious Awakened Protector, Bodhisattva All-Seeing
One,
And offer him outer, inner, and secret sacred supports.
I direct him using the path of creation, completion, and recitation.
Bless me with the accomplishment of whatever activity I undertake.

The ultimate dakini's heart counsel in vajra words
Is the Five Golden Doctrines' profound teachings.
With many hundreds of explanations and meditations' glorious
wealth,
Bless me, your child, that I become a mature, worthy vessel for the
Teachings.

From now until I attain enlightenment,
May I never be separate from you.
May I do whatever pleases you.
Bless me in meditation on this path.

Once you have blessed us and our dependents
With your compassion,
Bless us with the accomplishment of glorious supreme bliss,
Our basic nature, the luminous body of ultimate enlightenment.

This song expresses my spontaneous aspirations for Lama Shangpa's
Golden Doctrines. *Iti.*

TARANATA

DURING THIS AGE of conflict, Taranata was a great Buddha Vajra Bearer whose renunciation and realization were indistinguishable from those of Land of the Exalted's accomplished masters. In glorious Dévikotri, the wisdom dakini granted him her secret treasury, making him her principal spiritual heir and the great leader of the profound path of the extremely recent lineage. His [monastic] name was Kunga Nyingpo, although he was renowned as the noble omniscient master Taranata.

Among the many vajra songs he imparted, at the age of twenty-three he sang this to encourage himself while living at Samding:

Om Svasti!

Three Jewels, my place of refuge, to you I respectfully bow
And speak these words that well up in my mind:

I claim to meditate in a mountain retreat;
This makes a good impression in others' eyes.
Yet if I examine myself, my mind has not mixed with the Teachings.
How can this be genuine practice of the sacred Teachings?
The time has come to undertake heartfelt practice.
Banish plans for this life, o heartless one!

I've busied myself teaching Buddhism, supervising others' study and
    reflection,
But when slight misfortunes occur, I spurn the sacred Teachings.
I'm known as a scholar, yet I waste my own human life.
How can someone like me be a holy spiritual guide?
The time has come to tame my own mind.
Point your finger at yourself, o heartless one!

I see how fleeting things are in this wheel of life
But don't believe it a bit and lack contentment.
I have no confidence to depart from this life,
Yet I don't really consider death; I'm as careless as a madman.
The time has come to prepare for the next life.
Turn your mind to the Teachings, o heartless one!

I need nothing I don't already have, yet I harbor anger and desire.
Toward my qualities, my pride stands as tall as Supreme Mountain.
I still conform to social norms, though no one is pleased.
I have done so little, yet I expect so much.
The time has come to renounce the eight worldly concerns.
See whatever arises to be of equal flavor, o heartless one!

For the good of my spiritual life, I can't give up even a little sleep.
Thinking, "Later this year, or the next," I procrastinate.
I want signs of experience to appear immediately, without cause.
I haven't controlled my wish for food, fame, and fortune.
The time has come to focus my will on a single point.
Deeply reject your hopes and fears, o heartless one!

After adolescence, youth fades and decays.
Circles of relationships return help with harm.
Still, my mind remains open and untroubled.
I make plans for this life's affairs in ignorance.
The time has come to wholeheartedly abandon activity.
Train your mind to be impartial, o heartless one!

Those who have the title of spiritual master don't practice the
    Teachings.
There isn't one disciple who keeps the tantric commitments.
Most people have neither modesty nor shame.
In this evil time of the decay of the Buddha's doctrine,
Whatever you do to help others
Is usually no help at all and harms you instead.

Others will benefit continually
When I gain stability in the Teachings.

Therefore, I will give up the seeming benefit of others that sometimes
   appears in this life
And hold my own benefit as supreme.
To live my life devoted entirely to the sacred Teachings:
That's right! Now I should seriously consider it!

This song of the essential introduction to the nature of mind was sung
to Taranata's best disciple, the faithful one from Gangkar, Nyima Namgyal.

Lord Buddha Vajra Bearer in the form of an accomplished master,
Even to hear your name is very meaningful.
Turn my, your disciple-child's, mind to the Teachings.
Treasure of compassion, to you I pray.

Now that you have gained a human life
And met a qualified spiritual lord,
If you do not apply yourself to meditation,
There is danger that you will live a meaningless life.

The sovereign of experiential cultivation is devotion.
The sovereign of conducive circumstances is disillusionment.
The sovereign of activity is nonaction.
The sovereign of settling in evenness is natural arising.

This profound instruction of the four sovereigns
Is the qualified spiritual master's speech,

All accomplished masters' heart-essence,
And Taranata's experience.

Meditation on form is partial;
It cannot help in times of suffering.
Such teachings for life's happy times
Are said to be expedient means to guide meditators
But cannot place enlightenment within their grasp.

To see your own naked face,
You need devotion toward a qualified spiritual lord.

Sweet talk that the master is the Buddha,
And attachment to beauty—
That everything he does must be seen as good—
Constitute devotion that is of thought rather than deed;
It is an appearance that masks doubt.
Even if a person begins well with the thought "I will practice the
    Teachings!"
These are only words, not sight of the meaning.

The spiritual master has no partiality toward a buddha or a sentient
    being.
Within his enlightened mind's single essence—
The unborn body of ultimate enlightenment—
Even if his actions are faulty, those faults are useful.
His benefit to beings is impartial and very vast.

If his blessings enter you, that's fine; if not, that's also fine.
If you gain accomplishment, that's fine; if not, that's also fine.
With a firm decision, pray,
"I have no other place of refuge."
Settle in evenness, inseparable from his enlightened mind.
How can meditation be prevented from arising?

The wish for happiness in collecting food and clothing
Impedes your virtuous practice and is a big distraction.
That distraction, which some call "conducive circumstances,"

Is not what a meditator needs.
Strong renunciation and disillusionment
Are companions when you live alone.
In physical sickness, they are your nurse.
Distracted thoughts of food and clothing
Amount to "conducive circumstances" for turning back [on the
    spiritual path].

All you have done so far has caused rebirth in the wheel of life.
Now, relax yourself in nonaction.
That's how you'll reach the eternal fortress.
Even if you're diligent in mentally created virtue,
You won't reach that eternal, unchanging state.
With the vital point of the absolute expanse without death or
    transition,
You can settle your mind in natural repose
And thereby attain the changeless state.

Allow things to arise of themselves, without contrivance:
Lack of contrivance and recognition are crucial.

In mind's natural clarity, without thoughts,
Lucidity is radiant and empty.
If you recognize its nature,
It is the body of ultimate enlightenment.

When you recognize your own nature,
However impressive your thoughts' illusory manifestations might be,
However numerous the ways happiness or suffering arise—
Everything is the body of ultimate enlightenment's pervasive display.

There is then no difference between presence or absence of thoughts.
The natural defects of mind's stillness or movement are destroyed.
Like ice melting into water,
Whatever appears is vividly your own mind.
After the moment of appearance, nothing follows—subject or object:
All arises unimpeded from emptiness alone.

From the buddhas' three bodies of enlightenment above
To the realms of hell below,
Don't impede any arising.
Let whatever emerges be without formulation,
Beyond the domain of verbal expression.
Your mind will experience the great bliss of intrinsic awareness.

Enhance that experience by virtuous practice with formulation.
Everything is Great Seal's pervasive display.
By completing the dual cultivation of means and knowledge,
You realize the mind of enlightenment.

To cultivate this experience is like nectar;
To speak of it is empty pretense.
I ask you to put this into practice in your own mind.
I invite you to serve yourself at the banquet of experiential
    cultivation.

This song gives oral counsel, an admonition to encourage renunciation:

Namo Guru Vé!

I prostrate before my spiritual father, Buddha Vajra Bearer,
And express here the few words that flow from my heart:

This life's appearances are like rainbows;
Don't chase after them, I beseech you.

These appearances and what is made by mind are one;
Don't be attached, grasping them as separate, I beseech you.

If your awareness does not arise without attachment,
There is a danger that your meditation will become a white lie.

If you don't firmly control your own mind,
There is a danger that you'll waste your life in meaningless acts.

If you don't focus entirely on your own benefit,
You'll fool yourself with the seeming appearance of helping others.

This human body you have right now
Is very difficult to attain repeatedly.

Once you are reborn in the three miserable existences,
You'll have no chance whatsoever to meet the sacred Teachings.

Now, if your foot slips, you'll fall,
To become like a stone in the depths of hell.
That's the result of virtue and experiential cultivation
Put off for later—
Negative acts and faults pour down like rain.
Think of this and devote yourself to the Teachings.

Aging's suffering will soon come;
Once sickness and unwanted circumstances appear,
It is hard for the Teachings
To draw a mind tormented by suffering to the path.
I ask you to devote yourself to the Teachings while you're happy!

Now, during our human lives,
Our country's and region's changing fortunes,
Our spiritual masters' and teachers' lives,
Our monastic companions' and tantric brothers' and sisters' destinies,
And our parents', friends', and foes' situations
All expose the innate faults of impermanence.
Each passing year, month, and day
Is an instructor who teaches impermanence,
Evokes disillusionment, and is right beside us.

We will eventually have to leave behind
Any act we do at any time during this life—
Give up activity, my child, and meditate.

Your body is impermanent; its flesh and bone part ways.
As precious as this body is to you,

It will finish as a heap of bones.
All the wealth you accumulate with diligent greed
Will be gained and shared by who knows whom?
Even the clothes and food you now own
Are the shroud and dry food of a corpse.
Even if you amass great power and armies,
When the unpredictable time of your death arrives,
You will give up wealth, power, dominion, and possessions
And see yourself wander in the three miserable existences.
Impermanence is the common nature of composite phenomena.
Think about this and devote yourself to the Teachings.

Train in universal love and compassion
And maintain lack of attachment toward whatever appears.
In this life, the next, and the intermediate state,
What is always precious in every circumstance
Is confidence in your father spiritual master:
Put your trust in him.
Make heartfelt prayers to him, I beseech you.
Surely you will never be deceived.

Disengagement, compassion, devotion,
And lack of distraction within nonattachment—
If you can be diligent in these four points,
You will reach the summit of your aspirations.

At Daryul Draknak, the realized one of Gyalzang named Rinchen Tashi asked for advice and received this song in reply:

To my spiritual masters I bow!

My child, there is no difference between appearances and mind.
Settle without contrivance, regardless of what arises.

Compassion and emptiness are two sides of the same coin.
Don't relax your grip on compassion,
And don't let emptiness become nihilistic nothingness.
To cultivate these two in union is very important.

If a "great meditator" gives his attention
To wrong choices in relation to cause and effect,
Spurns renunciation in which we need nothing whatsoever,
Presents Great Seal as vain talk of emptiness,
Becomes divorced from universal altruism,
And engages in non-Buddhist techniques of channels and circulating
      energy,
He may be skilled in deceiving foolish people,
But he strays from the path that pleases the Buddha.

My child, practice as the Buddha taught,
Cause for attainment of enlightenment.
Therefore, don't busy yourself with wishes to be seen as good;
Conform to the Teachings in body, voice, and mind.

If your view is high and wide,
Your conduct meticulous and timely,
Your meditation continuous and without distraction,
These three will make the fruit ripen.

Those who strive for food and drink with vain words
And trick others as they travel the country
Cannot accomplish even the odor of a great meditator:
I beseech you to stay in a mountain retreat.

How can attachment to news and gossip
Accomplish the voice's power of true words?
If you're able, recite secret mantras;
If not, it's best to remain silent.

If you conform or try to please others with unvirtuous acts,
You might meditate, but your desire and anger will increase.
Such bonds are difficult to renounce, even if you intend to do so—
Cut them vigorously and leave them far behind.

When some slight experience arises,
If you cling to it as positive, demons will carry you away.
Like a person climbing a mountain who can tumble into a ravine,
It's important to be careful during the ascent.

Don't waste your spiritual masters' oral counsel:
Cultivate the experience of what you've received.
Don't become haughty or self-promoting;
If you meditate single-mindedly, feel content with that!

This song was sung in response to a request for advice from some meditators in Latö Balung:

Namo Guru!

Sovereign master, my sole spiritual father, sufficient in yourself,
To you I continually pray.
Turn my disciple-children's minds to the Teachings.
Bless them with realization of mind that embraces all space.

Now that all conducive circumstances are gathered
And you have met a qualified spiritual lord,
You receive many profound instructions:
Don't waste them meaninglessly, I beseech you!

To trust this body, a heap of flesh and bones,
And to hold to it as lasting are wrong.

Don't delay your virtuous practice.
Apply yourself to it immediately.

Pretentious persons with no meditative experience,
Carried away by nihilistic chatter of emptiness,
Are in danger of entering into sterile, negative talk:
To be meticulous about cause and effect is very important.

With uninterrupted intense devotion,
Fervently pray to the spiritual master,
But don't be attached to that as real.
There is no spiritual master apart from your own mind.

Without recognition of your own nature, you'll wander along the
    wheel of life.
It is very important to foster nonaggressive compassion.
Unreal delusion can deceive you
With happiness and suffering—regard them as dreams.

Without contrivance, your own mind's ordinary knowing
Is the body of ultimate enlightenment.
Understand whatever discursive thoughts appear to it
To be like waves on water.

However meticulous you are about your conduct,
Don't be false and hypocritical in the slightest.
It's important to remain in harmony with the Teachings.
I banish each "great meditator" who transgresses the Teachings with
    the sound of *pé*!

For continuous meditation day and night,
It's crucial to remain without action, without activity.
Maintain effortless vigilance.
If you let yourself slide into stupidity, the outcome will be uncertain!

The result, the Buddha of your own mind,
Is not found in pretentious emptiness, but on the fundamental basis.
Without falling into the ravines of hope and fear,

You need decisive certitude [in the basis].

Whatever appears is the body of ultimate enlightenment.
In this, it is said that you should not make biased distinctions.
However, such false "pure vision" can lead you astray:
Preserve your spiritual master's lineage!

One time, when Taranata was staying at Yoru in Tsang, all appearances arose as teachers to introduce the nature of mind. He then sang this vajra song:

Om Svasti!

At this time of flowers during the Ox year
Here in Yoru, a land where what is auspicious increases,
I, an adept free from bias, recall in my heart
My noble spiritual master's kindness.

Previously, from time immemorial, I did not find freedom;
Until now, I wandered along the wheel of life.
Here, where existence has no bounds nor limits in depth,
You are the precious one who sends sentient beings to enlightenment.

My parents of the six realms are kind,
But there isn't one of them who helps me reject life's circle.

None gives me lastingly useful guidance.
For such heart advice, I go to my master.

The time when this body, a heap of flesh and blood,
Will be destroyed is unpredictable.
I ask those who have nowhere to escape to after death
To focus their awareness within themselves.

In fear of death, I searched for a spiritual master.
I applied myself, as if touching my bone to rock, to every practice.
Now, when I die, my mind will be completely at ease.
Don't you need to prepare such a comfortable mind?

The first, the moon's phases and four seasons' changes;
The second, shifting patterns of high and low classes, of wealth and
    want;
And the third, negative changes in the country and region—
These three are the same instructor, who teaches that composite
    phenomena are impermanent.

The first, work in the fields that never ends;
The second, unkind acts in return for kindness done;
The third, salty water that doesn't quench thirst—
These three are the same instructor, who teaches that activity is sense-
    less.

The first, hurly-burly of village busyness;
The second, insects' insignificant occupations;
The third, ephemeral clouds that separate and circle—
These three are the same instructor, who teaches that cyclic life is
    directionless.

The first, a rainbow's formless appearance;
The second, a clear-sounding, nonlocalized echo;
The third, a nonexistent yet pleasant or troubling dream—
These three are the same instructor, who teaches that appearances
    are the mind.

The first, outer appearances, a magical moving wheel;
The second, inner awareness, gate for mind's appearances;
The third, the sphere of emptiness, free from identifiable
    characteristics—
These three are inseparable, like water poured into water.

Once a little experience in meditation is born,
Whatever appearances arise, however they arise, introduce the mind's
    nature.
Whatever we do in body, voice, and mind enriches that experience.
To think of that: Ah la la!

Now what is left of this human life
I dedicate to experiential cultivation,
Hold to my secluded mountain retreat,
And accept whatever arises as my path.

Very kind, precious spiritual master,
It could be said that your blessings in the past have been
    immeasurable,
But please bless me again:
Lord of the Teachings, I have no other refuge!

I, Taranata, sang this song when the sight of the country's changes
seemed to introduce me to the mind's nature.

When he was leading a vajra feast circle at Yardrok Taklung, this song arose as the inherent sound of the vajra inner channels.

Namo Mahamudra-ya!

In the space of the unborn expanse,
The wisdom of awareness manifests its impartial display,
Shining as the stars and planets of knowledge, love, and power.
Illustrious lord spiritual master, Buddha Vajra Bearer,
This beggar respectfully prays to you.
Compassionate one, please bless me.

In the pure realm above
Dwells an eternal body endowed with a mind of great bliss.
He is known as Buddha Vajra Bearer,
Said to be chief of all configurations of enlightenment,
But in fact he is nowhere else but here—
My root spiritual master.
My sole father, by your kindness and compassion,
I have gained a little stability.

My decisive confidence in the fundamental basis,
The uncontrived, innate state of the abiding nature,
Gives me the experience of joy.
Within the natural, vivid appearances that arise in mind's clarity,
There is nothing that cannot appear.
This liberation at the moment of arising
Is the contemplative practice of self-liberation, is it not?

This full recognition of my own nature, without distraction,
Is what is known as tranquillity.
This not finding an intrinsic nature, that mind is rootless,
Is insight's transcendent knowledge, is it not?

Once I know my own mind and the spiritual lord's to be inseparable,
To behold the face of ultimate enlightenment presents no difficulty.
To perform the contemplative practice of seeing your own
    enlightened face,

Develop devotion [toward your master,
Who] is never joined to nor separated from you.

I have attained a free and fully endowed human life,
I have met Buddhism in general,
I have received tantric instruction in particular,
And, especially, [I have gained instruction
In] the profound meaning of this awareness—
Signs that I previously cultivated a little merit.

My mind has turned a little toward the Teachings,
A qualified spiritual master nurtures me,
I have gained certainty in Buddha's discourses and tantras,
And at present I have no biased anger or desire—
These mean that I will be happy wherever I live.

I care not for this life's deceptive happiness,
Nor for praises and pleasant-sounding flattery;
And I haven't aspired to power or influence—
These mean that my mind is always at ease.

To become a spiritual person, I renounced three things:
Worldly, outer pretense of spirituality,
Pleasant speech voiced with negative intent,
And helping others with the aim of my own profit.
This as well is due to my spiritual master's kindness.

Master, I pray to you again:
Compassionate one, please bless me.
Lord, by your compassionate blessings,
Now and at all places and times
May all circumstances be perfectly auspicious.

The Essence of Ambrosia, oral profound instruction related to the stages of the path of the glorious Shangpa Golden Doctrines:

Namo Guru Vé

In the expanse, space of the unborn,
The sacred circle of unbound radiance spreads,
Emitting a hundred lights of enlightened compassion—
Spiritual father, Buddha Vajra Bearer, to you I bow.

Lord, from your compassion's clouds,
A steady rain of oral instruction
Pours on the field of my mind
And nourishes a harvest of fruit—meditative experience and
   realization.
If you are fortunate [disciples], take this fruit from me.

The great, glorious one known as Buddha Vajra Bearer
Enounced infinite numbers of tantras, among which five constitute
   the essence.
The one direct path that gathers many profound instructions
Is known by the name Six Doctrines of Niguma.

That essence of sure and secret ambrosia,
All mother dakinis' secret words,
Is nectar flowing from the mouth of my spiritual father, my master.

Today I the vagrant yogi,
Whose lifestyle is to beg aimlessly
And who acts in unpredictable ways,
Will sing a vajra song of the essential meaning
In this glorious celestial palace of Rigong.

At the crown of the head, energy center of great bliss,
The symbol of the unborn, sign of the syllable *Ah*,
Produces a stream of nectar.
The vital point of focus is certainty that this purifies
Faults, negative acts, and obscurations.
The name of the practice is the Purifying Ah of Inner Space.
This constitutes the preliminary practices' key point.

Within the support, the vajra body, vital essences circulate in the
    channels.
The key point of the basis is four energy centers,
Used now for burning and melting,
And movement of the four joys in your own body.
This is the key point of the tantras' sure secrets.
When conditions unite skillful means and transcendent knowledge,
The basis, your innate mind, is introduced
And the vital essences move through the four joys' descent and return.
This is called the activity, Fierce Inner Heat.
What is called the instruction for the other's body
Is the most vital point for integrating pleasure on the path.
I meditated on bliss and emptiness as inseparable.
You who are gathered here should also cultivate inseparable bliss and
    emptiness.
If you want to attain enlightenment in one lifetime,
There is no other path, o fortunate ones!
Concentrate on this single practice, self-igniting heat and bliss, I
    beseech you.

Integration with the path of outer appearances as illusory is this:
The body appears, but it is just the mind's own appearance.
This self-appearance naturally arising as the deity
Is like an illusion, without an intrinsic nature.

This is the essential meaning of the instructions on Illusory Body.
I also practiced this:
I purified desire and anger's appearances in their own ground.
The knotted snake of my firm belief in reality's solidity has uncoiled.
Destroy your belief in reality as solid, I beseech you.

Based on the vital instructions for immediate directed intent and
  transformation,
[To see reality as] the impartial radiance of awareness's own display
Liberates the bonds of clinging to it as substantial.
In this, training without set patterns is the key point.
This is called the instruction in Lucid Dream,
Useful for all those who practice Illusory Body.

Gaze at the basis, your own primordial, enlightened face,
With the contributory condition of intense devotion
And the auspicious connection created by the vital instruction
That joins the mind and circulating energy.
The mind's vajra nature, great luminosity,
Is engendered with effort during the day
And arises by itself at night in the appearance of clarity.
From clarity, emptiness arises—
This is called clear light of inseparable clarity and emptiness.
By blending the bliss of melting with the innate state,
The experience of bliss alone is purified in itself;
This is called clear light of inseparable bliss and emptiness.
In the primordially pure nature of mind,
The two obscurations' false pretense vanishes.
This is clear light endowed with two purities.
In the presence of Lord Buddha Vajra Bearer,
I requested instruction and resolved my doubts in this,
The path's result, Clear Light.
Having received the instructions, I didn't leave it at that:
I cultivated their experience, blending it with my own mind.
My vague concepts of meditative experience were purified
And I gained the eternal land of unchanging realization.
You too should single-mindedly meditate upon Clear Light.

The vital instruction of the wondrous magic of mind and circulating
    energy
Sends the one-pointed mind aloft
And trains in directed intent,
To see what appears as the intermediate state.
Make pure vision toward what arises your path.
These are called teachings in Transference of Consciousness and
    Intermediate State,
Vital instructions for beginners.

In uncontrived mind's innate essence,
Rest within the wide open, naked state of whatever arises.
Remain within the freshness of uncontrived body, voice, and mind.
This is called instruction for natural repose.
Meditate within clarity and an uplifted state;
Be relaxed, uncontrived, and uncontrolling.
The meditator who recognizes what arises in the mind
Finds it is liberated in its own ground.
This is called instruction in natural liberation.
Recognition of the primordial, natural place of these three—
Clarity, emptiness, and their union—
And the mind's resting or movement, whatever occurs,
Is called instruction in enlightenment's three bodies' self-arising.
Movement dissolves into movement-emptiness;
The line between meditation and postmeditation collapses and
    vanishes.
Many are widely knowledgeable in the discourses and tantras,
And it could be said that many are chiefs of specific doctrines,
But few can state, "There is no other meaning than this!"
This Great Seal of natural liberation
Is what I consider to be the discourses' and tantras' essence.
I cultivated its experience like that;
You should do the same.

All that appears is one within unlimited pure vision.
In the integrated path of devotion toward whatever appears,
The spiritual master, root of devotion, arises.
The spiritual master and the deity are inseparable;

Within that state, the deity is one with self-arising magical illusion.
Instruction in unlimited pure vision,
Affirmation of the self-arising of mind's uncontrived, relaxed
     radiance,
Is what is called the three paths of integration.
I trained in unlimited pure vision;
You should do the same.

Skillful means, those meditations' unceasing vital point, is pure
     vision.
The appearing aspect of mind's clarity and emptiness—the deity's
     body—
And the unchanging bliss of innate awareness
Have, from the beginning, not come into being.
Whatever is unborn will never cease.
At present, the kind spiritual master introduces us to the mind,
Whose nature is unborn and undying.
The name of this instruction is the immortality of your own mind.
It encompasses alone the essence of creation and completion.

To bind three things—circulating energy, thoughts, and mind—
Into the absolute expanse is experiential cultivation's key point.
Physical exercises' direction adds to experiential cultivation's energy.
Unhindered enjoyment of the other's body
Without loss of vital essence brings natural liberation
And introduction to the four joys in the absolute expanse.
This instruction is called the immortality of your own body.
Perfect self-control of your mind and circulating energy, o meditators!

The sole vital point for the immediate accomplishment of the four
     enlightened activities
Is the practice of devotion
Toward the spiritual father, the kind master,
And Swift Awakened Protector,
Who have two names but are ultimately not different.
Such devotion makes the expanse of the two accomplishments
     overflow
To spontaneously help beings.

Lord, qualified spiritual master, I offer this melody to you.
To all masters—from the glorious, great Buddha Vajra Bearer
To my spiritual father, my root teacher—
I offer this song in the melody of my experience.
To you gathered here, fortunate men and women,
I give this sublime taste of very secret ambrosia
As a joyous feast.
I, the unattached, vagrant wanderer,
Have the openness of the cultivation of equanimity.
I have smashed the fortress of my enemies, the eight worldly
  concerns.
I have reached the eternal ground of the innate state.
I gaze at the natural enlightened face of all phenomena.
I am not ignorant in the domain of religious technical terms,
But I have liberated into the absolute expanse
Any attachment I had to a positive wish for erudition.

My kind preceptor, who falsely appeared to be ordinary in body and
  mind,
Gave me this name:
Kunga Nyingpo.
My spiritual father,
Who introduced me to the mind's nature,
Who kindly sends human beings to enlightenment,
Gave me this name: Taranata.

Today I have spoken to you from my heart.

I sang this song in my twenty-fifth year [1599], during a vajra feast circle held in front of the self-manifest [statue of the] Protector, at the sacred
place of the Glorious Protector in Rigong. *Iti.*

When this noble omniscient master's supreme accomplishment manifested, its natural expression in activity guided boundless numbers of beings. During that time, he sang this vajra song of the seven auspicious signs:

Namo Guru!

From ultimate enlightenment's natural experience, great bliss,
Unlimited compassion's altruistic acts arise.
Spiritual father, Buddha Vajra Bearer, at your feet I bow.
Bless those gathered here, I pray.

This increase in impartial help for others
Is a sign of my mind arising as emptiness and compassion.

This self-introduction to the mind's nature
Is a sign that my devotion has reached culmination.

This lack of distraction at any time
Is a sign of my realization of mind's rootless nature.

This break in the continuity of arising thoughts
Is a sign of my realization of the mind's nonconceptual abiding
   nature.

This steady experience of bliss and emptiness
Is a sign of my taming the channels, circulating energy, and vital
essence.

This conduct without reference points
Is a sign of my calming the violent wind of the eight worldly
concerns.

This destruction of hopes and fears for attainment
Is a sign of my certainty that my own mind is Buddha.

The meditator endowed with these seven signs
Has reached the place where mind is blissful and happy within itself.

I am not unhappy; I am happy.
May all be auspicious with bliss and happiness.

LOCHEN GYURMÉ DÉCHEN

Lochen Gyurmé Déchen, nephew of the great accomplished master Tangtong Gyalpo, sang this song, a prayer of the Six Doctrines, called *The Rain of Great Bliss*:

Nama Shri Jnana Daki Nigupta-yé!

Lady of the celestial realms, compassionate one,
Chief of wisdom dakinis, Niguma,
When I, your child, pray fervently to you,
In your expanse free from formulations, please think of me.

Lady who reveals the sacred circle of great secrets,
Bestow now the empowerment of the four joys!

Lady who opens the door to the unborn state,
Clear away now my negative acts and obscurations with the
    purification practice!

Lady who emits fire from the short *Ah*,
Burn now my soiled aggregates and sense elements!

Lady who draws great bliss from the syllable *Ham*,
Bestow now coemergent wisdom!

Lady who reveals the natural experience of illusion,
Destroy now my attachment to the reality of anger and desire!

Lady who emanates and transforms during lucid dreams,
Cut now my bonds to supplementary delusion!

Lady who makes spontaneous luminosity arise,
Dispel now the darkness of my stupidity!

Lady who leads above at the time of departure [at death],
Guide me now to the celestial realms!

Lady who overcomes the appearances of delusion in the intermediate
  state,
Grant me now the invincible body of enlightenment's perfect rapture.

This prayer was sung by the religious teacher Gyurmé Déchen.

LOSAL TENKYONG

ZHALUPA RINCHEN LOSAL TENKYONG was spiritually nurtured by
the Vajra Queen [Vajra Yogini]. This opened his inner channels of
the supreme wisdom of meditative experience and realization. The following song of experience, called *The Wish-Fulfilling Jewel,* was sung as
notes to help himself recollect meditations on Great Seal Amulet Box:

The mother dakinis' chief is Niguma.
The inner, refined essence of her heart's ambrosia
Was transferred to words on a palm leaf and placed in an amulet box.
It is said that it became a beautiful ornament around the neck of Lord
  Kyungpo Naljor.

By the kindness of the lord protector inseparable from him,
My spiritual father, Lord of the Teachings, Venerable Tutob,
I received instruction in the progressive meditations
Of Great Seal Amulet Box, which I now express in notes to aid my
  memory:

The path's preliminary is the three modes of natural repose;
The main practice is liberation from the four faults;
The culmination is the spontaneous presence of enlightenment's four
  bodies' own face.
These constitute this excellent path's special characteristics.

Ah-Ho!
How wonderful!

Remain uncontrived, cease activity, be determined, be tight then
  relaxed.

High and low, near or far, [blend the meditation with] spiritual
activity, mantra, sound, and indeterminate behavior.
These constitute tranquillity meditation, concentration.

Search for the arising or cessation of an essence, an objective
appearance, and thoughts.
For each, make a special search for existence or nonexistence, a total
of six topics.
Certainty that the mind's nature is the absolute expanse is the
seventh.
With insight meditation, place the introduction to the mind's nature
in your heart.
These are the eighteen methods of meditation on the three modes of
natural repose.

Kyé-Ho!

It's so close—you don't recognize it.
It's so deep—you don't grasp it.
It's so easy—you don't believe it.
It's so noble—you don't comprehend it.

Now, ultimate enlightenment, enlightenment's perfect rapture, and
the manifest body
Emerge from the hollow of the mind's clarity, emptiness, and their
union.
The three bodies' inseparability is enlightenment's essential body.
They are complete in the display of mind's awareness-emptiness.

Its inner glow is expressed in devotion, compassion, and skillful
means.
Skillful means blend circulating energy and the phase of creation in
unison,
Tools to produce an immense enrichment of experience.
If obstacles emerge, use two techniques to dispel them.

In fear of losing my spiritual father's, my master's, wish-fulfilling
instructions

To the thieves of forgetfulness,
The monk Losal Tenkyong sang this
In a secluded retreat, a cave in glorious Zhalu Mountain.

This concludes the song of notes to aid recollection of Great Seal
Amulet Box meditations.

JAMYANG KYENTSÉ WANGPO

URING THE EXTREME degeneration that marks this time of conflict, this master's life is as rare and as very significant as [the blossoming of] an *udumvara* flower.²¹ A wondrous, supreme manifestation of enlightenment, masterful lord of the seven transmissions, his outstanding, unparalleled life of freedom made him renowned throughout the horizon of the Himalayas by the name of Jamyang Kyentsé Wangpo. Vast and extensive vajra songs naturally overflowed from the repository of his expansive wisdom. Among them, one appropriate for this collection is called *The Flower of the Awareness Holder*, a spontaneous vajra song in praise of the inner life of freedom of the master of accomplishment Tsöndru Zangpo [Tangtong Gyalpo]:

Ah-Ho!
How wonderful!

The inner flame consumes the three existences at one time.
To it, the syllable *Ham* generously gives a share of nectar.
This burning and melting produces enlightenment's wisdom body,
    dissolution into the central channel.
Transcendent perfection of Fierce Inner Heat's bliss-emptiness,
    to you I bow.

Familiarity with the running chase of white and red drops of vital
    essence
Produces ethical conduct of satisfaction in the four changeless joys
And purifies supplementary delusion in its own ground, the sound
    of enlightenment's speech.
Transcendent perfection of Lucid Dream's clarity-emptiness,
    to you I bow.

Drinking waves of the nectar of unborn, perfect quiescence,
Makes the incomparable, wondrously gorgeous lotus
Of patience toward the profound meaning blossom fully,
    enlightenment's vajra mind.
Transcendent perfection of Clear Light's awareness-emptiness, to you
    I bow.

An intellect familiar with all phenomena's lack of reality,
Together with diligent application,
Surpasses positive and negative bias and reaches the expanse of
    spontaneous qualities.
Transcendent perfection of Illusory Body's appearance-emptiness, to
    you I bow.

Ultimately there is no coming nor going, no craving nor grasping,
Yet on the relative level, meditation on application to the vital
    circulating energies
Accomplishes the infallible celestial realms' enlightened activity.
Transcendent perfection of Transference of Consciousness's sensation-
    emptiness, to you I bow.

Transcendent knowledge realizes any appearance of delusion in the
    intermediate state of becoming
To be sacred form, mantra, and the body of ultimate enlightenment.
[This knowledge] makes the integrated body of perfect rapture
    emerge.
Transcendent perfection of Intermediate State's experience-emptiness,
    to you I bow.

In brief, familiarity with the six transcendent perfections' definitive
    meaning,
Inseparable from the six vajra doctrines,
Produces enlightenment's inexhaustible body, speech, mind, qualities,
    and activity.
Eternal, sacred transcendent perfections, to you I bow.

This movement of respect's warming sun
Opens the lotus flowers of words that please awareness holders.

Through this smiling play, may I accomplish a state inseparable from
　you, lord protector,
And may I further your life of spiritual freedom.

This song of praise to the inner life of freedom of Tangtong Gyalpo,
emanation of Lotus-Born Master and lion among an ocean of accomplished meditators in the cool region [of the Himalayas], employs the six
vajra doctrines taught by the wisdom dakini Niguma. I composed it as a
prayer near a place blessed by this master, Shri Dzala Sarvata iron bridge,
while crossing the gently moving Brahmaputra (Lohit) River in a mechan-
ical boat decorated with wood carvings.

The Ladder of Definitive Meaning, a spontaneous vajra song that gathers profound subjects:

É Ma Ho!
How wonderful!

Beyond dualistic experience, reality's original nature
Is free from all formulation, the innate character of luminosity.
Embraced by unchanging great bliss,
[Emptiness,] the sublime aspect of all circumstances, dances in my
　heart.

The concealed meaning, the secret nature,
Revealed in the essence of accomplished awareness holders' realization

Is not something I have seen, yet this vajra melody arises of itself
And flows now in streams of profound joy.

These masters fully realized and mastered the vital instructions
Of the definitive meaning—the vajra body's abiding nature.
They developed the wisdom of bliss and emptiness
And, having seen it, taught the path of means, the profound phase of
   completion.

[The vajra body's] framework is the channels; its movement, circulat-
   ing energy;
Its vital essence, the supreme mind of awakening.
These three, throughout a complete dance of formation, abiding, and
   destruction,
Remain as natural great wisdom's supports.

All knots in the three channels and the four energy centers
Are the three syllables[22]—skillful means, transcendent knowledge, and
   neuter.
The circulating energies are vitality, effort, and equanimity.
The vital essence is the bliss and emptiness of embrace and union.
These three groups, in stages, naturally produce bliss, clarity, and
   absence of thought
And accomplish an auspicious connection to enlightenment's three
   bodies.

The channels' path is to become endowed with vajra qualities;
The channels' vital instruction is constraint by means of physical
   exercises.

Circulating energy's path is to hold vital energy in the vase;
Circulating energy's supreme vital instruction is four-part breathing.

The vital essences' path is the running chase of melting and bliss from
   Ah and *Ham*;
The vital essences' vital instruction is binding at the four energy
   centers.

Illusory Body's path is to view appearance-emptiness as the deity's
    body;
Its vital instruction is to appear as a manifestation without
    attachment.

Lucid Dream's path is firm control with directed intent at the time
    of sleep;
Its vital instruction is to remain within the unborn state upon arising.

Clear Light's path is to gather the universe and beings into
    luminosity;
Its vital instruction is to bind mind and circulating energy equally.

Intermediate State's path is to recall the threefold nature;
Its vital instruction is to always regard [appearances] as delusion.

Transference of Consciousness's path is to eject the essential substance
    through Brahma's gate;
Its vital instruction is to collect and restrain the mind and circulating
    energy.

The main and auxiliary stages of these practices
Thus gather the stage of completion's profound subjects.
In other words, control of circulating energy produces the experience
    of clarity;
Control of vital essence produces bliss.
As their results are different, they are taught separately.

The phase of completion without concepts and forms
Reveals the meaning of luminosity, primordially unborn, like space.
Not bound by the self of phenomena or of the individual,
It abides in supreme emptiness.
Therefore, Great Seal exceeds the intellect's bounds;
It is the essential meaning that cannot be conceptualized.
As soon as the holy master introduces the mind's nature,
Naked seeing arises and you gain liberation within your own nature.
Likewise, use vital instructions for the support—
Circulating energy, mind, and vital essence—

To subdue any experience that emerges.
Thus, inconceivable luminosity, what is supported, will arise.

Concerning this, noble Tilopa said:

> If those with lesser minds cannot dwell in the ultimate,
> Grasp the key points of circulating energy and aim for
> awareness.
> Use various styles of gazing and techniques for concentration,
> Be firm until you can remain in awareness.
> For example, if you examine the center of space,
> Your grasping to its edge or middle ceases.
> Likewise, if mind examines the mind,
> Concepts and sense experience cease, you rest undisturbed,
> And see your intrinsic nature—unsurpassable awakening.

As he said, based on firm application
Of the profound, secret path's skillful means,
According to your share of diligence and capability,
You reach the supreme, essential meaning of liberation in the three
times.

This definitive meaning, the awareness-holding dakinis' oral transmis-
sion,
Is not an experience that has arisen in my mind.
Since I fall to the lowest rank of those who practice by intention
alone,
It is inappropriate for me to have uttered these teachings.
Thus, in the presence of the Three Roots' sacred circle,
I openly acknowledge the mass of faults there may be
In this vajra music that rose of itself.
What virtue it may have
I dedicate that all beings may dwell in Great Seal.

A Cloud of Magical Offerings, a spontaneous vajra melody of sound and emptiness:

Ah-Ho!
How wonderful!

The basis, the place of liberation,
Where the eight collections' delusions disperse,
Is the glorious mountain.
Circle of awareness-holding dakinis,
Playful dance in magical luminosity, to you I bow.
To delight spiritual heroes and dakinis,
I sing this song, an offering of the melody of sound and emptiness.

In the voice of infinite pure channels,
I sing the song of the phase of creation, appearance-emptiness.
The collection of conceptual delusion's aggregates and sense elements
Dissolves within the bodies of the three seats' deities.

In the voice of circulating energy that plays in the central channel,
I sing the song of mantra recitation, clarity-emptiness.
All attachment to sounds and words' intrinsic characteristics
Dissolves within scripture and realization.

In the voice of the great bliss of the vital essence,
I sing the song of the four joys, bliss-emptiness.
All bonds of ordinary obscuring emotions
Dissolve within the luminosity of union.

In the voice of inexpressible intrinsic awareness,
I sing the song of settling in the innate state's spontaneous expanse.
All dualistic thoughts' myriad forms
Dissolve within simultaneous arising and liberation.

In the voice of the *kati* crystal channel,
I sing the song of rainbow drops.
All marks of aggregates' and sense elements' solidity
Dissolve within the exhaustion of phenomena beyond the mind's
    domain.

In the voice of the three gates' equality,
I sing the song of creation, completion, and Great Completion.
All thoughts of existence and transcendence as two
Dissolve within the expanse of the effortless result.

In the voice of a wretched, insensitive practitioner,
I sing the song of various empty sounds.
All spiritual life, my plans and wishes to meditate,
Dissolve into sloth and procrastination.

This is my offering of the definitive meaning's melody.
This is my song of disappointment with my own mind.
By its virtue, may all sentient beings without realization
Spontaneously achieve the essence of their intrinsic awareness.

JAMGON KONGTRUL

THE FOLLOWING SONG, *The Melody of the Kalavingka Bird*, sung in the voice of certainty, presents the glorious Shangpa Golden Doctrines' vajra subjects, such as the profound path of the Niguma's Six Doctrines. It was sung by the one praised by authoritative individuals as a master whose life the Buddha foretold—Jamgon Buddha Vajra Bearer, Karma Ngawang Yönten Gyatso:

Lineage of seven jewels, from Buddha Vajra Bearer;
Golden garland of bodhisattvas at the point of culmination,
    nonhumans who assume human form;
And my illustrious root spiritual master, who bestowed naked enlight-
    enment,
At your lotus feet I bow: Make my experience and realization
    increase, I pray.

É Ma!
How wonderful!

On this essential path, I have excellent fortune—
I keep as my heart's wealth and as my mind's central concern
Buddha Vajra Bearer's oral transmission, the wisdom dakinis' secret
    words,
This lineage's accomplished masters' experience, and my root master's
    spiritual legacy.

In this Tibetan Himalayan region, the religious kings', translators',
    and scholars' kindness
Caused the gems of the discourses' and tantras' doctrines
    to spread widely.

Among them, the accomplished masters' unbroken lineage that
    produces signs of experience,
The learned and accomplished Kyungpo's Golden Doctrines, is more
    valuable than a wish-fulfilling jewel.

Sukasiddhi and Niguma taught the tantras' five ultimate subjects
In a fivefold sacred circle of wisdom that illuminates the secret,
    supreme path.
Their spiritual children, the lineage that preserves their tradition of
    teaching and meditation, are bodhisattvas who dwell on the stages
    of awakening.
[Once you receive this lineage's instructions,] blessings will arise even
    if you don't meditate!

When you merely hear the great garuda's name,
You cease to ponder the state of lesser birds;
The splendid magnificence of the name Kyungpo's Golden
    Doctrines[23]
Impedes respect toward ordinary individuals' conceptual writing.

Millions of recitations of mantras done with benighted words in
    benighted mouths
Can't compare to the degree of signs gained from moments of medita-
    tive experience in these doctrines.
Months and years spent turning the wheel of conceptual studies
Do not bring a fraction of the transcendent knowledge provided by
    experiential cultivation of these subjects.

These days, due to [declining] times, determined meditators are rare,
Yet if you bring consistent and steady effort to experiential
    cultivation,
With strong certainty in these teachings that cannot be doubted,
Supreme accomplishment will quickly be yours: this was the wisdom
    dakinis' final promise.

Because I lack courage in meditation, my experience and realization's
    power is incomplete

And, due to my feeble enterprise and strong distraction, I live far
    from manifest signs of meditative heat.
Yet, due to positive karmic connections, I gained trust and confidence
    in these doctrines—
To be devoted to them, as dear to me as my life and my heart, seems
    innate to me.

In the Golden Doctrines' jewel treasury, the five great tantras' inner
    essence
Is known as the illuminating root, Niguma's Six Doctrines.
These teachings engender on a single seat the sprout of meditative
    experience and realization.
Such outstanding instructions lead to supreme results in the course of
    a single lifetime.

The syllable [*Ah*], primordially unborn, is the gate for all phenomena
    of existence and transcendence.
It arises at the energy center of great bliss; its purifying nectar washes
    away negative acts, obscurations, sickness, and demons.
This cleansing provides an experience of naked clarity and emptiness.
This skillful technique, the Purifying Ah of Inner Space, constitutes
    the preliminary practice that strikes the vital point.

There is no path of means to accomplish enlightenment in a single
    lifetime other than the union of bliss and emptiness.
For this reason, your own body is the skillful means.
To tame wild inner channels and wild circulating energy, the wildfire
    of Fierce Inner Heat acts quickly—
After three weeks of meditation, you can circle your shoulders with
    white cotton.

Within the vajra body's support, the inner space of the three main
    channels and four energy centers,
The closed vase of four-part breathing makes the *Ah* and *Ham* blaze
    and melt.
Their movement is instantly embellished with the four joys.
This path of means, the spontaneous combustion of heat and bliss, is
    the heart jewel of India and Tibet's accomplished masters.

Eating the food of inner heat nurtures the young body of bliss and
  emptiness.
Wearing the clothes of inner heat makes heat and bliss blaze
  unbearably.
Sitting on its seat and riding its horse allow you to travel wherever
  you wish.
This extraordinary practice is the enlightened intention of
  uncommon, unsurpassable, sovereign tantras.

The path of devotion to the spiritual master makes what appears
  arise as unreal.
Appearance-emptiness, the deity's body, arises of itself; you see
  whatever appears as magical illusion.
Although this is the essence of Illusory Body, there are few who can
  really gain it.
The spiritual master, lord of accomplishment, has reached the core of
  that experience.

When you are free from four undermining conditions, existence's six
  realms arise as a magical illusion.
When you apply the eight vital instructions and threefold directed
  intent, you will know sickness and demons to be illusory.
Six collections of qualities arise and the knotted snake of reification
  uncoils.
These [instructions] are nectar for beginners' hearts.

To naturally grasp the appearances of supplementary delusion, you
  employ instructions for the vital essence's four empowerments.
If you can't grasp dreams, nine unmistaken vital instructions allow
  you to grasp [the appearances of] delusion upon meeting them.
Then you train spontaneously in the natural display [of dreams] by
  means of the vital instructions of training, replication, and
  transformation.
You will see the definite appearances of places and train in Lucid
  Dream's ultimate freedom—

Effortless, natural arising of the deity's body and its ultimate
  dissolution into clear light.

This represents the summit of the many profound teachings that
  vigorously cut through supplementary delusion.
These teachings that quickly transport even a shepherd to
  enlightenment
Come from the kindness of the spiritual master, the Buddha, with
  whom I have a slight connection.

Impermanence, disillusionment, conduct, sacred substances, the path
  of means, and prayer
Form the root, branches, leaves, flowers, and vines that grow
To produce subtle and deep clear light, the fruit you grasp, integrated
  as enlightenment's three bodies.
The meditation is clarity and emptiness; the postmeditative state
  merges bliss and emptiness, day and night.

Thus, the lamp of Clear Light illumines the dark room of stupidity's
  sleep.
Through the connection of gathering the mind and circulating energy
  and, particularly, by the spiritual master's blessing,
You will find inseparable bliss, clarity, and emptiness—profound,
  peaceful, and unformulated clear light—
Hidden within every circumstance, breaking the seeming boundaries
  of dualistic experience.

[Transference of Consciousness] to ultimate enlightenment's body
  sends consciousness to the nature of reality; of the body of rapture,
  to the deity of union.
[Transference of Consciousness] can be done through the force of the
  master's blessing or as flawless upward transference to the celestial
  realms.
These are done according to your level of capability at the time of death.
All present-day tantric practitioners perform this practice of creation
  and completion.

The clear light of the body of ultimate enlightenment, the victors'
  body of rapture,
The unimpeded, self-arising manifest body, and the general, faultless
  vital teachings

Bring liberation in the three intermediate states, according to your
   level of capability.
If you prepare during the period of leisure, your practice will be effec-
   tive when the busy time [death] arrives.

The preliminary practice of the three modes of natural repose fosters
   tranquillity and insight.
The main practice, the profound pointing-out instruction, naturally
   frees the four faults.
The culminating practice is knowledge that the union of clarity and
   emptiness arises naturally as enlightenment's three bodies.
This path of Great Seal forms the trunk of the doctrines' tree.

The oral transmission from the two wisdom dakinis and Métripa
Includes effortless, natural repose in the essence, accompanied by the
   elephant's gaze.
This produces the freshness of ordinary knowing, free from all
   grasping.
Enlightenment's three bodies arise nakedly—you find enlightenment
   in the palm of your hand.

Unlimited devotion's knowledge that whatever arises is the spiritual
   master is the first.
Unlimited pure vision's knowledge that appearances and sounds have
   the nature of deities and mantras is the second.
The integrated practice of lack of reality, knowledge that appearances
   and mind are a magical illusion or dreams, is the third.
These three are called "branches," but in fact they constitute the core
   of all discourses and tantras.

Vajra Yogini's two forms have the moon's and vermilion's glow.
Meditation and the sublime prayer's power make streams of their
   compassion flow.
Once you train in the four circles' lamps that liberate desire into bliss
   and emptiness,
The beautiful coemergent female buddhas greet you in the celestial
   realms' gardens.

Your mind never comes into being, nor does it cease or die.
Your body's nature is inert matter; the basis for the term "death" does
 not exist.
By binding the mind and circulating energy in the absolute expanse,
 steered by physical exercises,
You gain the fruit on the wide, plentiful plain of all four
 uncontaminated joys.

The spiritual master and the Protector inseparable guide the great
 manifestations of enlightenment's five bodies
And thereby bestow in a matter of months or years the four activities
 and supreme accomplishment.
In particular, in the form of Swift Protector, Powerful All-Seeing One,
 they grant protection from fear in the intermediate state.
With gestures of devotion and compassion, I treasure them as my
 eternal heart gem.

Buddha Shakyamuni's doctrine has conventional and definitive
 truths, each true in its own context.
The profound teachings of accomplished masters' lineages can be said
 to be great within their own schools.
However, others don't have even the name of the learned and
 accomplished Kyungpo Naljor's Golden Doctrines.
Those of us who drink the essence of ambrosia aren't tempted when
 offered beer.

Although my behavior is unpredictable, my mind dwells in the
 ultimate state.
Although I seem brainless, I confine myself in the nature of reality.
Although my speech is contrived, my character dwells of itself in the
 fundamental truth.
Thus I have not been able to remain impartial: behold this vagrant's
 writing!

In this life and in all my lifetimes, may I wrap the wish-fulfilling jewel
 of the Golden Doctrines
In the splendid cloak of my heart and thus reach the place of victory,
 vajra union.

There, may I see without duality and become a refuge to liberate
  beings whose numbers fill space.
May I swiftly accomplish this through the compassion of my root and
  lineage masters.

The omniscient *mahaguru*'s [Kyentsé Wangpo's] very meaningful vajra
tongue stretched [in speech] and nurtured the stem of my devotion. As a
result, my voice's lotus uncontrollably blossomed in this bee's song of profound meaning. A false semblance of a renunciant, servant of Péma,[24]
[named] Yönten Gyatso Lodrö Tayé, sang this in the retreat grove,
Dévikotri, on the left flank of Tsadra Rinchen Drak.

CONCLUSION

At the completion of the songs, sung with the strength of devotion and the energy of experience and realization, arrange offerings for a vajra feast. Perform the offering ritual, from the [initial] consecration to [the distribution of] the remainders, as described in the meditation text of the Five Deities of Supreme Bliss. Acknowledge faults to the feast's guests, request their patience, and, if you have a sacred support, perform the permanent residence prayer.

As a dedication of merit and an aspiration, recite this prayer, known as *Kyungpo Naljor's Sealed Dedication*:

Lord of the Teachings,
Endowed with enlightenment's three bodies
And the ten forms of knowledge;
Spiritual masters, deities,
Dakinis, protectors, and all [sources of refuge]—
Please lovingly remain here to witness my dedication.

In this life and in other lifetimes,
May any virtue I do,
In thought, word, and deed,
Effect this for the benefit of all sentient beings:

May I turn my obscuring emotions to the spiritual path.
May I take control of appearances.
May I attain enlightenment's three bodies.
For my own benefit, may I accomplish ultimate enlightenment.
For others, may enlightenment's two form bodies
Increase in enlightened acts for beings' benefit
Until the wheel of life empties.

May I appear wherever and in whatever form can guide others
And thereby accomplish great beneficial deeds.

May I guide my disciples with the right means at the right time.
May I be skillful in creating auspicious connections.
May connections to me be positive and significant.
May the seas of existence run dry.
May sentient beings attain the clear light of ultimate enlightenment.

Just as all buddhas of the three times
Performed dedications,
May I accomplish this dedication.

Until I attain enlightenment,
May I belong to an excellent clan, be healthy, and have clear senses.
May I practice the Teachings with mindfulness and ethical conduct.
May I be respected by all.
May I fulfill others' every hope and wish.

Until my awakening becomes manifest,
May harm from sicknesses, demons, impediments,
Humans, wild animals, cannibal spirits,
And the four elements
Be totally pacified.

May my longevity and merit increase
And my glory and wealth grow
Until my fame fills the skies.

May whatever I do in thought, word, and deed
Be helpful to sentient beings:
May the seas of existence run dry
And may sentient beings attain perfect enlightenment!

Further, recite *The Sealed Prayer of Auspicious Fortune*, that all times and directions be filled with the glory of virtue and excellence:

> Your enlightenment's qualities are perfectly complete, as massive as
>   Himalayan mountains;
> Your blessing's rivers satisfy your fortunate disciples.
> You reveal our own minds to be coemergent wisdom:
> May the auspicious fortune of the sublime spiritual master, Lord of
>   the Teachings, abide!
>
> You watch over meditators as your own children.
> You remain as close to us as our shadows.
> You bestow accomplishment upon those who keep their
>   commitments:
> May the auspicious fortune of the hosts of deities abide!
>
> You follow those of us who keep the commitments,
> And you accomplish various forms of enlightened activity—
> Pacifying, enhancing, magnetizing, and overpowering—as we request:
> May the auspicious fortune of the protectors and guardians abide!
>
> In the continual experience of great bliss,
> Appearing existence is self-liberating, like a magical illusion or dream.
> Without mental activity, in the expanse of clarity and emptiness,
> May the auspicious fortune of Great Seal's bliss and emptiness abide!
>
> Whether persons rely upon and make offerings to us
> Or treat us with contempt,
> The incomparable mind of awakening places them all on the path:
> May its auspicious fortune abide!
>
> Like the course of a mighty river,
> May the magnificence of all those who attain the state of auspicious
>   fortune
> In both existence and transcendence
> Bring eternal auspicious fortune to all sentient beings!

May our merit increase to rise like massive Supreme Mountain!
May our great fame pervade everywhere, like the sky!
May beings enjoy long life and freedom from sickness, and may benefit for others be accomplished spontaneously!
May the auspicious fortune of the supreme sea of enlightenment's qualities abide!

COLOPHON

T HE PRECIOUS Oral Instruction Lineage considers the singing of vajra songs to be extremely important. However, since this historical tradition of the Shangpa Instruction Lineage has not spread widely, texts of its accomplished masters' songs have become as rare as daytime stars. Therefore, I gathered these songs mainly from the masters' life stories and supplemented them with some songs, as appropriate, from recent lineage holders. Thus the sublime essence of ambrosia from the entire lineage's profound doctrines now swirls within the golden receptacle of my virtue from previous lifetimes.

Karma Ngawang Yönten Gyatso Lodrö Tayé composed this text in the secluded retreat of Dévikotri at Tsadra Rinchen Drak. May this work cause the historical tradition of the glorious Shangpa Instruction Lineage to spread and increase in all times and directions.

May virtue increase!

DEDICATION OF THE FIRST EDITION

The self-manifest, self-arising, indestructible sound
From Lord Buddha Vajra Bearer, the dakinis,
And the lineage's accomplished masters in succession
Is meaningful to hear and the source of all blessings.

Therefore, for adepts who dwell in the two phases' meditations
Or for individuals imbued with wholehearted faith and devotion,
To undertake the recitation of these vajra songs of realization
Causes the Shangpa lineage spiritual masters' billowing clouds of
    blessings to gather.

Hosts of deities' heavy rains of accomplishment pour continuously.
Dakinis and protectors remove impediments and accomplish
    enlightened activity.
Benevolent local protectors are delighted and increase our brilliant
    glow.
Malevolent local spirits become meek and are doused with the mind
    of awakening's nectar.

The energy of meditative experience develops and realization is
    enriched.
The seed of freedom is planted in those endowed with faith.
To cause such very meaningful fruit to ripen,
I have linked this garland of gems

With the golden cord of my faith.
The pure, noble intention of my sponsorship
Has fashioned this single woodblock from which many copies can be
    printed.

By this virtue, may I and others, all incarnate beings,

And chiefly those with whom I have a connection, be immediately
    free from obscurations.
May the supreme mind of awakening's two aspects
Arise effortlessly in our minds, and may our enlightened nature mani-
    fest.
May we fully achieve the accomplished masters' lives of freedom

And then take miraculous birth in a lotus in Blissful Pure Land.
May we receive Buddha Boundless Light's supreme prediction [of our
    complete enlightenment],
Quickly traverse awakening's paths and stages, and with limitless
    enlightened activity
Place all sentient beings, whose numbers reach the bounds of space,
    in the state of awakening.

May we become similar to the perfect Victor Limitless Light.
By the immense intention and powerful aspirations
Of the spiritual masters and the victors and their heirs,
May the prayers made here be blessed with fruition.

The aspiration prayer to dedicate this edition has been written in verses
equal in number to the auspicious signs [eight]. The writer who had this
positive intention is the *kusali* [renunciant], Lodrö Tayé.

May virtue increase!

THE SONGS OF KALU RINPOCHÉ

Blessings Fall as Rain[25]
A Supplication to One's Lama

Homage to the Lama!

The myriad forms and appearances, interdependent yet unobstructed,
Arise in the outer world as my symbolic teachers;
Indescribable is the harmonious dance of magic.
From this state, experiencing the natural freedom of visible space, I
    supplicate you:
Bless me with the fulfillment of Nirmanakaya,
Enlightenment manifesting skillfully in the world of form.

The varied sounds and voices, unimpeded from cause and condition,
Arise to my senses as mantra, my audible companions;
Inconceivable is the symphony of melody and song.
From this state, experiencing the natural freedom of audible silence, I
    supplicate you:
Bless me with the unfolding of Sambhogakaya, enlightenment free
    from limitation.

The panorama of thoughts in the unutterable expanse of awareness
Arise in my own mind as my intuitive guide;
Vast and pervasive is the display of thought and memory.
From this state, blissful and luminous and open, I supplicate you:
Bless me that I may realize Dharmakaya, enlightenment pure and
    simple.

Thus the whole universe—visible, audible, and conceptual—
Pointing out to myself and others the direct apprehension of the
    underlying reality,
Is nothing but the gesture of my lama.
Ever conscious of your kindness, I supplicate you:
Grant me the realization of the fundamental nature of all.

The entire host, a vast ocean of the three roots
Which dance like mirages, responding to my devotion,
Are not separate in the least from my venerable lama.
From the state where all qualities are perfect and complete, I
    supplicate you:
Bless me that my mind may merge with yours;
Inspire me to renounce ego's hold;
Bless me that I may experience true contentment;
Bless me that I may develop loving-kindness and compassion;
Bless me that I may give rise to sincere devotion;
Bless me that I may cut off pervasive thoughts;
Bless me that I may pacify confusion in its own ground;
Bless me that I may perceive ultimate reality, Mahamudra;
Bless me that I may attain Buddhahood in this very life.

From this time on, until enlightenment is reached,
With pure discipline as my ornament,
Enriched with the awakening attitude, equanimous to all,
And fulfilling the stages of transformation and consummation,
May I, the disciple, reach full enlightenment, inseparable from the
    teacher!

Thus, Karma Rangjung Kunchab spoke this sincere and heartfelt song
of the phenomenal world as one's lama, entreated by the diligent practitioner Lama Karma Shérab. May it serve to fill his heart with the lama's
blessing!

E Ma Ho!
How wonderful!

Remain relaxed, without clinging or contrivance
Within mind's nature, like space,
Free from any reference point
And with the vigor of vivid, mindful awareness.

Whatever outward or inward movement of thought arises,
Don't lose hold of the vital inner glow of the expanse of mindfulness.
Don't fabricate [mental states].
Rest your mind as it is—
It will be liberated into the absolute expanse.

Recollection stirs thoughts.
Recollection itself is the inner glow within the nature of mind's
    expanse.
Those three are inseparable, like waves and water—
Mind's nature is a vast sea;
Recollection is the sea's wetness, its inner glow;
Thoughts are its waves.

Rest in an uncontrived state and they become inseparable.
You don't need to create this inseparable state:
It exists primordially. Rest within it.

Don't strive with thought; remain uncontrived.
If you contrive and hold a reference point,

The view and the viewer will separate
And impede meditation.

Without contrivance, transformation, or reference point,
Rest your mind as it is: that's it!
When that continues without interruption, you will gain the result.

For the benefit of others, I, the one known as Lodrö,[26] wrote this based on my own experience. May it prove virtuous!

Fortunate brother and sister companions whose commitments are
    pure,
You have reached the path to freedom in a single lifetime.

This body of ultimate enlightenment, the mind's nature, awareness-
    emptiness,
Is endowed with all the positive qualities of freedom and maturity.

Not shrouded by the darkness of ignorance,
Not scattered by the winds of distraction,
Not polluted by clinging to meditative states—
If you don't lose hold of the vigor of unformulated awareness,
And if simple knowing's inner glow has not faded,

Even if you view and examine appearing forms,
You will not find a moment in which they transcend appearance-
    emptiness.

Even if you listen to and grasp audible sounds,
They will be vivid sound-emptiness, without attachment.

Even if you smell and linger on myriad fragrances,
Your awareness of sensation-emptiness will be fresh.

Whatever sweet and delicious tastes you savor,
Your knowing of taste-emptiness will be pure and empty.

Even in the expanse of sexual union's touch,
Your awareness of bliss-emptiness will be unimpeded.

Even if you are never free from sickness and pain,
They become sensation-emptiness in your basic nature.

Even if you spend your time in deep sleep,
Your awareness in empty clarity will be naked.

Regardless of what thoughts of attachment or anger arise,
They become arising-emptiness in their lack of a basis.

There is no other key point than this—Ah la la!

A deity's form higher than appearance-emptiness,
Mantras to recite higher than sound-emptiness,
Ultimate enlightenment higher than awareness-emptiness—
Search where you will for these, you'll not find them!

Without impeding thoughts of the six senses,
Grasp awareness in its own ground
And enjoy the six sense domains without attachment—
No other offerings than these complete the cultivation of merit and
    wisdom!

Your outward, seeming behavior can be pure and excellent,
Yet if you do not lose hold of the nature of mind's inner glow,
Your view, meditation, and conduct will be magnificent.

Relative behavior is misleading:
Even if you act disregarding what is clean and unclean, like dogs or
    pigs,
And your behavior seems incoherent, like a madman's,
When you remain within awareness-emptiness,
You are the equal of India's accomplished masters.

If you do not move from ultimate equanimity,
Whatever you do is the act of a buddha,

Wherever you live is a pure land,
And your every companion is a deity of appearance-emptiness.

Om Svasti
Namo Guru

By the blessing of the Three Roots, the spiritual master, and
    protector,
And by the force of our conduct in the splendid sea of the two
    accumulations,
May all those gathered here have long lives free from sickness,
And may we not be separated for an instant until we reach
    awakening!

May the fortress of our enemies, the eight worldly concerns, be
    demolished from its foundations,
May we know food, wealth, and possessions to be like magical
    illusions,
May we be freed from the chains that bind us to friends and family—
May we reach the capital city of our Oral Instruction Lineage
    ancestors!

May we not harbor pride of rank or learning,
May we never wish to compete with those above us or have contempt
    for those below,
May we never entertain thoughts of the five poisons that kill the life
    force of freedom—
May our minds turn toward awakening!

In secluded mountain hollows, in a fathomless wilderness,
Having left worldly affairs far behind,
May we live relaxed and joyful, content with what comes our way,
Treasuring only the essence of our own minds!

With the lifestyle of acting like small children, without attachment,
And not moving from the inexpressible meaning that transcends the
    intellect,

May we gain mastery of the mind of awakening, awareness.
For it, what appears, what arises, becomes meditation!

May all seemingly solid phenomena arise as the deity's illusory body,
May all verbal expression dissolve into mantras' sound-emptiness,
May every thought arise as great wisdom:
In this lifetime, may we attain the state of Buddha Vajra Bearer!

Sarva Mangalam Bhavantu

Om Svasti
Namo Guru

My child, if you go from here to practice the Teachings,
Your old father has a few words for you, from his heart.
Cherish these always in the center of your mind.

My child, to make this free and fully endowed human life
    meaningful,
You'll need to sincerely recall death.

To continue wandering aimlessly,
You'll need to rely on yourself and no one else.

To stay alone in mountain retreats,
You'll need to reduce your activity of gifts and offerings.

To be happy anywhere you stay, without choosing,
You'll need uninterrupted meditation and forbearance.

Toward your spiritual master, Buddha of the three times,
You'll need faith without fatigue or disillusionment.

In the phase of creation's clear appearances of the deity,
You'll need the confidence of knowing them to be your own mind.

In the phase of completion's abiding nature of mind,
You'll need the continuity of rest within natural repose.

Toward your kind parents, the six kinds of beings,
You'll need uninterrupted love and compassion.

Toward phenomena that are like a magical illusion,
You'll need to destroy clinging to their reality.

Toward the harm of demons who cause obstacles,
You'll need fearless rest within natural repose.

To accomplish the spiritual master's blessings,
You'll need to keep them within you, without arrogance.

To practice the Teachings correctly,
You'll need to cut your bonds of attachment at their roots.

I sing this short song of twelve needs,
These delicious and nutritious words,
For my child who is going away to meditate.

Not forgetting your old father,
Know all appearing existence,
Including thoughts of happiness, suffering, or in between,
To be the spiritual master's display:
Please travel to that place!

You who learn these words from my heart,
Should promise yourself never to forget them:
You will thereby accomplish great things in this life and the next!

In all places, times, and circumstances,
The protector of the teachings, Swift Protector,
Will surely guard you like a mother her child.

I offer you my prayers that your life be long and without sickness,
And that you accomplish all your wishes in harmony with the
    Teachings.
May you practice as long as you live!

Lama Rangjung Kunchab spoke this to Gonya Tokden. May it prove virtuous!

Incomparably kind root spiritual master,
Body that unites all victors and their spiritual heirs of the three times,
Illustrious leader of every sentient being, myself and others,
From the bottom of my heart, I pray to you.
Bless me that I train in love, compassion, and the mind of awakening.
Bless me that I see the innate enlightened face of my abiding nature.

Lama Kalu spoke this in response to my child-disciple Tsöndru.

The spiritual master's auspicious fortune is the exhaustion of all faults
    and the perfection of all qualities.
The profound Teachings' auspicious fortune is to reveal the sublime
    path, free from error.
The disciples' auspicious fortune is to enter the correct path:
May the ultimate auspicious fortune, the merging of the master's and
    disciples' minds, abide!

Listening's auspicious fortune is a heart rejuvenated with profound
    instruction.
Reflection's auspicious fortune is the collapse of delusion's false
    cavern.
Meditation's auspicious fortune is sight of awareness's own face:
May the result's auspicious fortune, actualization of ultimate
    enlightenment, abide!

Erudition's auspicious fortune is knowledge of all things to be
    accepted or rejected.
Noble conduct's auspicious fortune is freedom from all faults.
Excellence's auspicious fortune is the beauty of every positive quality:
May the auspicious fortune of magnificence, victory over faults,
    abide!

Teaching's auspicious fortune is to bring others, faithful persons, to
    maturity.

Debate's auspicious fortune is victory in battle with the obscuring
  emotions.
Composition's auspicious fortune is to reach perfection in the view
  and meditation:
May the abiding nature's auspicious fortune, spontaneous help to others, abide!

The auspicious fortune of the basis is a noble, altruistic intention, a
  single white cloth.
The path's auspicious fortune is that all you do becomes the spiritual
  path.
The result's auspicious fortune is the accomplishment of your own
  and others' benefit:
May all-pervasive auspicious fortune entirely pervade all space!

Sarva Mangalam Javentu

THE SONGS OF BOKAR RINPOCHÉ

The Queen of Spring's Song to Ease Troubled
Minds, Advice for Us All

Namo Guru Vé

All noble buddhas of the three times'
Wisdom, love, and creative power
Converge in you, paragon of all families of enlightenment, beings'
    lord protector,
My supreme guide, lord of the Teachings,
Illustrious mighty one among victors, Karmapa,
Ultimately inseparable from my kind root master, to whom I bow.

At all times—in this life and the next—watch over me with your
    compassion:
I have no one else to turn to!

My previous acts and merit have not been weak:
My life is full and free, my spiritual guide is qualified,
And I received Lord Shakyamuni's essential doctrine.
In this present moment, the best of all worlds,
I don't cultivate the experience of genuine Teachings
But throw this human life away in fleeting distractions.
The deeds I've done form a wide canopy of unvirtuous acts—
When I die, I'll be wracked with regrets.
Thinking of this, I'm utterly discouraged with myself.

People of this degenerate time are busy and preoccupied;
They are unreliable and very unstable.

Ignorant of the consequences of their acts, they live unaware
Of vows, tantric commitments, modesty, or shame—
They lead themselves and others to eternal calamity.
The Jewels are an unfailing refuge;
Apart from them, I've not found a reliable companion—
I've lost hope in everyone.

We pride ourselves on shouldering the burden
Of the doctrines of scripture, realization, teaching, and meditation
    practice—
Excellent education, spiritual activity, monastic lifestyle,
And flourishing projects for others' good—
Yet the impurities of our wish for fame and fortune, and the eight
    worldly concerns, taint it all.
How could this be correct Buddhist practice?

To our conceit toward what we've requested and received of the
    Teachings
We add complaints when putting them into practice.
I wonder if our good-looking guise of spiritual acts
Will ever result in what we wish to attain for eternity?

Now we should be more than a little kind to ourselves
And consider the lives of our lord Kagyu ancestors.
If we don't sincerely nurture the Teachings in our hearts,
The teachings we repeat with our mouths—
Turning from attachment, the mind of awakening, and the phases of
    creation and completion,
As lovely as rainbows—can enthrall our audience,
But when misfortunes occur,
We find we are but ordinary persons.
Thinking of this, I'm sincerely ashamed.

To wish to liberate others
Without freeing our own mind
By cultivating the ultimate—what folly!

Granting empowerments and teaching with arrogant self-assurance

Smothers others and ourselves with burdensome faults and violations
    of tantric commitments.
To live alone and uninvolved entails few faults:
I should ponder that well, fool that I am!

I have not the fortune to replicate the lives of my Kagyu forefathers,
Who wandered in secluded mountain retreats,
Devoting themselves to single-minded meditation.
Yet my lord spiritual master, all buddhas incarnate,
Has lovingly granted me his essential oral instructions:
May I not waste them
But devote myself to diligent practice!

May our feet stand firmly in clear-sighted turning from attachment
In sincere, intense application
To the four common preliminary practices.
May our minds turn to the sacred Teachings.

May we use the four special preliminary practices
To complete the two accumulations and cleanse the two obscurations.
Especially, may the profound path of devotion
Bless us that the Teachings become our spiritual path.

The highest Vajra Way's profound instructions
In the two phases, and in the paths of means and liberation,
Cleanse attachment to delusion's ordinary appearances.
In this lifetime, may we attain the state of integral purity,
    enlightenment's four bodies.

Sing with devotion, never separate from your father spiritual master,
The body of ultimate enlightenment, Vajra Bearer;
Your fervent songs draw his mind's vajra wisdom—
The blessed ultimate lineage's realization moves to you.

In the continuity of the spiritual master's mind and your own as one,
Look back, look at this very mind.
Mind is not existent, it is emptiness—
Its form, color, and substance do not exist,

Yet it is not nonexistent: anything at all can arise within it.
Its luminosity forms the basis of existence and transcendence.
Its noncomposite nature transcends the intellect.
No words or terms can express it.
In the domain of individual, intrinsic awareness,
This naked, ordinary knowing
Is the entire Canon's discourses' and tantras' meaning,
The victors of the three times' essential realization,
Called "Great Seal of the body of ultimate enlightenment."

Words can only indicate this view;
Its meaning, the abiding nature, is experienced by means of
    meditation.
Based on that experience, we gain realization.
Realization leads in this lifetime to manifest enlightenment.

For this, we need an authentic introduction to our innate essence.
Don't consider that we must rid ourselves of thoughts;
Don't deliberately create a nondiscursive state.
Settle in continual evenness
In this relaxed, ordinary knowing—
Without distraction, without meditation, without action.

Single-minded clarity without thoughts
Forms the basis of tranquillity meditation.
Tighten the focus when dull; loosen it when agitated.

In insight, gazing at the mind's abiding nature
Destroys its seemingly identifiable characteristics.
Come to an inner conclusion concerning its real nature.

The inseparable union of tranquillity and insight is Great Seal.

How precious it is to gain stability in this
By means of a lineage-bearing master's pith instructions
And our own meditative experience!

The peerless king of skillful means

Is devotion's supplications to the spiritual master,
Accompanied by thoughts of impermanence, disillusionment, and
    compassion.
Never apart from this union of skillful means and transcendent
    knowledge—
Vital, supreme instruction for dispelling hindrances and enriching
    experience—
May they dissipate delusion on the path.

May we traverse at once the inner paths and stages,
Along the twelve levels of contemplative practice, three on each of
    four,
Until reaching nonmeditation, the great body of ultimate
    enlightenment.
May the immense creative power of experience and realization reach
    culmination.
May appearances of delusion arise as great wisdom.
May the formulations of existence and transcendence be purified in
    the basic nature.
May the characteristics of affirmation and denial be freed in their own
    ground.
May desire in the view, meditation, and conduct be exhausted.
May the luminosity of the basis and the path, mother and child,
    merge.

In this lifetime, may we fully achieve the two goals, for others and
    ourselves—
The epitome of enlightenment's four bodies and five wisdoms,
Powerful Buddha Vajra Bearer.

May I now accomplish what I have always wished for:
To reach the capital city of my Kagyu ancestors!

In Darjeeling district's Mirik retreat center, Garden of Joyous Union
(Zungjuk Gatsal Ling), a sublime sacred place blessed by Lord Métripa, the
lamas of the three-year, three-fortnight retreat, led by Adzin Choktrul Rinpoché, who has awakened to his holy heritage; and others, including Ladak
Lama Tashi Döndrub, Nyishang Lama Tashi Wangdu, Gangkar Lama

Purbu Tashi, and Lama Pasang Dorjé, made offerings to repeatedly encourage me: "You must write the vital points of experiential cultivation in the form of a song."

It's impossible for a song giving profound advice to others to emerge from someone like me, who is nothing more than an ordinary, self-centered individual. Yet, so as not to deny the intentions of those who made the request and despite my not having cultivated this experience, I kept in my mind only the unfailing blessings of the Kagyu masters endowed with the tantras and wrote this on October 1, 2002, in the retreat center. I, Karma Ngédön Chökyi Lodrö, who bears the title of Bokar Tulku, pray that this will prove helpful to those who rely on me.

Sarva Mangalam

The **Nada's** *Own Sound: A Vajra Feast Song to Enrich Adepts' Experience*

Ah-Ho!

Great bliss of intrinsic awareness—spiritual master of ultimate reality;
Wisdom's display, enlightenment's three bodies—infinite hosts of the
  Three Roots' deities;
Natural repose, fully and primordially free from all change or
  movement—the innate, basic nature:
Please come to this feast gathering, a festival of uncontrived, exposed
  awareness-emptiness.

Accept these feast offerings of the pleasures of appearing existence,
  gods' and humans' finest possessions;
Enjoy them in the great wisdom of integral union, appearance-emptiness without attachment.

Accept these feast offerings of the five meats and five nectars, pure
  forms of the five families' male and female buddhas;
Enjoy them in great equanimity toward marks and concepts of
  cleanliness or filth.

Accept these feast offerings of *Ah* and *Ham*'s blazing and melting, the
  essential substance of your own body's skillful means and
  transcendent knowledge;
Enjoy them in the coemergent festival of great bliss-emptiness
  without attachment.

Accept these feast offerings of mental activity, my own mind arising
  unhindered as any appearance of existence and transcendence;
Enjoy them in the great pervasive expanse, the intrinsic display of
  awareness-emptiness without clinging.

Spiritual heroes and dakinis of pure sacred places and regions, outer,
  inner, and other—
Enjoy this feast gathering, a festival of great, uncontaminated bliss-
  emptiness.
Bind our aggregates and sense elements within the unobscured
  essential substance of our bodies' channels, circulating energies,
  and vital essence.
Make changeless coemergent wisdom manifest now.

Above, the vajra master, my noble master imbued with kindness;
Between, brothers and sisters with pure commitments, my vajra companions;
Below, fortunate men and women, persons with pure faith and
  devotion—
Accept the wisdom ambrosia of these feast substances with no
  attachment to ordinary appearances,

Apparent existence in infinite purity, the display of sacred form,
mantra, and wisdom.
Enjoy them as inseparable from the nature of reality, free from
craving, attachment, and choosing among them.
In the Highest Pure Land of Dense Array, endowed with the
magnificent five certainties,
May I gain manifest enlightenment in the realization shared inseparably between teacher and disciple.

The chief of France's Kagyu Yiga Chödzin, Lama Shérab Dorjé, accompanied by Lama Orgyen Wangdu and the retreat master Lama Tenpa
Gyatso, presented me with offerings and insistently encouraged me [to
compose a song]. Merely to avoid refusing their requests, I, Karma Ngédön
Chökyi Lodrö, who holds the title of Bokar Tulku, have formulated these
aspirations.

A Short Song of the Six Similes to Satisfy the Heartfelt Yearning of Devoted Disciples

Fortunate men and women, who have karmic affinity with the
Teachings,
You gained a free and fully endowed precious human life,
Met an authentic noble spiritual master,
And received vast and deep teachings for spiritual maturity and
liberation.
Now exert yourselves in cultivating meditative experience,
I beseech you.

Your spiritual master is like the sun in space—
When your doubts or wrong views do not cloud him,
His compassionate light shines continuously:
In yearning faith and devotion, pray.

Your pure vision is like an eye—
When your pride or critical thoughts do not blind it,
All beings are mines of noble qualities:
Train in universal pure vision, I beseech you.

Your development of the mind of awakening is like a potent seed—
When plans for your own good do not spoil it,
It grows into perfect awakening:
Always meditate on the two aspects of the mind of awakening.

Your self-clinging is like an unseen enemy—
When you lose hold of the antidote of mindfulness,
You will never escape the den of suffering:
Therefore, please subdue your own mind.

Your mind's nature is like an endless ocean—
When waves of clinging to appearances do not disturb it,
It has a single flavor, the essence of reality:
Dwell without acceptance or rejection, affirmation or denial, I
  beseech you.

Your mind is like a wish-fulfilling jewel—
When delusion's impurities do not taint it,
It produces all you need and desire:
Always meditate on Great Seal.

At all times—in this life, the next, and in between—
The spiritual master's enlightened mind and your mind
Are not separate in your intrinsic awareness.
In natural repose, without distraction or clinging,
Make manifest the primordial body of ultimate enlightenment.

I, Karma Ngédön Chökyi Lodrö, who holds the title of Bokar Tulku, composed this *Short Song of the Six Similes to Satisfy the Heartfelt Yearning of Devoted Disciples* according to the wishes of the residents of France's Nigu Ling Retreat Center.

Namo Guru!

When singing supplications of yearning
In devotion without a trace of doubt
To your father spiritual master, Buddha of the three times,
Settle in the oneness of his mind and yours.

In continual love and compassion
For your mothers, all sentient beings of the six kinds,
Live life with all thoughts and deeds turned toward others' good.
Always meditate on the mind of awakening's two aspects.

All appearing existence, primordially pure,
Is eternally existent sacred form, mantra, and wisdom, inseparable.
Make realization of this your contemplative practice.
Dwell only within infinite purity.

These three—devotion, pure vision, and the mind of awakening—
Are the path of contemplative practice's essence.
Adepts imbued with all three
Never leave Great Seal.

The basis—two truths as one—Great Seal.
The path—two accumulations as one—Great Seal.
The result—enlightenment's two bodies as one—Great Seal.
May you quickly realize integral union—Great Seal.

I, Karma Ngédön Chökyi Lodrö, who holds the title of Bokar Tulku, composed this according to the wishes of the residents of Naro Ling, the retreat center at Kagyu Ling, France.[27]

Wide Wings That Lift Us to Devotion: A Supplication

Spiritual master, think of me! Think of me!
Source of blessings, root spiritual master, think of me!

Spiritual master, think of me! Think of me!
Epitome of all accomplishment, root spiritual master, think of me!

Spiritual master, think of me! Think of me!
Agent of all enlightened activity, root spiritual master, think of me!

Spiritual master, think of me! Think of me!
All refuges in one, root spiritual master, think of me!

Turn all beings' minds, with mine, toward the Teachings.
Bless me that all stages of the faultless path—
Renunciation, the mind of awakening, and the correct view—
Genuinely arise in my being.

May I dwell untouched by the faults of pride and wrong views
Toward the Teachings and the teacher of freedom's sublime path.
May steadfast faith, devotion, and pure vision
Lead me to fully achieve the two goals for others and myself.

The human tantric master introduces my intrinsic essence.
The master in the Joyful Buddha's Canon instills certainty.
The symbolic master in appearances enriches experience.
The ultimate master, the nature of reality, sparks realization of the
    abiding nature.

Finally, within the state of the master inseparable from my own mind,
All phenomena of existence and transcendence dissolve into the
    nature of reality's expanse;
The one who affirmed, denied, and clung to things as real vanishes
    into the absolute expanse—
May I then fully realize the effortless body of ultimate enlightenment.

In all my lifetimes, may I never be separate from the true spiritual
    master.
May I enjoy the Teachings' glorious wealth,
Completely achieve the paths and stages' noble qualities,
And swiftly reach the state of Buddha Vajra Bearer.

In 1995, in response to requests from two translators, Lama Tcheuky and Lama Namgyal, on behalf of my foreign disciples, I, Karma Ngédön Chökyi Lodrö, who holds the title of Bokar Tulku, wrote this at my home in Mirik Monastery. May it prove meaningful.

PART 2

THE SHANGPA MASTERS
AND THEIR LINEAGE

BUDDHA VAJRA BEARER

PERSONS UNFAMILIAR with Tibetan Buddhism might question the plethora of deities that appear in its rich tantric landscapes: If this is Buddhism, where is the Buddha? Sacred tantric art and literature overflow with colorful forms, yet they often seem to exclude Buddha Shakyamuni. Here, for example, at the beginning of the collection of Shangpa masters' songs, the place of honor is offered not to Shakyamuni but to Vajra Bearer—pictured as dark blue and long-haired, wearing regal ornaments and a crown, sometimes alone and sometimes in sexual union, a buddha who seems a universe apart from the serene sage all Buddhists revere. Nevertheless, practitioners of tantra see Buddha Shakyamuni and Buddha Vajra Bearer as two forms of a single enlightenment. One later Shangpa master, Mokchok-pa Kunga Ö, begins his *Biography of Buddha Vajra Bearer* by explaining the relationship between these two buddhas:

Of the 1,002 buddhas who appear during this Fortunate Eon, three appeared previously [before our Buddha]. Our present era is that of the Victor Shakyamuni's doctrine. This teacher took birth as Siddharta, son of King Shuddhodana and his consort Beautiful Goddess of Illusion [also known as Mahamaya]. He demonstrated twelve acts, including that of manifest enlightenment.

On an inner level, this teacher was Vajra Bearer. For the benefit of disciples (beginning with Indrabhuti) who harbor desire [as their principal emotion], he taught the four classes of tantra and other instructions. During such teachings, an entourage of wrathful male and female deities, and bodhisattvas on awakening's tenth stage encircled him. His teaching occurred during the lowest time of existence; its location was the place created by transcendent virtues, the magnificent configuration of all buddhas, Vajra Queen's vagina.

Why is the teacher called Vajra Bearer? Because he maintains vajralike concentration within the nature of reality, he is known as Vajra Bearer. As is said:

> Why is he called Vajra Bearer?
> Whoever is endowed with all buddhas' wisdom
> And mind of awakening
> Is the Victor Vajra Bearer,
> Chief of all transcendent buddhas.

Therefore, the Buddha who perfected renunciation and realization is outwardly Shakyamuni and inwardly Vajra Bearer. Their common nature is the body of ultimate enlightenment; they epitomize the three bodies of enlightenment. (*The Collection of Shangpa Masters' Biographies*, pp. 2-4)

Therefore, in general, tantric practitioners reflexively recognize Vajra Bearer as the form Buddha Shakyamuni displayed when he taught tantra. A doctor at the office might greet and treat patients while wearing street clothes, but in the operating room the same doctor can be virtually unrecognizable in surgical dress. Vajra Bearer is none other than Buddha Shakyamuni dressed appropriately for the teaching of tantra. The two forms reflect different activities, not a distinction in hierarchy. Although Buddha Vajra Bearer has an ethereal, superhuman form, "the body of enlightenment's perfect rapture," many Buddhists believe that Shakyamuni himself was not merely a human being who attained enlightenment during one lifetime. We consider him a sublime manifestation of an enlightenment gained elsewhere, who demonstrated Buddha's acts in this world and who fashioned his teaching to be accessible and beneficial specifically for the beings of our historical era. Kunga Ö describes this view of Buddha Shakyamuni's spiritual journey in the same text:

> How can the three bodies of enlightenment be complete within a single individual? The chief of the Buddhist doctrine, Shakyamuni, attained enlightenment in the past, incalculable eons ago. That achievement constituted his attainment of ultimate enlightenment. His two form bodies of enlightenment [the bodies of perfect rapture and manifest enlightenment] are as stated in *The Descent to Lanka Discourse*:
>
>> The perfect Buddha [demonstrated] the attainment of enlightenment there;
>> One of his manifestations [demonstrated] the attainment of enlightenment here. (*Ibid.*, pp. 17-18)

The author goes on to explain that Vajra Bearer is the perfect Buddha who demonstrated enlightenment in the form of enlightenment's perfect rapture "there," specifically the Highest Pure Land; and that Shakyamuni is the manifestation who exhibited enlightenment "here," in this world. This portrayal of Shakyamuni is at obvious odds with common Buddhist versions of him as a man who attained enlightenment during his lifetime. Yet, for tantric practitioners, if Buddha was born a manifestation of enlightenment, his attainment of ultimate enlightenment had to have preceded his birth. Kunga Ö writes:

> Which [of enlightenment's three bodies] is attained first? It is that of ultimate enlightenment, followed by the two form bodies, in stages. The opposite order is impossible. (*Ibid.*, p. 15)

For readers unfamiliar with the three bodies of enlightenment or in need of a reminder, since they are mentioned repeatedly in this collection of songs, Kunga Ö provides this outline:

> The three bodies of enlightenment can be divided into three categories: the three bodies of the intrinsic basis; those of practice on

the spiritual path; and those that arise naturally as the result.

First, the three bodies that abide in the basis [are twofold]: Sentient beings (the inner contents of the universe's environment) naturally possess the complete three bodies of enlightenment—death is the body of ultimate enlightenment; life is the body of perfect rapture; and birth, the manifest body. Chapter 10 of *Matrix of Mystery Tantra* states:

> The body, speech, and mind of the sentient beings of the three realms
> Unite Vajra Bearer's body speech, and mind; meditate on equanimity.

The universe's outer environment also naturally possesses the complete three bodies of enlightenment—space is the body of ultimate enlightenment; the four elements are the body of perfect rapture; and their manifold appearances, the manifest body...

Second, the spiritual path's three bodies are as follows. To rest the mind within its spacelike purity is the body of ultimate enlightenment; to have the mind's sacred circle [of deities] arise is the body of perfect rapture; and to perform [such visualizations] as to emit light from the deities' sacred circle and to gather it back is the manifest body...

Third, the three bodies that arise naturally as the result are as follows. When the three bodies naturally present in the basis are engaged in spiritual practice guided by the spiritual master's teaching, they naturally arise even without having been wished for. For example, when crops are properly tended and rice grows, its husks form at the same time. That is to say, from the body of ultimate enlightenment, like space, appearances of the form bodies of enlightenment, equal to the bounds of space, will arise to benefit disciples, sentient beings in numbers equal to the bounds of space. (*Ibid.*, pp. 10-12)

Thus Buddhas Shakyamuni and Vajra Bearer, forms that appear for beings' benefit from the same source, the ultimate body of enlightenment, are likened to husks that have grown along with rice.

Each of these buddhas is commonly assigned a number, but for very different reasons. Shakyamuni's four refers to the fact that he is considered the fourth historical buddha to appear in this era's series of 1,002; whereas Vajra Bearer's six indicates that he gathers in his sole person the qualities of enlightenment's five families. Kunga Ö writes, "Vajra Bearer, the sixth, unites the five families of enlightenment." For the same reason, we sometimes see references to Vajra Bearer as the "lord who pervades," implying that he masters enlightenment's every facet, including its many forms of wisdom and what are called its families.

Finally, songs often begin with homage to the spiritual master as Vajra Bearer. Although such homage is perfectly sincere, it is not meant to be taken as a historically verifiable fact, except in the cases of such extraordinary masters as Niguma and Sukasiddhi. Rather, it is an expression of faith that needs no independent confirmation of the sort Himalayan tantric Buddhists are fond of giving, such as affirmations that the Dalai Lama and Karmapa are incarnations of Bodhisattva Great Compassion. To my knowledge, no reincarnate master has ever been recognized as Vajra Bearer incarnate, yet all spiritual masters are cherished and worshiped in prayer by their disciples as none other than Vajra Bearer, temporarily in human form. So prevalent is this faith-induced identification of one's own spiritual master with Buddha Vajra Bearer that Kunga Ö comments on it. He first finds support for the practice in a tantra (although he mentions another buddha, Vajrasattva) and then warns us not to take such pure vision to the point of expecting our own Vajra Bearer to compose new tantras:

> Should you think that it is inappropriate for [Vajra Bearer] to appear in ordinary [human] form, having assumed the five psychophysical aggregates that arise from karma and obscuring emotions, *The Vajra Tent Tantra* states:
>
> > Why is he called Vajrasattva?
> > That buddha has assumed the form of a spiritual master.
> > With the intention to benefit sentient beings,
> > He lives in an ordinary [human] form.
>
> [You might think that] if that individual is Vajra Bearer [incarnate], it would be appropriate for him to teach [new] tantras. [However, this is not the case.] Tantras [must be taught in the context of

the] five magnificent aspects of the teaching [the teacher, location, time, audience, and teaching]: [if such an individual were to enunciate new tantras now,] the [magnificent] time would be contradicted, as this present time is the period of the doctrine's decline. Further, one doctrine cannot have two Teachers. (*Ibid.*, pp. 20-21)

This last line reaffirms that Shakyamuni and Vajra Bearer cannot be dissociated, since their different forms and distinct teachings do not count as separate Teachers or initiators of the Buddhist doctrine, but as one and the same Buddha.

NIGUMA

THE SHANGPA INSTRUCTION LINEAGE is a Tibetan synthesis of diverse Indian tantric Buddhist meditations. The Indian masters who contributed to this lineage's spiritual treasury had but one thing in common, a Tibetan disciple named Kyungpo Naljor. What we call the Shangpa lineage reflects his spiritual fortune, values, interests, and preferences. He received extensive instructions from 150 teachers but did not include most in his core lineage. Of the chosen few, Kyungpo Naljor valued most the teachings of two women, Niguma and Sukasiddhi.

These two Kashmiri women are commonly referred to as wisdom dakinis. The Tibetan equivalent of the term "dakini," *kandro* (mkha' 'gro), can be used to designate both women and men, beings either worldly or spiritual. For example, when Kyungpo Naljor first met Niguma, she claimed to be the leader of cannibal dakinis, what in another day and age we would call witches. In fact, however, she was a wisdom dakini, an appellation that situates her attainment at the level of perfect, complete enlightenment.

Those who are curious to learn of Niguma's story are quickly confronted by what appears to be a failure of Indian and Tibetan historians—the life story of this woman, one of the most remarkable masters Buddhist India produced, seems to have been left unrecorded. Perhaps she was the wild, silent type. Certainly she was not an unknown teacher in her day; for example, Marpa visited Niguma each time he went to India, the first time at the advice of Naropa. *The Life of Marpa* relates:

> Naropa said, "On the shores of the poison lake in the South, in the charnel ground of Sosadvipa is Jnanadakini Adorned with Bone Ornaments. Whoever encounters her is liberated. Go before her and request the *Catuhpitha*. You can also request of the kusulus there whatever teachings you desire."
>
> Having arrived in the charnel ground at Sosadvipa, Marpa met

this yogini, who was living in a woven grass dome. Offering her a mandala of gold, he supplicated her. She joyfully gave him the full abhiseka and oral instructions of the *Catuhpitha*. (pp. 32-33)

Decoded, this story recounts Marpa's first meeting with Niguma, the wisdom dakini (*jnanadakini*), who gave him the full empowerment (*abhiseka*) and meditation teachings for a deity practice called Four Seats (*Catuhpitha*), not included among her teachings that Kyungpo Naljor passed on within the Shangpa tradition.

Niguma occupies the same place in the Shangpa Instruction Lineage as Tilopa does in the Marpa Instruction Lineage, next in line after Buddha Vajra Bearer (a position she shares with Sukasiddhi). I have never read any discussion of Tilopa's marital status or family background, and in the above account, Naropa introduced her as a master in her own right, without reference to himself. Yet thousand-year-old doubts persist: was she Naropa's wife-consort? We read this in the introduction to *The Life of Marpa*:

> She was Naropa's wife before he renounced worldly life to enter the dharma, and later she became his student and consort. Finally, she became a great teacher herself and her lineage of teachings was taken to Tibet (though not by Marpa) and continues to this present day. (*Ibid.,* p. xliii)

Within the Shangpa tradition's old texts, there is some evidence that Niguma was a direct disciple of Naropa; however, the practices they shared did not become part of the Shangpa core transmission. All accounts affirm that a direct relationship existed between Naro and Nigu, yet the honorific word Tibetans use to describe it is ambiguous. *Cham-mo* (lcam mo) can mean either sister or wife. Unless a text is found that describes their life together we will never know which it was, although it hardly matters. The reader is advised, however, that the word will be translated here as "sister," as this seems to me more coherent in the contexts it appears (such as in Jamgon Kongtrul's supplication to Niguma below), and it is also Bokar Rinpoché's preference.

In the Shangpa tradition's collections of the early masters' life stories, Kunga Ö's *Biography of the Wisdom Dakini Niguma* covers a mere six pages, most of which amount to verses of praise. Only the following words are pertinent to her life:

This wisdom dakini was born the daughter of the great Brahmin Shantivarma [Zhiwé Gocha] and the Brahmini Shrimati [Palgyi Lodrö]. Her name was Shrijnana [Palgyi Yéshé]. She was pandit Naropa's sister and a member of the Brahmin caste.[28]

During three previous incalculable eons of time, she actualized her training on the spiritual path. In the continuity of that path, during this lifetime she received a little instruction from a few accomplished spiritual masters and, based on their teaching, directly saw the truth of the nature of reality. Her illusory body of obscuring emotions appeared as a pure body of enlightenment. Having reached awakening's three pure stages, she actually met the great Buddha Vajra Bearer and received from him the full four empowerments of Great Way tantra within an emanated sacred circle of deities. The wisdom of her understanding of every sacred teaching, such as Buddha's discourses and tantras, profound instructions, and treatises, flowered to include direct [knowledge and sight] of the nature and multiplicity of all phenomena. She reached awakening's tenth stage, Cloud of the Doctrine. Her obscurations of knowledge became finer and finer until no veils remained; she became one with enlightenment, an epitome of the three bodies of enlightenment. She reached perfection in renunciation and realization, the achievement of her own goal. Her enlightenment's two form bodies appear for the benefit of others until the end of existence and bring benefit to beings in ways that can purposefully guide them. In particular, she watches over those who preserve her lineage with a compassion that knows no distance; she blesses them and ensures the success of their enlightened activity. (*The Collection of Shangpa Masters' Biographies*, pp. 40-42)

These few paragraphs indicate her extraordinary realization but do not satisfy some meditators' yearning for a good read. Naropa's search for his master and the twelve arduous years he spent following him have been well documented. Has Niguma suffered at the hands of male historians? I think not. Kyungpo Naljor treasured her teaching as well as that of Sukasiddhi. He related Sukasiddhi's story in full, and there is no reason to believe that he didn't do the same for Niguma. Her "story" may be as simple as this: she was born in Kashmir, met some accomplished masters, and, unlike her brother, attained full enlightenment quickly and easily. What her biographer related may be exactly all there is to know about her. She had no need for heroics, she made no mistakes, and no obstacles littered her path to enlightenment.

Niguma far exceeded the stage of awakening of all but a very few before or after her in that she received a large corpus of instruction directly from Buddha Vajra Bearer. In *A Supplement to the History of the Lineages*, Taranata relates that she gained realization after just one week of meditation:

> The account of the wisdom dakini Niguma as the sister of Naropa and so on is well known everywhere. It should be added that she received a few instructions from the master Lavapa of the East. After meditating with the master for one week, she became a wisdom dakini, who exhibited a rainbowlike physical form and attained spiritual realization that reached awakening's eighth stage. It is said that Lavapa of the East's body dissolved into light, leaving only a palm-sized portion of the crown of his head behind. He was also known as Lavapa the Younger.
>
> She is called Nigu, Nigupta in Sanskrit, said to mean "definite secret" or "definitely hidden," although her name is really from the dakinis' symbolic language. From her, the great accomplished Kyungpo Naljor, endowed with five ultimate teachings, received many of the tantric transmissions known throughout the Land of Exalted Ones [India]. In particular, her special instructions included the Great Empowerment of Illusory Body, which she bestowed to him on the night of the fifteenth day of the fourth lunar month, by the light of the full moon. The following morning, she taught him the entire Six Doctrines in his dreams. He later received these instructions from her in waking life twice, a total of three times. (pp. 2b-3a)

Niguma transcended human limits and attained a rainbowlike body, thus she is sometimes praised as a nonhuman being, i.e., a buddha or dakini. She has continually watched over those who preserve her lineage and has renewed the vitality of her instructions by appearing over the centuries to many of her spiritual children.

The supplication to Niguma that follows was written by Jamgon Kongtrul as part of a collection of supplications to the Shangpa masters,

A Garland of Udumvara Flowers: Supplications to the Lives of the Wonderful Lineage of Jewels, the Masters of the Glorious Shangpa Instruction Lineage. Kongtrul wrote to inform and to inspire, and usually included in each supplication the main events of each master's life. In Niguma's case, he had little choice but to depart from his seminarrative style. Instead, he praises her for having followed the path to enlightenment, without having "to rely on exhausting training," and he describes her realization of the view, tantric meditation's four stages of familiarization and accomplishment, postmeditation conduct, and the final result. Despite its lack of new information on Niguma's life, I have included this supplication in part to give non-Shangpa readers a chance to read something they have probably never seen before. Where else in this world can we read devotional supplications to a dark-brown woman as an enlightened being, a buddha, and as head of a living, worldwide spiritual lineage?

The Melody of Wisdom:
A Supplication to the Wisdom Dakini Niguma
by Jamgon Kongtrul

Vajra queen, mother of all buddhas,
Dark-brown woman wearing bone ornaments who flies through
    space,
You bestow supreme accomplishment on your fortunate disciples:
Noble Niguma, to you I pray.

You were born in the wonderful land of Kashmir,

In a sublime city
Known as Incomparable in the Land of Jambu,
Emanated through Madhyantika's blessing; to you I pray.[29]

In the family circle
Of the pure Brahmin, Shantivarma,
Narotapa and you, the wisdom dakini, were brother and sister—
Your karma ripened together like sun and moon; to you I pray.

You are the feminine form of true emptiness,
Sublime among all appearances, giving birth to all victorious
    buddhas.
Although you manifest in a worldly form,
You renounced any connection to existence through craving and
    grasping; to you I pray.

During incalculable past lives, you reached the far shore
Of awakening's paths and stages.
Thus, in this life, you gained the inconceivable, perfect freedom of
    self-manifest accomplishment.
Innate dakini, to you I pray.

You did not have to rely on exhausting training—
When some advice from accomplished masters entered your ears,
You understood all teachings.
Great bliss of natural liberation, to you I pray.

Knowledge of one subject—the tantras' subtle, profound meaning—
    led to your total liberation
And the flowering of your two forms of knowledge.
You saw directly and without obscuration the truth of the nature of
    reality.
Illustrious woman of accomplishment, to you I pray.

You bound your mind, eyes, and circulating energy within the
    expanse of emptiness,
Permitting you to see in the central channel the [empty] forms
    created by the spring vital essence.

Vajra illusory reflections, such as smoke, developed together.
You completed the branch of familiarization; to you I pray.

You used your breath to block dark circulating energies and made
　them descend to your belly.
You joined the vitality and descending energies equally at the six
　energy centers,
Blocking the movement of the six elements' sun and moon.
You completed the branch of proximate accomplishment; to you I
　pray.

You transcended the three seals to reach incomparable Great Seal.
The innate light of its unchanging, coemergent bliss
Created your ten-faceted illusory body, replete with all powers.
You completed the branch of accomplishment; to you I pray.

You blocked the twenty-one thousand six hundred circulating
　energies and attained that many forms of changeless bliss.
At the crown of your head, the mind of awakening became stable,
And you traversed awakening's stages in an instant.
You completed the branch of great accomplishment; to you I pray.

Through engaging in conduct that is enlightenment's direct cause,
You enjoyed many pleasures and were nurtured spiritually by Buddha
　Vajra Bearer.
Your fortune equaled his—your body of training's integral union
Works for beings whose numbers equal space; to you I pray.

You saw directly all phenomena without obscuration
And opened inconceivable millions of gates to meditative states.
You master the secret treasury of all victorious ones.
Consort of all buddhas, to you I pray.

Body of great bliss, emptiness and compassion inseparable,
Manifestation of blissful buddhas, sovereign of common and supreme
　accomplishment,
Powerful bodhisattva on awakening's tenth stage, glorious guide
　for beings,

Wearer of Bone Ornaments, to you I pray.

Sentient beings, our venerable mothers, wander along the wheel of
    life
In endless and fathomless seas of suffering.
With your universal great compassion,
Lead them to a pure land of flourishing, uncontaminated bliss, I pray.

Nurture fortunate persons who have entered the path;
Pacify all adversity, hindrances, and obstacles;
Continually enhance our experience and realization;
And bless us with the completion of awakening's five paths and ten
    stages.

(*A Garland of Udumvara Flowers*, pp. 3a-4a)

SUKASIDDHI

SUKASIDDHI'S ACCOMPLISHMENT equaled that of Niguma. Although they were both born in Kashmir, there is no record of any meeting between them. They are cited together only as teachers of the same disciple, Kyungpo Naljor, yet according to the Nyingma tradition, they are related from past lives. Jamgon Kongtrul writes in *The History of the Sources of the Profound Treasures and the Treasure Revealers* (p. 32b), that Niguma in a past life was none other than Mandarava, Guru Rinpoché's foremost Indian disciple. The identification of Sukasiddhi with Yeshé Tsogyal, Guru Rinpoché's foremost Tibetan disciple, and with her reincarnation as Machik Lapdrön, is well known.[30]

Sukasiddhi arrived at tantric Buddhism late in life. She lived as an impoverished housewife and mother of six children until the age of fifty-nine. She was thrown out of her home by her husband and children, who were irate at what they considered her misplaced generosity to a stranger who came begging at their door. She wandered westward to Oddiyana (Swat Valley in modern Pakistan), where she acquired a measure of grain, with which she made alcohol. Her business proved a modest success, and she allowed herself to again be generous, this time to a female adept referred to as Avadhuti-ma, who regularly bought alcohol for her companion, an adept in retreat. Sukasiddhi's gift of free alcohol intrigued the adept, Virupa, who asked whether his surprising benefactor wanted to receive Buddhist teaching. She did. Sukasiddhi's story relates that she brought as offerings to Virupa two containers of alcohol and some pork. Although this meeting predates the Muslim domination of India, pork and alcohol were far from what would have normally constituted suitable offerings for spiritual teaching, even to tantric masters. Nevertheless, Virupa was no normal master, and Sukasiddhi would prove an exceptional disciple.

Upon receiving empowerment and instruction from Virupa, Sukasiddhi, then a sixty-one-year-old, attained full enlightenment that very evening.

Like Niguma, her body became rainbowlike. Niguma is remembered as a wrathful, dark-brown woman who wore bone ornaments, whereas Sukasiddhi is portrayed as a peaceful, light-skinned sixteen-year-old.

Niguma's teachings make up the bulk of the Shangpa Instruction Lineage's meditation practices, yet it is Sukasiddhi who occupies the center of the sacred circle when Kyungpo Naljor's masters are recalled. Kyungpo Naljor himself testified to her central position, as quoted in *The Story of the Wisdom Dakini, Sukasiddhi, Whose Other Name [in Tibetan] is Déwé Ngö-drub [Accomplishment of Bliss]*:

> Among my four principal spiritual masters, Niguma, Rahula, the hidden yogi [probably Métripa], and Sukasiddhi, the kindest was Sukasiddhi. Her first great kindness was the bestowal of many transmissions. Her later great kindness was to be my secret consort and to grant me every empowerment. Her final great kindness was to give me directions for giving empowerment, along with profound instruction in meditation. Moreover, she said she would remain inseparable from me throughout India and Tibet, a very great kindness, and that meditators in future generations would gain accomplishment by experiential cultivation of this secret meditation she taught. (*The Collection of Shangpa Masters' Biographies*, pp. 56-57)

In fact, Sukasiddhi kept her promise to appear to future lineage holders, notably to each of the first four lineage holders after Kyungpo Naljor, and has thereby revitalized and added to the Shangpa teachings over the centuries.

If we compare Niguma and Sukasiddhi's contributions to the Shangpa lineage, Niguma's definitely outnumber those of Sukasiddhi, but both taught Great Seal and a series of meditations called the Six Doctrines (each very different from the other and from those of Naropa, although the subjects are the same).

Niguma's and Sukasiddhi's biographies have one thing in common. Both women reached as high a level of realization as any of the great Indian masters without the drama that we have come to associate with Dharma (Buddhist religious practice), particularly that of the early Marpa Instruction Lineage. In looking at the Marpa lineage masters' lives, we might wonder, "Does the path to enlightenment have to be so excruciating?"

Niguma and Sukasiddhi would answer, "No." While it's true that Naropa and Milarepa in particular had difficult spiritual lives, we should recall that they were particularly difficult characters. Before his awakening, Naropa had been a brilliant Buddhist university professor, one of the best of his time. Yet his tight, solid, self-assured mind was so unfit for meditation, or instruction in the mind's nature, that his teacher had him undergo hardships instead. For his part, Milarepa had practiced black magic and killed forty people before meeting his teacher.

Naropa and Milarepa were not average people and did not follow an average path to awakening. Their stories are well loved throughout the Himalayas, but Tibet's Buddhists also know many other "templates" for the path to enlightenment. While we might not be able to attain enlightenment in an evening or a week, as Niguma and Sukasiddhi did, we can absorb that possibility into our outlook. Things can be light and easy—we receive pith instructions from a qualified teacher and we give ourselves permission to allow the teachings to guide us to awakening. It could be as simple as that. And so it was for our two uncomplicated, straightforward dakinis.

New Buddhist converts must confront the inevitable influence of their former religion's presentation of the spiritual path, which in the case of the Judeo-Christian tradition is not necessarily good news. Whether or not new Buddhists actually practiced in that tradition, the pervasive influence of Judeo-Christian culture has given most of us a deep, reflexive expectation that a spiritual path will involve something along the lines of dark nights of the soul, suffering, painful ego death followed by glorious spiritual rebirth, and so on. While such a template seems incredibly dramatic and foreign to Buddhism, it is perfectly "normal" if we recall that Western culture, both religious and secular, has been deeply influenced by the idea of original sin, the opposite of Buddhism's intrinsic enlightenment or primordial purity. Niguma and Sukasiddhi were unburdened by such debilitating expectations; they were "pure" Buddhists who did what all Buddhists should—they became pure buddhas. Fortunately for them and for us, no one told them that enlightenment was beyond them or that the path had to be long and arduous.

The Melody of Great Bliss:
A Supplication to the Wisdom Dakini Sukasiddhi
by Jamgon Kongtrul

Bestower of uncontaminated, coemergent bliss;
Radiant with the full splendor of sixteen-year-old youth;
Leader of every assembly of dakinis in the three locations—
Venerable Accomplishment of Bliss [Sukasiddhi], to you I pray.

You manifested in a pauper's home in Kashmir
And trained in realization on the path.
Having completed the force of faith and great compassion,
You diligently gave gifts without attachment; to you I pray.

Millions of eons ago, you perfected the cultivation of merit and
    wisdom
And the result of your training manifested.
The awakening of your karmic connections
Made you renounce home life; to you I pray.

In the land of Oddiyana, source of great mysteries,
Men were spiritual warriors; women, female warriors.
Just by your reaching the center of that gathering,
The power of your enlightened potential awakened; to you I pray.

You demonstrated the skillful means of illusory conduct as a vendor
    of delicious alcohol.

You gave twice-strained rice alcohol to a female adept.
This created a connection through faith
With a tantric practitioner in the forest; to you I pray.

Noble Virupa accepted you as his disciple
And gave you the full four empowerments into secret practice.
Instantly, your ripened karmic body of sixty-one years
Became that of a sixteen-year-old maiden; to you I pray.

Taking the inner path, you truly traversed in a single moment
The major vajra stages of awakening,
And you appeared in an uncontaminated, vajra rainbow body.
Powerful one of the celestial realms, to you I pray.

You became the manifest form of coemergent wisdom, Buddha
    Selfless One,
To remain until the end of cyclic existence.
You watch over the three realms' beings during the six periods of day
    and night.
Honored female buddha, to you I pray.

You manifestly bless those who pray to you
And lovingly watch over your children who preserve your lineage,
    never parting from them.
You bestow common and supreme accomplishment in a matter of
    months or years.
Powerful one of great compassion, to you I pray.

Vajra Yogini, perfection of transcendent knowledge,
You appear to help beings in a body that has form.
The exquisite flower of your body, which one never tires of seeing,
Blooms with the marks and signs of physical perfection; to you I pray.

In the Teaching's infinite gates, which have the nature of emptiness,
You speak according to beings' dispositions.
Your speech, invincible sweet sound in every situation,
Flows imbued with the sixty tones of Brahma's voice; to you I pray.

Inseparable bliss and emptiness, the true vajra of space,
Pervades all animate and inanimate life.
Your sublime enlightened mind of luminous Great Seal
Is coemergent and uncontaminated; to you I pray.

Epitome of the qualities of freedom and maturity,
You have an inconceivable life.
Just hearing your voice inspires uncontaminated bliss.
Sublime wish-fulfilling jewel, to you I pray.

You unite in pleasure with all victors and bodhisattvas.
Your emanations reach the four elements' limits.
Like an excellent vase, a gem, or a wish-fulfilling tree,
Your enlightened activity is spontaneously present; to you I pray.

Your compassion knows no distance and embraces all equally.
You guide fortunate persons on the path to the celestial realms.
Your loving face wears the conscientious smile of compassion.
Friend to all beings, to you I pray.

To your child who preserves the lineage and who prays to you,
Show your loving face and joyfully grant me your supreme prophecy.
Bestow the empowerment of great vajra wisdom,
And bless me that I merge inseparably with you.

(*A Garland of Udumvara Flowers*, pp. 4a-5a)

MÉTRIPA

M OST WESTERN BUDDHISTS first heard the name of Métripa in connection with another great Tibetan master, Marpa. Within the Marpa Instruction Lineage, the Six Doctrines transmission flows from Naropa; the Great Seal transmission comes from Métripa. Kyungpo Naljor counts Métripa as one of his principal masters, the source of two major cycles of instruction, Six-Armed Protector and Great Seal. The Shangpa tradition's Great Seal teachings unite three streams of instruction: Niguma's three aspects of natural repose constitute the preliminary practice; Métripa's self-liberation of the four faults, the main practice; and Sukasiddhi's integration of enlightenment's three bodies on the path, the culmination.

According to *The Blue Annals* (p. 842), Métripa's dates are 1007 or 1010–1087. Tantric Buddhism in that period in India was a small world—as Kongtrul mentions below, Naropa converted Métripa to Buddhism; Métripa himself was the teacher of Atisha, Marpa, Kyungpo Naljor, and many other great Indian masters. The following biographical supplication gives us a picture of this master's life outside his enormous impact on Tibet's Kagyu lineages. Kongtrul seems to have drawn his information for this supplication, and those to Dorjé Denpa and Rahula, from Taranata's *A Mine of Jewels: The Amazing and Excellent Lives of the Sevenfold Transmission Lineage-Masters.*[31]

The Melody of Love:
A Supplication to the Great Lord Métripa
by Jamgon Kongtrul

Lord Métripa, your great qualities reach the bounds of space
And your fame pervades India and Tibet.

You attained Great Seal.
Advayavajra, at your feet I bow.

Born to the Brahmin caste, you became a non-Buddhist scholar,
But when you met Naropa, you converted to Buddhism.
When you received all the empowerments and instructions you could,
Your previous karmic propensity awakened; to you I pray.

At Nalanda Monastery, you became a renunciant.
You approached many learned and accomplished masters,
Such as the omniscient one who lived during the time of conflict,
    Ratnakara-shanti.
You thereby hoisted the banner of renown as a great scholar; to you
    I pray.

Like a lion, you lived at the temple
And alternated periods of teaching and meditation.
During this time, you saw the mother of the buddhas Vajra Yogini
And received her prophecy and blessings; to you I pray.

You knew that the time had come for inner conduct, practiced
    secretly,
To aid your meditative absorption.
Before those who challenged you, you transformed alcohol and
    your consort
Into milk and a bell; to you I pray.

When the monastic community expelled you from its residence,
You sailed away on a skin you spread on the Ganges River.
Further, you gained countless other common
And extraordinary capabilities; to you I pray.

At that point, since you had not attained the ultimate,
You followed your meditation deity's advice
And went to the slopes of Glorious Mountain, where you joined
    Prince Sakara
In search of a master who had gained accomplishment; to you I pray.

Despite hardship, exhaustion, negative emotions, and fatigue,
You never gave up hope.
After six months of single-minded prayer,
You accomplished your wishes; to you I pray.

You met Shavari with the two noble women who served him.
He taught you with profound symbols
And nurtured you with empowerments and instruction.
He gave you permission to teach the meaning of the abiding nature;
    to you I pray.

The wisdom that sees the ultimate as it is arose within you,
And you became the chief of infinite numbers of spiritual heroes
    and dakinis.
In the central place [of Buddhist India, Bodhgaya],
You taught and widely spread instruction in mental nonactivity;
    to you I pray.

At Cool Grove, you entertained yourself with the practice of entering
    the dead,
And Mahakala accomplished your every wish.
You practiced gazes, emanated many forms of yourself,
And remained in retreat in the forest; to you I pray.

You brought many fortunate Indian and Tibetan disciples,
Such as Gangadhari, Ratnadévi,
And the four great masters, to spiritual maturity
And had them travel to the pure expanse; to you I pray.

After death, you attained Great Seal's supreme accomplishment.
Your sublime wisdom body pervades all space.
In the north [Tibet], the stream of your enlightened activity of the
    tantras' essence
Flows until the end of the Buddha's doctrine; to you I pray.

Métri-gupta, powerful lord, son of the victors,
Think of me, your child, with compassionate love

And bless me with the realization of the innate state
Of inconceivable, coemergent Great Seal.

(A Garland of Udumvara Flowers, pp. 5a-b)

The two women mentioned in this prayer, Gangadhari and Ratnadévi, also number among Kyungpo Naljor's teachers. Taranata mentions that Ratnadévi's wisdom and realization were said to equal Métripa's, whereas Gangadhari's was half theirs. Taranata also repeats some age-old gossip, that the disciplinarian who mistakenly expelled Métripa from Vikramashila Monastery was none other than Atisha (982 - 1054). Further, "It is said that to purify the obscuration [from having lacked pure vision, Atisha later] received teachings from the lord [Métripa], went to Tibet, and continually made *tsa-tsa* molds." (*A Mine of Jewels,* p. 8a) By use of a nonhonorific for "it is said," Taranata makes it clear that his source for the story is less than authoritative, yet it seems to reflect what some in India believed.

RAHULA

RAHULA WAS UNIQUE among Kyungpo Naljor's Indian gurus in that he visited Kyungpo Naljor while he was in retreat in Tibet. This master demonstrated many miracles, including flying through the sky when he left Kyungpo Naljor for Bodhgaya in India, where he had an appointment that same day! Rahula contributed some Six-Armed Protector practices to the Shangpa lineage, as well as his trademark meditation, the Integrated Practice of the Four Deities. The four deities united in the single meditation are Six-Armed Protector, Vajra Yogini, Two-Armed All-Seeing One, and Tara.

Like Métripa, Rahula is not entirely unknown to students of Tibetan lineages, for he also numbers among the masters of one of the main contributors to Tibet's Buddhism, the great Indian master Atisha. In *Atisha and Tibet* (p. 72), Alaka Chattopadhyaya cites three sources that concur that Atisha received empowerment from Rahula-gupta (also named Rahula-guhya-vajra) at a place called Black Mountain; she then points to Black Mountain as probably a hill in the region of Rajgir (p. 73).

Taranata's account of Rahula in *A Mine of Jewels* does not include details of his early life but does mention the two terrible hardships he underwent. According to Taranata, "It is said that both [trials] purified the obscuration incurred from having disobeyed his master's command." (*A Mine of Jewels*, p. 15b) Kongtrul calls the discipline Rahula's master enjoined him to undertake "*avadhuti* conduct," whereas Taranata names it as total renunciation. Both would imply giving up all trappings of status and social standing, which Rahula hesitated to do.

The Melody of Jewels:
A Supplication to the Great Accomplished Master
Rahula-gupta-vajra by Jamgon Kongtrul

The heap of many fine jewels in three collections [letters, words,
    and terms]
Produces your qualities, a Massive Mountain that rises high at the
    center of the four continents.
Venerable Rahula-gupta,
Your life was foretold by millions of sublime deities; to you I pray.

In southern India, in the region of Élabhisha,
The special land of Vajra Dakini,
You were born like the purest grass
Among the aristocracy of Bhiraji town; to you I pray.

At your birth, light, sweet sounds and fragrances
Accompanied emanations of the four deities, who manifested forms
    of wisdom.
You began your life with these virtuous signs
And became known as a divine bodhisattva; to you I pray.

Until the age of twenty, you trained in the sacred Teachings.
At twenty-one, you suffered pain from a vajra thorn.
The lord of yoga and the four deities blessed you,
Told you that this illness would exhaust your previous bad karma,

And foretold that you would go to the celestial realms in this lifetime;
   to you I pray.

While you performed fasting practice for five days
Before the self-manifest [image of] Tara, your parents bound you in
   chains.
Vajra Yogini freed you, blessed you,
And gave you a prophecy; to you I pray.

Like a lion, you received in a tantric temple
The complete basic training of Shakyamuni's [order].
From many scholars and accomplished masters,
You received the entire corpus of discourses and tantras; to you I pray.

When you meditated on the profound tantras' meaning,
Your spiritual master encouraged you to engage in *avadhuti* conduct,
But your pride in your learning made you delay.
Later, you practiced single-mindedly
But couldn't reach accomplishment.
You then followed the advice of [the master] Guna-akara
And cut your tongue and limbs with a razor.
At that moment, you saw the four deities,
Who healed you; to you I pray.

Powerful All-Seeing One, Vajra Yogini,
Noble Tara, and Swift Awakened Protector
Taught you whenever you wished
And granted their blessing and accomplishment; to you I pray.

You followed the advice of Jnana Sagara
And submerged yourself in water for seven days.
Leeches sucked your blood and you nearly died,
Completely exhausting your karmic obscurations; to you I pray.

Encouraged by the advice of accomplished meditators,
You traveled to the Himalayan region by means of your
   miraculous powers.

Manifesting wondrous feats, you visited the learned and
    accomplished Kyungpo Naljor.
Beginning with the blessing of the four deities,
You bestowed various profound instructions and meditations.
You placed some fortunate persons within your emanated sacred
    circle [of empowerment],
And then you left for Land of the Exalted,
Arriving there instantly; to you I pray.

On the perfectly stable vajra ground in the south,
You renounced distraction and established your place of meditation.
You attained the sublime accomplishment of Great Seal
And the state of an immortal awareness holder; to you I pray.

On the wooded hill known as Black Mountain,
You dwell in a vajra rainbow body.
You have arrived at the end of training,
A wondrous and excellent sublime master of accomplishment; to you
    I pray.

May I too thoroughly exhaust the two obscurations' impurities,
And may wisdom's sun arise within me
To vanquish the darkness of ignorance's momentary delusion.
During this lifetime, may I accomplish the state of a vajra awareness
    holder.

(*A Garland of Udumvara Flowers*, pp. 7a-8a)

DORJÉ DENPA

ALTHOUGH JAMGON KONGTRUL does not accord Dorjé Denpa a separate section in the collection of songs, he deserves a specific mention. A master whose life Buddha foretold, Dorjé Denpa (whose name is sometimes cited as Vajrasanapa in probably reconstructed Sanskrit) preserved the Buddha's doctrine at the site of Buddha's enlightenment; thus we know him as "he of the Vajra Seat," rather than by his formal Buddhist name, Punyakara. He was the first main teacher Kyungpo Naljor met on his travel in India; the disciple records their exchanges in song.

Dorjé Denpa seems totally unknown in the West, but according to Tibetan oral history (which I have been unsuccessful in finding in print, in Tibetan or English) he should be recalled for at least one event. He offered a vajra feast in Bodhgaya and invited in prayer all the accomplished masters of India. Those who appeared on that occasion, among the thousands of possible enlightened guests, have been remembered as a group, although their attendance at that vajra feast on that day is the only event that linked them—the eighty (or eighty-four) mahasiddhas, the great accomplished masters of tantric India.[32]

According to *The Blue Annals*, a number of Tibetans traveled to India and sought instruction at the feet of Dorjé Denpa. The book also credits Atisha after arriving in Tibet with sending a Tibetan to India to meet Dorjé Denpa (p. 1021). Certainly, it is clear from Kyungpo Naljor's account of their first meeting (in the songs above) that Dorjé Denpa was well acquainted with the Tibetans and their weaknesses as new Buddhists. One such story can be found in *The Blue Annals*, on the subject of Dorjé Denpa's transmission to a Tibetan translator (La-tö Marpo) of the meditation of Bodhisattva Great Compassion, which he had received from Virupa.

> When [La-tö Marpo] came to Dorjé Denpa, he presented him half
> of the gold and asked him to bestow the method with which he

could remove hindrances in this life, and obtain enlightenment in the next. Dorjé Denpa imparted to him the meditation mantra of the Great Merciful One, and (to stress its secret nature) he introduced a bamboo tube into his ear, and through it repeated "Om mani padmé hum." He thought in himself: "This mantra is repeated throughout Tibet by all old men, women, and even children. This doctrine seems to be a common one." The teacher perceived (his doubts) and gave him back the gold. (p. 1027, round brackets in the original)

At that point, Marpa the Translator intervened and advised La-tö Marpo to return to Dorjé Denpa and make amends for his initial lack of receptivity. This he did and gained accomplishment in meditation, although he remained a troublesome student. Therefore, when Kyungpo Naljor meets Dorjé Denpa, the Indian master's first comments concerning Tibetans' foibles are probably founded in his own teaching experience rather than in clairvoyance.

The Melody of Self-Arising:
A Supplication to the Great Master Dorjé Denpa

Like the sun, you dispel darkness from beings' intellects;
Like the moon, you bring the circles of love and knowledge to
    fullness.
Lord of Shakyamuni's doctrine, Dorjé Denpa,
Venerable Punyakara, to you I pray.

At Malabar, a place of power and wealth in Land of the Exalted,
Virtuous signs of blessing arose in a Brahmin's home
Where the conduct of purity was practiced
And nonvirtue was naturally renounced; to you I pray.

Glory of the doctrine, you took rebirth intentionally
Without attachment to your excellent caste, body, and possessions.
Your innate intelligence
Led you to meditate for your own and others' benefit; to you I pray.

You saw existence's happiness and wealth as a dream—
Disillusionment raged in your mind like fires at the end of time.
At Nalanda you renounced home life.
Accomplisher of all noble goals, to you I pray.

The force of your training in previous lifetimes
Kept you from committing natural faults,
And even in dreams you did not associate yourself with vows'
    downfalls.
Mighty, ultimate foe-destroyer, to you I pray.

In the exalted land's east, west, and center,
You received a host of accomplished masters' heart-essence.
Your ocean of learning filled with the jewels of analysis,
And you became the source of many essential teachings; to you I pray.

In knowledge of the ten subjects of study, you were peerless.
Particularly in the outer and inner tantras
You relinquished hesitation and became an omniscient master.
Lord of transcendent knowledge, to you I pray.

You gained a fortunate inheritance from one million teachers;
Your jewel treasury of direct instructions was unfathomably deep.
Erudite and accomplished master, who gathered the nagas' wealth
    from all sources,
You preserved it for others' benefit; to you I pray.

In Magadha, source of the fortunate eon's victors,
You preserved Shakyamuni's doctrine with the confidence of one
   whose awareness is liberated.
Like the moon's orb amid the stars,
You led the Spiritual Community; to you I pray.

You attained the state of a fearless master of the Teachings
And assumed the throne at the Heart of Great Awakening.
Foretold by the Victor by the name of Dorjé Denpa,
Your fame spread throughout the world; to you I pray.

The single path trod by all victors and their spiritual heirs,
The supreme mind of awakening, was in you as stable as the massive
   central mountain.
Like cooling moonlight it touched all impartially.
Chief among the Victor's children, to you I pray.

You gained full mastery of the secret treasury
Of common tantras and of special ones, such as *Ocean of Jewels,*
And you had full control of the two accomplishments' glorious
   wealth.
Sovereign holder of the vajra, to you I pray.

With incomparable activity of awakening
You fully guided your disciples impartially.
You made your region's environment and beings very auspicious
And every connection to you meaningful—
Those who saw or heard you were moved to faith; to you I pray.

In Shakyamuni's capital city, you preserved his activity.
You were the crown ornament of all accomplished masters from India
   and Tibet.
The world, including the gods, pays homage to you.
Lion among humanity, to you I pray.

May I dwell within the bounds of ethical conduct, reach the bounds
   of learning, reflection, and meditation,

Train in the mind of awakening, accomplish beings' benefit
   impartially,
And be a sun of Shakyamuni's doctrine.
May I quickly accomplish sublime individuals' state of complete
   liberation!

(A *Garland of Udumvara Flowers,* pp. 5b-6b)

KYUNGPO NALJOR

To this point, we have examined some aspects of the lives of Kyungpo Naljor's Indian masters. Two remarkable facts emerge from any study of this period. First, most of these teachers were interrelated and most were connected to Atisha, as was Kyungpo Naljor. Despite their disparate birthplaces in India, the men mentioned thus far all took monk's vows at Nalanda Monastery and spent some time at Vikramashila Monastery. Such an illustrious gathering at these two institutions was probably due to the fact that tantric colleges were rare in India, even at the height of Buddhist India's tantric phase. There may in fact have been other major institutions for the transmission, study, and practice of tantra, but these monasteries (as well as Odantapuri) were located in northern India, relatively near Bodhgaya, where all Tibetan pilgrims eventually gather.

Second, the Tibetans who traveled to India at the same time as Kyungpo Naljor returned home with most of what we now call Tibetan Buddhism. Of Tibet's eight major lineages of meditation practice, only the Ancient Instruction Lineage (Nyingma)[33] predated this period and only one other, Intensive Meditation and Accomplishment (Nyendrup), came later. This brief confluence of Indian masters and their Tibetan disciples shaped Tibet's spiritual landscape forever. Consider these contemporaries of Kyungpo Naljor:

Rongzom Chökyi Zangpo (1012–1131) is still revered and studied as one of the greatest Nyingma scholars ever; he taught Marpa.

Rinchen Zangpo (958–1055), one of the most important translators of the later period, met Kyungpo Naljor with Atisha. His work formed part of the basis of the Buddha's Word as Instruction (Kadampa) lineage. Dromtön (1005–1064), Atisha's main Tibetan disciple, founded that lineage's monastic institutions.

Drokmi the Translator (d. 1064 or 1074) traveled to India and studied with Virupa (Sukasiddhi's teacher), among others. His transmissions became the basis for the Path and Result (Lamdré) teachings of the Sakya School. He was another of Marpa's teachers.

Marpa (1012–1097), founder of what Kongtrul calls the Marpa Instruction Lineage (Marpa Kagyu), studied with some of the same teachers as Kyungpo Naljor, including Niguma and Métripa.

Machik Lapdrön (1031–1129), founder of the Severance (Chö) Instruction Lineage, never journeyed to India, but she lived during this crucial period.

Gyi Jo Dawé Özer (eleventh century, dates unknown), Ra Lotsawa Dorjé Drakpa (1016–1098), and Dro Shérab Drakpa (eleventh century, dates unknown) will never be household names, but these three translators were responsible for the initial introduction of Kalachakra to Tibet. Gyi Jo Dawé Özer was the first of the three. His return from India (in 1027) with the first translation of a Kalachakra tantra is remembered by all Tibetans, as their sixty-year-cycle calendars then began. These master meditators and translators were the founders of the Six Applications Lineage (Jordruk), based on Kalachakra.

Finally, Padampa Sangyé, founder of the Pacification of Suffering Lineage (Zhijé) ended Tibet's astounding eleventh century with what some say was his second visit, in 1091–92. He would teach Machik Lapdrön, Milarepa, and many others.

Thus, much of Tibetan Buddhism was produced from the cross-Himalaya exchange during this short window of time. We have no record of India continuing to produce masters of eleventh-century caliber, and Tibet seems to have waited a century or so before hitting spiritual high tide again in the thirteenth century.

What causes and conditions contributed to this crucial era? On one side of the border, the Muslim invasion of India had begun, although the situation was not as disastrous as it would become. Later generations of Indian masters fled to southeast Asian countries, some even to Tibet (among them, the Kashmiri pandit Shakyashri among them, who stayed in Tibet 1204–1214). The Muslims did not single out the Buddhists for persecution, nor did they eradicate other faiths from the country—Hinduism continued to thrive. Yet Buddhism suffered far more than Hinduism when foreigners unlikely ever to convert ruled India. With the end of royal patronage, Buddhism's major institutions, which had been on a scale of modern universities, withered. It is also possible that the heavy demands Buddhism makes on all its adherents—disengagement, renunciation, study, contemplation, meditation, impartial compassion, and impeccable nonviolence—seem more reasonable to common people during times of relative peace, leisure, and prosperity. Even in the land of its birth, Buddhism was not as rooted in the soil and people's lives as Hinduism. By the end of the eleventh century, Buddhism's bright, blessed days in India were ending; it was time to find new homes.

On the Tibetan side of the border, the Yarlung dynasty collapsed with a popular uprising in 869, and the country would remain without a central government until 1252. That year, the Mongols designated the Sakya lama Pakpa Lodrö Gyaltsen (1235–1280) as Tibet's ruler; in 1253, he returned to Tibet to begin his administration.[34] This event ended over 350 years of Tibetan life without a strong government, without demands for military or other service, and without the possibility of administrative or other government careers. Young, bright Tibetans could seek new horizons beyond their borders if they so wished. At the same time, China, a country with which Tibet long had a conflict-prone relationship, had also fallen into dynastic disarray. The Tang dynasty ended in 907, and the fragmented country would also wait until the Mongols for the next unifying administration (the Yuan dynasty was proclaimed in 1271). With peace in the east and no interference from the center, Tibet's Buddhist compasses at this time pointed south to India.

Kyungpo Naljor's exceptionally long life made him a contemporary of many of the great early masters of the later spread of Buddhism in the Himalayan region.[35] He practiced and gained realization in both the pre-Buddhist Tibetan religion Bön and the Ancient Instruction Lineage before setting out for Nepal and India in search of more teachings. There, he studied with 150 masters, Niguma, Sukasiddhi, Métripa, Rahula, and Dorjé Denpa foremost among them. No authoritative testimonial to the greatness of this master surpasses that of Jamgon Kongtrul, who expressed this opinion of Kyungpo Naljor in *An Impartial History of the Sources of Spiritual Instruction*:

> [Kyungpo Naljor's] attainment of accomplishment equaled that of the Indian masters Luyipa, Krishnacharya, and Ghantapa. In the Tibetan region it would seem that among the twenty-five disciples [of Guru Rinpoché] during the original [spread of Buddhism] or [among the masters] of this later period, no one has ever appeared

who equaled his mastery of scholastic erudition, accomplishment in meditation, miraculous powers, and enlightened activity. (p. 11b)

Kongtrul chose to voice this view in a text that described the history of Tibetan Buddhism and gave an overview of all its religious traditions. Looking back over more than a thousand years of the Tibetan experience of Buddhism, Kongtrul felt that Kyungpo Naljor was the finest accomplished master Tibet had ever produced, bar none.

Why is he so little known? His relative obscurity may be due to the relative obscurity of his lineage's institutions. The Shangpa Kagyu monastic lineage he founded never occupied much real estate space on the Tibetan stage after Kyungpo Naljor passed away. The Shangpa Instruction Lineage of teaching began as an exclusive one—Niguma asked that her entire corpus of teachings be passed on to just one disciple in each generation until the fifth Tibetan lineage holder, a seal that remained unbroken until the thirteenth century, providing enough time for most other traditions to have spread far and wide by many fully invested lineage holders. In the Shangpa lineage, only one person per generation was the authorized lineage bearer, and he would pass the entirety of the teachings on to just one person during his lifetime. This restriction probably acted as a damper on institution building.

After the eleventh-century period of travel to India and collection of teachings, Tibet settled down to building homegrown Buddhist centers in the twelfth century. Kyungpo Naljor was the only Tibetan to participate in both of these pivotal undertakings. To give a short outline of the founding of Tibetan Buddhist institutions during this second wave, Atisha's main disciple Dromtön founded Radreng Monastery in 1057, the start of the Kadampa Lineage. Kön Könchok Gyalpo founded the Sakya Monastery in 1073 to begin that school. In 1121, Kyungpo Naljor founded a monastery at Shang, beginning the Shangpa Kagyu. The same year, Milarepa's main disciple Gampopa founded the Daklha Gampo Monastery and with it the Dakpo Kagyu. It should be mentioned, since this information is so often given incorrectly, that the Shangpa Kagyu lineage was never one of the many subsects of "the" Kagyu lineage, from the point of view either of teachings or of monastic institutions.[36]

Kyungpo Naljor began his career as a translator and seeker of Indian gurus, a contemporary of Marpa. After his travels were over, Kyungpo Naljor meditated in retreat in Tibet for many years, a contemporary of Milarepa. Close to the end of his life, he founded a series of religious institutions in Tibet as a contemporary of Gampopa. While scholars may question Kyungpo Naljor's birth year, no one disputes the incredible span of his life and experiences.

As great as he was, Kyungpo Nalor found himself sometimes frustrated by the realities of life in so-called spiritual communities. His main student, Rinchen Tsöndru, found that this aspect of his master's life followed him; disheartened, he walked away more than once from the community he headed. This may be fitting, since Kyungpo Naljor never measured his success by the number of students or offerings he attracted. If he had, he would never have left behind his relative success as a teacher at the age of fifty to make the first of his many arduous journeys to India. Each time Kyungpo Naljor traveled to search for or to visit his masters, he went laden with gifts of gold. At first, he accompanied these gifts with requests for teaching; later, he made difficult and dangerous journeys to India only to express his gratitude to his masters with more offerings. Thus, his lineage's teachings became known as the Shangpa Golden Doctrines.

If we remain true to their spirit, the spread of Buddhism in general and the Shangpa Instruction Lineage in particular cannot be measured by acres of land, tons of brick and mortar, or head counts in assembly halls, but by changes of mind and heart. In Buddhism, these can happen only when a teacher meets a disciple and they commit to the transmission of the teaching and to one another. From the perspective of land, walls, and head counts, the Shangpa lineage went straight downhill from Kyungpo Naljor's time, but if the lasting purity of the teachings and the exceptional quality of the lineage masters are our criteria, Kyungpo Naljor's long life of spiritual freedom produced an enduring success as good as gold.

The Melody of Devotion:
A Supplication to the Erudite and Accomplished Kyungpo Naljor by Jamgon Kongtrul

In the Sage's doctrine, source of virtue and excellence,
You are unrivaled in the past, present, and future as a prodigious
   learned and accomplished master.
Amazing manifestation of enlightenment endowed with the five
   ultimate teachings,
Kyungpo Naljor, to you I pray.

Although you gained manifest awakening from the original moment,
Your uninterrupted compassion shows itself to those you guide
As miraculous forms that pervade space and the absolute expanse.
Epitome of all three bodies of enlightenment, to you I pray.

On the circle of Tibetan land, in the central province, at Nyémo,
The moment your manifestation of physical perfection's marks and
   signs appeared,
The accomplished master Amogha
Gave his blessing and made a prediction; to you I pray.

"This child, a reincarnate master, will travel to India.
He will collect the heart-essence of all scholars and accomplished
   masters
And lead beings to spiritual maturity and liberation.
He will guide his disciples with many emanations.
He will proclaim the Great Way's essence beyond extremes
And sound to the ten directions the lion's roar
Of the ultimate tantric teachings of indivisible bliss and emptiness.

"His body is that of Wheel of Supreme Bliss;
His speech, Mahamaya personified;
His mind, glorious Vajra Creator of Delight;

His sublime place of emanation, Matrix of Mystery;
And his secret place that holds bliss, Slayer of Lord of Death.
He will not only embody these deities' sacred circles
But will actually manifest them to his disciples.
Moreover, he will transform himself into various other deities
And guide countless numbers of difficult beings.

"He will live for one hundred fifty years,
And at the end of his life, as his final deed,
He will demonstrate many signs and miraculous displays
And depart to Blissful Pure Land.
He will attain enlightenment in that land praised by all buddhas
And turn the wheel of the Great Way Teachings.
All disciples of future generations who have faith in him
Will travel to that buddha's pure land: have no doubt of this!"

This said, the accomplished master left for India,
Flying like a bird through the sky; to you I pray.

You issued from the clan of the wondrous Great Garuda,
Blessed by Ever-Excellent Radiant Awareness, King of Luminosity.
You became learned and accomplished at writing, calculation, and in
    the mind section of Bön's teachings;
You nurtured disciples in that discipline; to you I pray.

From Jungné Sengé and Kor Nirupa,
You received Great Completion's three classes of instruction and guid-
    ance in Great Seal's principal texts.
In each doctrine, you became a second Teacher,
Perfecting your innate and acquired great talents; to you I pray.

Your training from previous lives impelled you to travel to Land of
    the Exalted.
At Vajra Seat, you met the second Buddha.
From him you received and thoroughly assimilated
Such teachings as the three collections and the four classes of tantra;
    to you I pray.

"In a former lifetime, the Victor foretold your life—
You were a listener who gained miraculous powers.
Therefore, Indian scholars, such as I, cannot act as your preceptor."
With these words, he showered you with inconceivable praise; to you
 I pray.

As the master foretold, you went to the Cool Province [the
 Himalayan region],
Where Buddha Boundless Light's manifestation, Langri Tangpa,[37]
Hoisted the victory banner of freedom's pure conduct.
Second Powerful Sage, to you I pray.

You traveled without material needs, carrying rare gems and gold
 powder,
And you disregarded your precious life when confronted with
 hardships
In the course of seven journeys to India and Nepal.
Great bodhisattva, to you I pray.

You approached one hundred fifty Indian scholars,
Of whom fifty were particularly learned and accomplished masters.
Four were especially exalted root spiritual masters,
And two were wisdom dakinis, who received direct teaching
From the body of enlightenment's rapture, the sixth Buddha Vajra
 Bearer.[38]
You pleased them, received their ultimate instructions,
Resolved your misunderstandings, and practiced single-mindedly
Until you attained common and supreme accomplishment; to you
 I pray.

In Sosa Park's acacia grove,
The Victor's consort, vajra queen Niguma,
Entrusted you with the single-disciple lineage, Buddha Vajra Bearer's
 secret treasury.
Lord of awakening's tenth stage, to you I pray.

In the place that brings happiness, Medicinal Grove,
Buddha Selfless One, Sukasiddhi, bestowed empowerment and
 prophecies,

And gave you uncommon blessings with the ambrosia of her
   teaching.
Regent of the sixth buddha, to you I pray.

In the sacred circle emanated by Advayavajra,
You received empowerment and prophecies.
From him, Lord Métripa, you received instruction in Great Seal and
   the Protector.
The doctrine's protectors became your servants; to you I pray.

At Vajra Seat, you held a large offering festival.
For ten days, amazing signs and portents multiplied.
Gods, humans, scholars, and meditation masters praised you in unison.
Incomparable one in three worlds, to you I pray.

All lamas, deities, dakinis, and protectors
Converge in Swift Awakened Protector,
Who overtly promised to be the destined deity
Of you and your lineage; to you I pray.

The accomplished master nurtured by the four deities, Rahula,
Visited you, bringing teachings.
You received inexpressible numbers of tantras, practices, pith
   instructions, and activity rituals.
He performed incredible miracles; to you I pray.

You bestowed empowerment in many emanated sacred circles.
You turned back the onslaught of enemies and obstructors with an
   emanated army.
Gentle Splendor taught you a treasure chest of visualizations
And you overtly expelled sickness and demons; to you I pray.

When you emanated Lord of Death's messengers and divine goddesses,
You induced disillusionment and inspired interest in those who held
   phenomena to be permanent.
You passed unhindered through rock and displayed single and
   multiple forms
And other illusory, magical appearances; to you I pray.

Consistent with the prophecies of your masters and the dakinis,
  you went to Shang.
Beginning with Zhang-zhung, you constructed one hundred eight
  monastic centers.
You covered the earth with study, teaching, meditation, and
  accomplishment.
Lamp of the Teachings, to you I pray.

Your body actually appeared as Vajra Creator of Delight and the nine
  emanated deities,
With the Five Tantras' Deities at five points of your body.
Your emanations taught
On one hundred eight thrones; to you I pray.

In answer to the gods of the Four Great Kings' supplication,
For seven months you nourished yourself with the food of
  concentration.
You sat cross-legged in space
And turned the wheel of Great Way Teachings; to you I pray.

"You've fulfilled your masters' wishes, satisfied the gods, liberated
  humans,
And furthered the Buddha's doctrine!"
With a shower of flowers and the sounds of "Ah la la!",
The gods made this proclamation; to you I pray.

Your emanations dispelled the jealousy in a large monastic college.
During a famine, seeds you planted in the morning on the wide
  plains
Bore fruit in the afternoon,
Nourishing many persons; to you I pray.

In the Highest Pure Land, in Blissful, and Potala,
The Great Mother, Buddha Boundless Light, and Great Compassion
Granted you the Three Aspects of the Unborn, the longevity practice
  Vase of Ambrosia,
And Universal Compassion; to you I pray.

You traveled to the sacred places of Willow Leaf and Oddiyana,
Where Lord of Secrets and yoginis gave you empowerments.
They bestowed secret tantras, and instruction in blazing and
    gathering.
You mastered any meditative state you desired; to you I pray.

Tanglha, Shampo, Unheated,
And other great, powerful gods offered you their heart vitality
    mantras.
You gave them empowerment, bound them with oaths, and installed
    them as the doctrine's guardians.
Sublime, glorious Héruka, to you I pray.

In the fertile earth of your disciples from central, western, and eastern
    Tibet,
Méutön Drimé formed the trunk of transcendent knowledge;
Yorpo Gyamo, the spreading branches of altruism;
Ngultön Rinwang, the flourishing leaves of compassion;
Latö Könkar, the gorgeous flowers of loving-kindness;
Zhangom Chöseng, the essential sap of luminosity;
And Mokchok, the ripened fruit of Illusory Body and Lucid Dream.
As masters and dakinis predicted,
These were the six ultimate disciples equal to you,
Leaders of the ultimate congregation, one hundred eighty thousand
    persons,
Whom you taught and brought to spiritual maturity over a number
    of years.

At the end of your ultimate life span, one hundred fifty years,
The Four Classes of Great Kings, the king of celestial musicians, and
    many other worldly beings
Pleaded with you not to transcend suffering.
You compassionately considered their request
And gave them teaching and prophecies; to you I pray.

Buddha Boundless Light displayed the design of the pure land of
    Great Bliss

And proclaimed, "You are a bodhisattva in your final life.
You will attain manifest awakening in Blissful Pure Land.
Whoever trains in your footsteps
Or merely hears the name of Buddha Boundless Light
Will be reborn in Blissful
Through great miraculous power."
He predicted that the next three holders of your lineage
Will attain awakening in Joyous and other pure lands; to you I pray.

"No one has vital instructions like the teachings of my lineage.
Therefore those of highest, middle, or common capability
Will attain enlightenment in the body of ripened karma, in the body
    of habitual patterns, or in the intermediate state."
You made this sure promise; to you I pray.

"Those who have faith should pray to me in Blissful Pure Land:
You will be born there without any doubt!"
Having said this, you displayed multiple forms of yourself.
Epitome of the ten powers, to you I pray.

You assumed such manifest forms as the Five Tantras' Deities
And the Four Deities of Blessing, and you granted the sacred Teachings.
The heavens filled with rainbows and the sound of music;
A rain of flowers fell; to you I pray.

In the midst of amazing signs, you left for Blissful.
To lead the faithful, you emanated limitless kinds of relics,
Such as sacred images, relics, and auspicious circles.
Master endowed with the four modes of liberation, to you I pray.

For three weeks, these wonderful signs multiplied.
At the site of your remains, deities and dakinis made visible offerings;
Lights shone in the four directions.
Master comparable to the Buddha, to you I pray.

From the ocean of your life of inconceivable freedom,
I have drawn a drop in faith for this supplication.

By its power, may you accept and bless me and all those to whom
   I am related,
That we actualize your life of freedom during our lifetimes.

Noble Kyungpo, trustworthy sublime refuge,
Sit on a lotus and moon seat at the crown of the heads of all beings
And in your unceasing loving-kindness
Bestow upon us common and supreme accomplishment.

(*A Garland of Udumvara Flowers,* pp. 8a-10b)

RINCHEN TSÖNDRU

T HE SHANGPA LINEAGE forms part of what we call the later spread
of Buddhism in Tibet. The great scholar Butön marks the beginning of that period as 973, when a man called Lachen Gongpa Rabsal took
monk's vows; Dromtön, Atisha's main disciple, considered that it began in
978, when Gongpa Rabsal granted ordination to ten men from central
and western Tibet.[39] The event of that ordination is important both for the
continuation of the monastic vows' lineage and for the fact that the ten
returned to central Tibet and founded monasteries throughout the region.
What happened later to these second-wave institutions is a story rarely
told, but I believe it had an impact on the development of the Shangpa lineage. Here is an account told by a modern Tibetan historian:

> The [ten monks] gradually returned to central and western Tibet
> but were unable to stay in Lhasa, so they journeyed to [Tibet's first
> monastery] Samyé, where Lumé Tsultrim Shérab took possession
> of the Kachung Temple, Rakshi and his brother took possession of
> the Gégyé Jéma Ling Temple, Dring Yeshé Yönten took possession
> of the Kamsum Zangkang Ling Temple, and Ba Tsultrim Lodrö
> and his brother took possession of Samyé's central temple.
>
> Later, they gradually traveled to Lhasa. In upper central Tibet,
> Lumé constructed a temple called Morchak-déu and he resided
> there. (*The Collected Works of Dungkar Lozang Trinlé*, p. 533)

Four of Lumé's disciples each constructed temples and monastic residences; together they were known as Lumé's group. Among the three other
men from central Tibet who first stayed at Samyé, Ba Tsultrim Lodrö and
Dring Yeshé Yönten each constructed a monastery in Penpo, near where
Kyungpo Naljor meditated in retreat when Rahula visited him. The last of
the group of four, Rakshi Tsultrim Jungné, also founded a monastery.

These four groups became known in Tibetan shorthand as "Lumé's, Ba's, Rak's, and Dring's groups."

After the initial generation of founders, relations between these four groups degenerated quickly, as Lozang Trinlé relates:

> These four groups—Lumé, Ba, Rak, and Dring—gradually spread to and developed in Lhasa. During the middle of the eleventh century and at the beginning of the twelfth century, battles were fought many times among these four groups. In the Fire Dog year of the second sixty-year cycle, 1106 in the general calendar, a battle was fought at Samyé between Lumé's congregation, and Ba's and Rak's congregations. As a result, most of the temples surrounding Samyé's main temple were burned; the "iron mountains" and the perimeter walls were leveled. (*Ibid.*, p. 534)

One of the Kalachakra translators who had traveled to India, Ra Dorjé Drakpa, otherwise uninvolved in the dispute, hired five hundred workers, who worked continually for two years to repair the damage, at an expense of one hundred thousand measures of grain. This did not end the sad events:

> Further, in the Iron Dragon year of the third sixty-year cycle, 1160 in the general calendar, a long war between the four groups mentioned above broke out at Lhasa, Yarlung, and Penpo. During this time, parts of the main temple in Lhasa [later to be called the Jokang], Ramoché [also in Lhasa], and Tradruk [temple in Yarlung] were ravaged by fire and severely damaged. On that occasion, a disciple of the Doctor from Dakpo [Gampopa], Dakgom Tsultrim Nyingpo [1116–1169] negotiated a settlement between the warring parties and repaired both the large and small temples in Lhasa. (*Ibid.,* p. 535)

These are not pleasant stories to repeat or to reflect upon, even now. Yet we can imagine that these events and the tensions underlying them flavored the atmosphere during the lives of Kyungpo Naljor and Rinchen Tsöndru, particularly the latter, who never evinced any interest in empire building.

These two masters met late in Kyungpo Naljor's life; he sent the young

man away to study with other teachers. Years later, when Rinchen Tsöndru returned to report on his stellar progress in meditation, Kyungpo
Naljor thought that he was lying and dismissed him. As he did so, Buddha Boundless Light, and many deities and dakinis visited Kyungpo Naljor
and informed him that the seemingly impertinent youngster was the lineage holder he had waited so long to find. He called Rinchen Tsöndru
back and gradually gave him the entire Shangpa lineage during the nineteen months he had left to live.

Kyungpo Naljor suggested that his protégé act as his attendant in order
for them to have the proximity that would allow the transmission process.
Rinchen Tsöndru's worries at that moment are curious: "I can't be your
attendant among these wild and very powerful Khampas and monks."
(*The Collection of Shangpa Masters' Biographies*, p. 164) He felt intimidated
by the persons around his teacher; soon thereafter, at Kyungpo Naljor's
death, disputes erupted between the great master's many disciples from
eastern, western, and central Tibet over the fate of their teacher's remains.
Despite Kyungpo Naljor's explicit advice to preserve his body, they cre-
mated it.

I mention this because the so-called Shangpa Kagyu monastic lineage
seems to have been centered at Shang only for a few years between its
founding and the death of its founder. Kyungpo Naljor never enthroned
Rinchen Tsöndru as the head of his institution; he told him to go into
retreat and to meditate alone. Later in life, at no time does Rinchen Tsöndru, nor any of the main "Shangpa" masters, report being invited to
assume responsibility for Shang Monastery; only the last of the lineage's
"seven jewels" visited it (in the thirteenth century), and then only close to
the end of his life. Shang Monastery continued to function, but it seems
to have been irrelevant to the Shangpa Instruction Lineage, for only one
master at a time held the entire lineage and all of them lived and taught
without directing the monastery that lent its name to their teachings.

No Shangpa master was purely—that is, exclusively—Shangpa. Each
received and meditated upon a wealth of Buddhist teachings, both before
and after they received the Shangpa transmission. Each taught others but
maintained the same ecumenical approach as they had developed in their
training. They taught from a variety of lineages, according to others' needs,
and did not concern themselves with establishing institutions and admin-
istrations that would outlive them. This is the story of Rinchen Tsöndru's
life; his lineage descendants would follow his example.

When Kyungpo Naljor died, Rinchen Tsöndru first meditated for two years and then went to Gampopa for further guidance. Gampopa told him they had often been teacher and disciple in past lives. Their reunion moved both to tears. Although Gampopa was able to provide some instruction, he informed his new disciple that he had taken a vow to no longer impart Naropa's Six Doctrines. The two circumvented this promise by meeting in a dream, since Rinchen Tsöndru had already gained mastery of lucid dreaming. During the year they spent together, Gampopa's main contribution to Rinchen Tsöndru's spiritual life was complete instruction in Great Seal that led him to certainty in the view.

At their parting, Gampopa told his disciple to go into retreat and not to concern himself with the spiritual community's work, let alone worldly work. Rinchen Tsöndru stayed for twelve years in retreat at Mokchok, after which some students gathered. Eventually their numbers outgrew the retreat place and Mokchok-pa (Rinchen Tsöndru's nickname) founded a small monastery, which he maintained with mixed feelings for the last decade and a half of his life. Rinchen Tsöndru was a meditator at heart, and his autobiography relates his dream experiences more than details of his active life. Both Niguma and Sukasiddhi appeared to him in visions; the fact that Niguma did so when Rinchen Tsöndru was performing a ritual of offering to Gampopa led him to comment, "Spiritual masters all share the same life force; only cultivation [of merit and wisdom] and devotion are important, I think." (*Ibid.,* pp. 200-201)

It is in Rinchen Tsöndru's life that we find the Shangpa lineage's lasting character, lifelong dedication to all tantric teachings impartially, expressed through renunciation and meditation.

The Melody of Wonder:
A Supplication to the Incomparable Mokchok-pa,
by Jamgon Kongtrul

Victor's heir who spontaneously accomplished the two goals,
Master prophesied by the dakini,
Indisputable lord of accomplishment, illustrious Mokchok-pa,
Venerable Rinchen Tsöndru, to you I pray.

You were born at Lhapu, Shang, within the Shéu clan.
You entered Buddhism and relied correctly on your spiritual master.
Having resolved your misunderstandings, you meditated.
A definite certainty was born within you; to you I pray.

Moved by having met a man whose study made him insensitive to the
    teachings,
You vowed to search for profound instruction.
From Khampa Aseng, you received sovereign tantras'
Profound creation and completion practices; to you I pray.

From Venerable Burgom, you received Noble Réchungpa's creation
    and completion practices.
When you meditated upon them,
You displayed signs to your enemies, saw Noble Vajra Yogini's face,
And attained meditative states; to you I pray.

From Könkar, Yorpo, Dorjé Gyal, and other masters,
You received many source texts' profound instructions, mainly of the
    transcendent perfection of knowledge.
In particular, the great, accomplished master Kyungpo accepted you
    as his disciple.
You pleased him in many ways; to you I pray.

Not withholding anything, Kyungpo gave you every profound
    instruction
He received from his four root masters, to whom he offered gold.
Further, he gave you his single-disciple transmission.
You always saw his body as that of the tantric deities; to you I pray.

You actualized illusionlike absorption.
You knew the one that liberates all; your wisdom's display unfolded.
You tamed all evil spirits
And made many beings happy; to you I pray.

You saw the face of Buddha Immutable, the two wisdom dakinis,
Indrabodhi, Vajra Yogini,
And in particular Héruka—
They gave you deep and vast sacred Teachings; to you I pray.

When you arrived in the presence of the incomparable Dakpo,
    Gampopa,
He said that you had been his disciple-child in many lifetimes; he
    treated you lovingly.
He led you to direct sight of ultimate enlightenment's naked body.
Your realization and liberation occurred simultaneously; to you I pray.

Gampopa entrusted you with the transmission of Great Seal's lineage.
Your meditative states' power became complete.
From that point forth, for as long as you lived, you never thought of
    this life.
Bodhisattva in your final life, to you I pray.

For twelve years at Mokchok Cliff,
You renounced human food and practiced single-mindedly.

Buddha Unmoving, the Four Deities, Awakened Protector,
And the dakinis visibly visited you; to you I pray.

During your celebration of Lama Shangpa's death memorial,
He and Buddha Boundless Light came to give you the Central
     Channel's Nectar.[40]
You saw the pure lands clearly, with buddhas as numerous as all atoms
On each atom; to you I pray.

Others could see emanations of your overpowering mastery.
When you sat in space, fortunate persons were moved to faith.
You accepted them, gathered countless disciples,
And brought them all to spiritual maturity and liberation; to you
     I pray.

To hear your name or voice, to see your residence,
Or to have faith and devotion toward you induced meditative states
And led limitless numbers of people to liberation.
Any connection to you was significant; to you I pray.

When you gave empowerment,
The Five Tantras' Deities visibly appeared at your five centers
And upon the sand mandala, seen by all fortunate persons.
Source of blessings, to you I pray.

From Blissful realm, Buddha's servants came to invite you,
But you did not agree to leave [to die].
For three years you stayed to turn the wheel of the Teachings,
To nurture your disciples-children; to you I pray.

"After this life, in the eastern pure land of Joyful, in the Radiant
     realm,
I will attain manifest enlightenment
And teach only the Great Way!"
You made this proclamation in a lion's roar; to you I pray.

"Those who preserve the lineage should turn their prayers to
     me there:

They will be reborn in that supreme pure realm!"
Having said this, you demonstrated boundless amazing miracles
And left for Radiant Pure Land; to you I pray.

Again, you returned on a path of light,
Placed the lineage's crown on beings' lord protector,
And entrusted the leadership of your family lineage to Shérab Répa
To prevent its interruption; to you I pray.

King of the Teachings, Noble Mokchok-pa,
Please give your compassionate, loving attention to my prayer.
Give me the blessing of your body, speech, and mind,
And lead me to Radiant Pure Land!

(*A Garland of Udumvara Flowers,* pp. 10b-11b)

CHÖKYI SENGÉ

I N *The Blue Annals*, Gö Lotsawa comments on the subject of the Shangpa lamas, "It is difficult to establish clearly the dates, months and the age of these teachers." (p. 746) To this day, the problem remains, although modern books cite Rinchen Tsöndru's dates as 1110–1170 and Chökyi Sengé's as 1154–1217.[41] I believe these to be approximate dates, the first based on whichever dates one accepts for Kyungpo Naljor. The latter set of dates is clearly inaccurate, as Chökyi Sengé had not met Rinchen Tsöndru by the time he was sixteen (which would be his age at Mokchokpa's death by these dates) and in fact lived far into his master's life.

Chökyi Sengé began his spiritual life much as his teacher had, by spurning a seemingly sensible approach to Buddhism: first a classical education, then meditation. That was not for him. In spite of repeated discouragement from his fellow monks, he persisted in meditation practice in retreat to the detriment of study and eventually met his chosen deity, Bodhisattva Great Compassion. In an exchange that reminds us of the great Indian master Asanga's first words to Bodhisattva Loving-Kindness after twelve years of hardship, Chökyi Sengé's initial reaction on seeing the bodhisattva was to complain. He had undergone severe hardships during three and a half years of solitary meditation and he questioned the aptness of the bodhisattva's name, "Lord, your compassion's not great at all!" he protested. Great Compassion explained that from the retreat's third day, he had never strayed from Chökyi Sengé's side, but that negative karma and anticipation of the joy of their eventual meeting had prevented the young man from seeing the bodhisattva.

Like the lineage lamas before him, Chökyi Sengé sought instruction from a number of lamas before meeting Rinchen Tsöndru. On the eve of their first encounter, Six-Armed Protector gave them both an indication that their meeting would prove to be crucial for the lineage. In later generations, this cue giving by the main protector of the Shangpa lineage was often repeated before the first meeting of the lineage holder with his future heir. This was even true for a twentieth-century Shangpa lineage holder, Norbu Döndrub, who dreamed that Six-Armed Mahakala carried a white scarf and went to welcome the new Shangpa lineage holder who, he said, would arrive the next day. Norbu Döndrub told his attendant in the morning to allow anyone who arrived at his isolated retreat place to enter, as this was an important guest. But by evening, no one had appeared. With some consternation, Norbu Döndrub questioned his attendant, "Didn't anyone at all come here?" The attendant replied that no one had arrived, except for a young boy with his possessions strapped on a yak and who spoke a dialect the attendant couldn't understand. As he knew his master was expecting an important visitor, he had sent the boy away. The fifteen-year-old boy was the future Kalu Rinpoché, who had arrived to prepare for his three-year retreat under Norbu Döndrub's guidance.

Rinchen Tsöndru gave Chökyi Sengé the entire cycle of teachings but never asked his disciple to assume responsibility for his circle of followers or his institution, such as it was. When monks from Chökyi Sengé's uncle's monastery called upon him to replace that late abbot, he felt more inclined to meditate in retreat, but Rinchen Tsöndru asked him to try to continue his meditation while assuming responsibility for the monastery, located in Kyergang. Just as Rinchen Tsöndru is often referred to by his retreat's place name, Mokchok, so Chökyi Sengé is called Kyergang-pa, after that monastery. We also sometimes refer to him in Tibetan as Öntön, "the nephew teacher."

Chökyi Sengé's autobiography mentions a number of mistakes he and others made and how they corrected them. His honesty remains helpful, as he confronts the same issues that meditators struggle with today: how to balance study and meditation, the error of teaching before one is ready, purity in motivation, impartiality, the need to keep meditative experience to oneself, and the pitfalls of judging others before having reached omniscience. He also continues the Shangpa tradition in the inner path of tantra; he was a dreamer, a lucid dreamer. Although the Shangpa lamas learned Fierce Inner Heat (*tummo*) as had Milarepa, they quickly gained mastery in it (for example, Kyergang-pa took one week to reach the stage where he could wear a cotton robe) and instead paid lifelong attention to their practice of Lucid Dream. All the early Shangpa masters present themselves in their autobiographies as avid dreamers.

One of the major contributions Chökyi Sengé made to the Shangpa lineage was made possible by his control of dreams. He went to visit Guru Rinpoché in the course of a lucid dream, and he asked for and received empowerment in a wrathful form of Bodhisattva Great Compassion called Hayagriva in Sanskrit, literally Horse Neck. This deity with an unflattering name is an important tantric meditation. Guru Rinpoché told Chökyi Sengé where he could find the master on earth who held the texts that corresponded to the empowerment he had just received. After having found the lama (named Nyémo Zhuyé), he returned in a lucid dream to seek Guru Rinpoché's confirmation that he had received the entire transmission. No, said Guru Rinpoché, the lama had withheld one part, which Chökyi Sengé then was able to receive. This may seem an unlikely story, but this meditation is still treasured by Shangpa meditators; it has become very popular and widespread in the Gélug tradition; Jamgon Kongtrul included the entire transmission in his *Treasury of Precious Rediscovered Teachings* (in Volume 25).

Chökyi Sengé also continued the Shangpa tradition of excellence. Kyungpo Naljor's Indian teachers said there was no disciple equal to him in India at that time. Kyungpo Naljor considered Rinchen Tsöndru's meditation to be better than his own; Rinchen Tsöndru in turn told Chökyi Sengé that "a cow has given birth to a *dzo!*" The cow, the lama, had given birth to a much larger animal, a dzo (a male cross between a yak bull and a cow), the disciple. In the series of Shangpa masters' biographies, Kyergang-pa's is the first in which this story is told, but it is repeated in each successive generation. Each great master repeatedly praises his foremost disciple as better than himself. On a human level, this is a very touching event, and for the lineage it situates all students' focus in the present, unlike some lineages that seem to collectively mourn their long-lost glorious past.

Another feature common to the Shangpa masters was their substantial offerings made to receive instruction. It was not enough for each master to have been foretold by the protectors or dakinis as the awaited lineage holder, he still was expected to make offerings for the empowerments and teachings he received. This was certainly true for Kyungpo Naljor, who offered much gold for the instruction he received, and despite the renunciant character of the lineage and the masters, each notes his diligence in making offerings. Three times, Chökyi Sengé offered all his possessions to Mokchok-pa, despite the strong protests and pointed lack of cooperation from the officials at his late uncle's monastery. (I remember Kalu Rinpoché also saying that he had offered all he owned to his teacher, Norbu Döndrub, three times.)

Jamgon Kongtrul's supplication to Chökyi Sengé contains references (in the second and third verses) to his past lives and to his attainment of full enlightenment after this life (at the end of the prayer). This master related some of his past lives and foretold his own and his close disciples' final attainment. Again, this display of clairvoyance was not uncommon in Shangpa masters, although they customarily restricted the information to their closest and most trusted disciples until after their death.

The Melody of Faith:
A Supplication to the Great Öntön Kyergang-pa
by Jamgon Kongtrul

Billowing clouds of your love gather in luminous space.
Your compassion continually rains on the fields of your disciples,

Ripening the fruit of the two accomplishments.
Kyergang-pa, Venerable Chökyi Sengé, to you I pray.

In Land of the Exalted, you were Prajna-varma and other masters,
Both famous and hidden adepts.
Your many emanations guided infinite numbers of disciples.
Lord of compassion, I bow my head to you.

In China, you led those of wrong conduct to the Teachings.
You gave instruction in cause and effect, emptiness, and compassion
To *tramen* spirits and monkeys, according to their needs.
Creator of manifestations suitable to others' needs, to you I pray.

Powerful All-Seeing One nurtured you in all your lifetimes;
You spontaneously accomplished the two goals.
Here in the Himalayan region as well, your many manifestations
Accomplished exalted enlightened activity; to you I pray.

Lord protector of beings, you were born in central Tibet.
You took renunciant's vows and learned the discourses in Kyergang,
    from the omniscient master Bal.
In Lubuk, from the accomplished master Chégom,
You received exalted maturing and liberating instructions; to you
    I pray.

You meditated during three and a half years of hardship.
Great Compassion and Slayer of Lord of Death
Showed you their face and blessed you,
Staying with you forever; to you I pray.

From Tsagom Penpuk-pa, you received the complete instructions
Of Réchungpa's and Lord [Atisha]'s lineages.
Events led you to directly realize your own mind
As the unborn body of ultimate enlightenment; to you I pray.

When you met noble Mokchok-pa, Awakened Protector greeted you
    and became your servant.
You were entrusted with the single-disciple lineage;

Your clinging to appearances as real collapsed.
Your meditative states' great creative power reached perfection; to you
   I pray.

All-Seeing One continually granted you sacred Teachings.
The Five Tantras' Deities gave you instruction in the profound
   meaning.
Many accomplished masters and dakinis taught you
And made prophecies; to you I pray.

When you traveled to your residence of Kyergang,
Awakened Protector and his entourage visibly went with you.
They carried offerings to the lama's residence
And served you respectfully; to you I pray.

With clairvoyance, you guided beings impartially.
Varuna offered you the nagas' jewels.
Three times, with perfect purity in the three spheres, you offered all
   you had
To please your master; to you I pray.

In Oddiyana, from Lotus Skull-Garlanded Adept [Guru Rinpoché],
You received Great Power Horse Neck's empowerment and
   meditation.
Following Lotus-Born's directions, you received the entire teaching
From Nyémo Zhuyé; to you I pray.

From Zhangom, around whom dakinis gathered like clouds,
And other masters, you received the Teachings' profound essence.
With only your meditation, recollection mantras, and water,
You nurtured countless destitute beings; to you I pray.

Emanated and returning light from Eleven-Faced All Seeing One
Purified your own and others' sickness, demons, and obscurations,
   and fostered meditative states.
Padampa Sangyé taught you Pacification of Suffering;
Vajra Creator of Delight's male and female deities taught you
   confession using the vowels and consonants; to you I pray.

"During the degenerate time, your tradition of meditation will spread
And [its followers] will continually see my face."
Great Compassion gave you this encouragement to teach disciples.
Master of others' benefit as vast as space, to you I pray.

After this life, you took miraculous rebirth in Blissful,
Received the Victor's teachings, then traveled to Oddiyana,
Where your tantric activity led many beings
To the state of a vajra holder; to you I pray.

From there, you traveled to Joyous, where in Buddha Immutable's
    presence
You perfected your pure conduct.
In the world of Lapis Light, you attained manifest enlightenment.
You lead those who preserve your lineage to that pure land; to you
    I pray.

"I will be the Transcendent Buddha Glory of Immaculate Space,
Live for one thousand years, have a following of nine hundred
    thousand,
And impart fifty-six thousand sacred Teachings."
Such was your fearless promise; to you I pray.

"To see, hear, remember, or be touched by me is significant.
Those who pray to me will become bodhisattvas on stages of
    awakening
In the eastern pure land." This you proclaimed,
Then entered into the evenness of the absolute expanse; to you I pray.

Compassionate Öntön, All-Seeing One incarnate,
Please quickly take your hook of compassion
To hold me and other disciples who have bad karma—
Bless us with the accomplishment of the two goals.

(A *Garland of Udumvara Flowers*, pp. 11b-12b)

SANGYÉ NYENTÖN

THIS LINEAGE HOLDER also sports an impressive portfolio of names. He is usually called Sangyé Nyentön (Buddha Teacher of the Nyen Clan), although this amounts to a family name and profession. He is sometimes referred to as Rigong-pa, the place of his main residence, much in the same way that Kyergang-pa and Mokchok-pa are commonly known by their meditation sites. Finally, this teacher had a nickname that alluded to his lifestyle, Bépé Naljor (hidden adept), and a purely Buddhist name, Chökyi Shérab, the name he used the least. It would seem from the evidence of the Shangpa masters that some Tibetans were slow to use their religious names (which most Buddhist Tibetans do now), preferring their family names or residence names.

Sangyé Nyentön received a Shangpa-style confirmation from his master: his practice surpassed that of his teacher. It is clear from his and other biographies that such comments reflect an appreciation for each young student's quality of meditation and its reflection in lucid dreams and visions. The masters never based their evaluation on outer calculations, such as the quantity of prayers or mantras recited.

Another theme of the Shangpa lineage continues in the life of Sangyé Nyentön—lack of concern for the lineage's institutions. Kyungpo Naljor had been a founder, an initiator on many levels; Rinchen Tsöndru was a meditator and a lay person. Chökyi Sengé was a more social individual who integrated his monastic responsibilities with his meditation. Nevertheless, he guided his sole spiritual heir to a lifestyle much different from his own. Before Sangyé Nyentön met his teacher, he had taken full monastic ordination and had done what neither Rinchen Tsöndru or Chökyi Sengé had ever managed—he completed a traditional Buddhist education. That could have marked a turning point in the lineage, from meditation cushions only to a full-service Buddhist monastery, such as so many other schools were busily establishing. To this point, the Shangpa lamas were obstinate meditators whose only concept of graduation was the moment when their naked, radiant awareness broke through the confines of meditation to reach liberation. To have a well-trained monk and well-educated scholar as the designated lineage holder was perhaps the sign of a new direction.

Instead, Chökyi Sengé seems to have viewed his disciple's credentials as a potential source of obstacles. Here is his advice to Sangyé Nyentön: "Be a hidden adept, drink alcohol, eat in the afternoon [to the contrary of monastic discipline], and associate with many kinds of people [not just monks]. People will say you don't care about monastic purity. Don't wear fine clothes and always sleep in ragged blankets. At the outset of practices, don't develop the mind of awakening and, at the conclusion, don't recite a dedication of merit. Don't teach the meditation texts or profound instructions widely. Present yourself as someone who knows nothing." (*The Collection of Shangpa Masters' Biographies*, pp. 310-311)

As much as we might appreciate this as advice to focus on liberation rather than to keep up appearances, Buddhist or worldly, it is clear that the speaker's primary concern was not the enhancement of the lineage's institutions. It sounds like a public relations disaster in the making. In fact, Sangyé Nyentön was misjudged by those far and near to the point that he needed to exhort his disciples to pure vision, to see the buddha within his unorthodox appearance and demeanor. This has been the fate of all realized masters who have acted outside Buddhist conventions; Indian and Tibetan tantric Buddhist lore is particularly rich in such nonconformist characters. While most Buddhists adore our monastic community of dedicated men and women, it is not true that all Buddhist masters extol the virtues of life within the monastic institutions themselves. Here are some lines that point out that for many, leaving home for a monastery was to leave a small home life for a large one:

> To remain in either [a lay or monastic] lifestyle creates a lot of activity and provides the basis for the deterioration of spiritual life.
>
> First, in a worldly lifestyle, partiality toward friends rather than foes, the needs of children and spouse, and worries concerning taxes and damages make you a servant to tonight's and tomorrow's food and clothing, thwart the completion of anything, blind you to life itself, prevent your feeling pleasure in anything, make the day without respite and the night without rest, and yet you never finish

your busyness. Thoughts of spiritual life become rare, and whatever you do becomes a wide arena for mingling with negative acts. The flames of your spouse's attachment and anger are searing, and the burden of your karmic debt to your children is crushing. Whatever you do, you become weighed down by an oppressive load of suffering. You suffer, but you cannot stand to see others in opulent circumstances. These events repeat themselves many times; spiritual life becomes distant.

Adopting the second lifestyle, that of an ordained person [in a monastic institution], also entails suffering. You renounce a small home for a big home. You strive at commerce and agriculture; you make horses and donkeys beasts of burden; you become preoccupied with increasing your wealth; you plan for your old age; and you give counsel to close relations. You become attached to craving for pleasure; you long for happiness in the enjoyment of food and drink; you lay plans for your residence and its protection; and you are distracted by never-ending activity. Day and night, your horizon is defined by your attachment or anger. You are burdened by the obligation to remember rank. Because of your worldly pleasures, your spirituality becomes a hypocritical, false image of study and reflection. Flames of your attachment, anger, and competitiveness tower; those attitudes' thorns always sting. Whatever you do is for this life's benefit; you always make hopeful plans. Master and disciple struggle with one another, without faith; you feel jealous competitiveness toward your spiritual brothers and sisters. The strongest part [of your character] is the mountain of your eight worldly concerns; the weakest, your behavior due to lack of study. So many faults separate your mind from spiritual life—authentic spirituality focused on freedom is very difficult! *The Transmission of Monastic Discipline* states:

> It is difficult to initially renounce home life, abandoning both large and small family duties. (*Treasury of Discourses and Tantras*, Section 3, pp. 8a-8b)

These words come from a text outside the Shangpa tradition, but they were first written about one hundred years after Sangyé Nyentön's life by Longchenpa, a Nyingma master who received the Shangpa teachings at a young age and whose words are sometimes quoted in later Shangpa lineage treatises. I think that the early Shangpa masters lived the meaning of these words and tried to steer their lineage toward single-minded dedication to renunciation, meditation, and freedom.

Chökyi Sengé also advised Sangyé Nyentön that he would be wiser to keep the ten good disciples his master foretold (eight men and two women) than to have tens of thousands of others. Again, such counsel helped preserve the Shangpa lineage values but did little for its public image and presence.

To the body of teaching identified as the Shangpa Instruction Lineage, Sangyé Nyentön added a number of supplementary meditations taught to him by Sukasiddhi and a series of exercises called the Immortal Body exercises, which he received from an adept called Latö Gönpo. For Sangyé Nyentön, these exercises untied a knot in his channels that had long produced what he refers to as a "blockage at my secret [genital] area." Unfortunately for us, the Shangpa lineage at some point crossed the line from carefree to careless, and the transmission for these exercises has been lost, although the text itself is extant. In the Tibetan tradition, it is not enough to have a book's clear explanation; each of us must receive the empowerment, reading transmission, and personal guidance in an unbroken lineage for the teaching to become alive. Jamgon Kongtrul reported in the nineteenth century that the transmission for these exercises had already been irremediably interrupted.

Sangyé Nyentön is also known for his close relationship with the Shangpa lineage's main protector, Six-Armed Mahakala. He was able to converse with the protector and his entourage as we speak to other human beings. Nevertheless, some of the minor protectors who are pictured around Six-Armed Mahakala were so eager to help him that he had to repeatedly ask them to not harm his enemies. In Jamgon Kongtrul's supplication to Sangyé Nyentön below, he mentions a statue of Six-Armed Mahakala that remained intact at Rigong until the Cultural Revolution. The statue was called a "self-manifest statue" as it was an emanation of the protector who sculpted and consecrated it. Many pilgrims, including Kunga Drolchok, Taranata, and Kalu Rinpoché, visited it over the centuries and marveled at its blessing and the continued purity of Rigong's atmosphere as a meditation place.

The Melody of Blessing:
A Supplication to the Great Sangyé Nyentön
by Jamgon Kongtrul

Buddha Vajra Bearer in the guise of a spiritual guide,
You perfectly completed every noble quality.
Hidden enlightened one, Nyentön Rigong-pa,
Chökyi Shérab, to you I pray.

In Yoldar, you were born in a family that resembles pure rice.
You had an innate, sincere attitude of detachment.
Not holding on to your body or possessions,
You perfected generosity; to you I pray.

With intense disengagement, you renounced home life to enter the
    doctrine.
You trained to become learned in the teachings of discipline, the Mid-
    dle Way, logic, and the transcendent perfections.
Guarding your superior training as if it were your eyes,
You perfected ethical conduct; to you I pray.

Sickness, demons, or misfortunes did not intimidate you;
For the sake of the teachings, you accepted hardship.
Repaying any harm with helpfulness,
You perfected patience; to you I pray.

With the lamp of outer study, you resolved misunderstandings;
You brought boundless intensity to your inner transcendent
  knowledge born from reflection;
In meditation without distraction, the result manifested—
You perfected diligence; to you I pray.

You were accepted by Öntön, Great Compassionate One,
Who gave you the entire single-disciple lineage of the dakinis' secret
  words.
You saw appearances, sounds, and phenomena as unreal, like
  rainbows.
The experience of illusion naturally arose; to you I pray.

Vajra Creator of Delight, Vajra Sow, powerful All-Seeing One,
And Exalted Tara granted you the Teachings' ambrosia.
In particular, Sukasiddhi introduced you to the mind's nature.
Your realization reached the bounds of space; to you I pray.

As you ordered, Awakened Protector performed enlightened activity;
Varuna acted as your servant and subject.
Many powerful worldly gods and demons requested empowerment
And you had them enter the Teachings; to you I pray.

Day and night, illusion, lucid dreams, and the deities' forms naturally
  arose.
Within your nondual wisdom of bliss and emptiness,
Thoughts of deluded appearances completely faded—
You perfected meditation; to you I pray.

Heeding [the Guru] Black One of the Charnel Ground's command,
Latö-pa traveled with miraculous powers from Land of the Exalted.
You received the exercises of immortality
And demonstrated freeing your secret hindrance into the absolute
  expanse; to you I pray.

Obeying your master's command, you lived as a hidden adept
At Rigong retreat, where you accepted fortunate disciples

And wandered through the victors' pure lands in the ten directions.
Lord of awakening's tenth stage, to you I pray.

The eighty accomplished masters visibly visited you,
Stayed for three days, and granted you empowerments and sacred
    Teaching.
They spoke prophecies, then left, flying through the sky.
Foremost child of the victors, to you I pray.

Your realization of the unborn state was continual, during and after
    meditation.
You saw phenomena lucidly, like the moon on water.
You gained empowerment and mastered the six forms of
    clairvoyance—
You perfected transcendent knowledge; to you I pray.

When thirteen bolts of lightning struck your body,
It became a flaming meteorite, adorned with flowers.
You sent back the dakinis' envoys and consecrated your body as
    indestructible
To guide your disciples; to you I pray.

Encouraged by the Goddess and noxious spirits,
When you received the materials for [a statue],
Awakened Protector's emanation sculpted the image then actually dis-
    solved into it,
Making the Protector's self-manifest statue; to you I pray.

"You have engendered unlimited devotion toward great Buddha Vajra
    Bearer
And will thereby attain manifest awakening.
I too will bless you in the future."
Sukasiddhi clearly told you this; to you I pray.

"Whoever sees you, hears your voice, or brings you to mind
Will never fall back into the wheel of life
And will be reborn as your disciple-child."
Your master and deities repeatedly foretold this; to you I pray.

When you momentarily completed your guidance of this realm,
You left for the eastern Strewn Flowers Pure Land,
Where you attained enlightenment as Buddha Glorious Lotus
And turned the wheel of the Teachings; to you I pray.

Knower of the world, Victor Nyentön-pa,
Look to us with your veil-free enlightened vision.
Bestow spiritual ripening on sentient beings such as I,
Who wander in our bad karma, bad bodies, and bad circumstances.

(A Garland of Udumvara Flowers, pp. 12b-13b)

SANGYÉ TÖNPA

AT THE BEGINNING of this collection of songs, Jamgon Kongtrul composed a two-line prayer to each of the major masters of the lineage. To evoke Sangyé Tönpa, he wrote,

> Noble Sangyé Tönpa, exemplar of the seven-jewel lineage
> And their lives of freedom, to you I pray.

Sangyé Tönpa (also known as Tsöndru Sengé or Chöjé Tönpa) was the last of the seven jewels of the Shangpa transmission that began with Buddha Vajra Bearer. He was the one to untie the vajra knot of the dakinis' seal, allowing Niguma's instructions to be taught in their entirety to more than a single disciple. Kongtrul cites him as the epitome of the seven, the one in whom the qualities of all were gathered, and it is difficult to feel otherwise when reading his story. The autobiography of this master meditator and visionary is almost entirely situated on an "inner" level, that of visions, lucid dreams, and clear light.

A few stories of his early years reveal him as a prodigy. At nine, he met an emanation of Machik Lapdrön and received her single-disciple transmission and a prophecy; his name is found in some Severance lineages. Later, at twelve years old, he confided to one lama his deep disillusionment with life; the lama remarked that the boy's acute alienation indicated either that he was a spiritual prodigy or that he had been possessed by a demon! Later, another master identified him as his lineage's predicted disciple, seventh in a line from an exceptional woman master. That lineage centered on the meditation of Buddha Infinite Life, whom Sangyé Tönpa was said to incarnate; it was founded by an Indian woman master known as Queen of Accomplishment, teacher of Milarepa's disciple, Réchungpa.

True to the Shangpa tradition, Sangyé Tönpa stressed the need to keep meditative experience secret and to remain steadfast within spiritual practice for one's entire life. The reader might assume from this and the absence of details of his active life that Sangyé Tönpa had few students. Not so; two supplementary biographies by his disciples reveal that he had students "from the seas of China to Jalandhara in India." One hundred eight disciples were "hidden adepts" foretold by Niguma when she visited Sangyé Tönpa and gave him a string of prayer beads made of 108 pearls. This was her reassurance that he could teach widely, that her secrets could finally be told to more than one chosen heir. The fact that Niguma calls the 108 "hidden" refers not to antisocial behavior but to the discipline of silence in relation to one's spiritual life. I believe that she did not envision them as public, active teachers, just as discreet meditators, content to practice rather than to preach.

Sangyé Tönpa confesses to some pride during his extraordinary exercises in control of lucid dreams, but he points out that as soon as his pride arose, his experience faded until he had rid himself of that stultifying attitude. Even the thought during lucid dreams that his offerings and elaborate dream creations were positive proved the occasion for a warning from an anonymous dakini that attachment to things as positive was a golden chain he could well do without.

Like his spiritual master, Sangyé Tönpa was a monk, although unlike Sangyé Nyentön, he adhered closely to the external appearance of discipline. Nevertheless, he too had to urge his disciples to look beyond his physical state. He reports that sickness troubled him most of his life, infirmity he blamed on doubts that he had entertained during a past life in India concerning tantra's third empowerment (that of wisdom engendered by an embodiment of transcendent knowledge). Sangyé Tönpa claimed to be an invalid by day and a buddha by night. He exercised extraordinary control during lucid dreams and in the clear light of deep sleep. His autobiography also provides vivid testimony to the strength of his devotion to his teacher. Nevertheless, he does not give any indication that he busied himself with institutions. He taught many disciples but did not found a monastery of his own. Close to the end of his life, he paid a short visit to Shang Monastery, the first of the Shangpa masters to do so since Rinchen Tsöndru's meeting there with Kyungpo Naljor.

In the Shangpa tradition, Sangyé Tönpa's life had been foretold for generations and he was designated repeatedly during his lifetime as the one who would take Niguma's teaching to the world. His qualifications for that task define the Shangpa tradition: perfect renunciation, outward discretion and simplicity, and a lifelong dedication to the fullness of inner realization. Although the full Shangpa Instruction Lineage was no longer closed to just one individual in each generation, those who received and preserved it did not alter the lineage's character.

The Lion's Melody:
A Supplication to the Protector of Beings,
Lord of the Teachings, Sangyé Tönpa
by Jamgon Kongtrul

Like a wish-fulfilling gem, you are the source of what we need and
    desire.
Just the sound of your name protects us from fear of the miserable
    realms.
Protector of beings, Tönpa, Lord of the Teachings,
Venerable Tsöndru Sengé, to you I pray.

At Karek, on a grassy plain, in the Yangal Karpo lineage of Shen Bön
You emerged from the womb bearing the physical marks and signs
    of perfection.
In every activity, your experience of the teachings increased.
Your karmic propensity from previous training awakened; to you I pray.

When you were nine, an emanation of Machik
Came to give you a mind empowerment of Severance.
She gave you oral instructions, a single-disciple lineage,
    and a prophecy.

Sole son of the dakini, to you I pray.

You viewed the prison of existence as a hellish fire pit.
With intense feelings of needing nothing and of disillusionment, you
   renounced home life.
With many tutors, you trained in the discourses and tantras.
Lion of Speech, to you I pray.

In the presence of the accomplished master Zangyul-pa,
You were recognized as the one foretold—
Emanation of Buddha Infinite Life, seventh in Queen of Accomplish-
   ment's lineage.
He gave you a single-disciple transmission; to you I pray.

When you arrived in the presence of master Sangyé Nyentön,
Many spiritual heroes and dakinis greeted you.
As an initial connection, he gave you teaching of the three bodies—
You saw the master as the Buddha; to you I pray.

You accomplished simultaneously illusion, lucid dreaming,
   refinement, emanation, and replication;
Your meditative states' great power was complete.
Your entire grasping to the reality of appearances collapsed into
   shreds.
Great destroyer of delusion, to you I pray.

From Buddha Vajra Bearer through the lineage of jewels,
The masters foretold that you would guide all their disciples.
You became the fortunate one who received the entire transmission
Of the Golden Doctrines; to you I pray.

During the day, Great Seal, ineffable, beyond the intellect's scope,
And during the night, self-manifest, spontaneous clear light endowed
   with three characteristics
Appeared naturally in union.
You completely perfected the Victor's three bodies of enlightenment;
   to you I pray.

Your body had no shadow; you saw unobstructedly
Sentient beings' thoughts during their lifetimes, in the past, present,
and future.
When you gave your attention to afflictions such as leprosy, demons,
and chronic diseases,
They were cured instantly; to you I pray.

When you gave empowerments, spiritual heroes and dakinis
Erected the mandala and showed their forms.
On hearing your name, humans entered the spiritual path.
On merely seeing your face, they experienced sublime meditation; to
you I pray.

At Samten Cliff, the dakini Niguma
Gave you a garland of one hundred eight pearls
To foretell the appearance of that number of hidden, accomplished
masters
You would bring to spiritual maturity and liberation; to you I pray.

Obeying your master's command, you gave teaching based on your
experience
To all impartially—high and low, good and evil, old and young.
Thus, your name's renown
Reached the far ocean's shores; to you I pray.

The Land of Jambu's six major regions and lesser regions
Filled with accomplished masters, your disciples.
You brought many hundreds of thousands to spiritual maturity,
An inconceivable life of freedom; to you I pray.

As foretold by the male and female masters of enlightenment's six
families,
The seven-jewel garland appeared and you untied the vajra knot.
You became the pilot of the ship to freedom
For as long as Buddhism endures; to you I pray.

To encourage those who cling to permanence,
You completed your work for beings' benefit.

In rainbow light, a rain of flowers, earthquakes, and wafting incense,
You left for the eastern Strewn Flowers Pure Land; to you I pray.

As a sacred support for gods' and humans' offerings,
You emanated unlimited numbers of amazing remains in the forms
of deities and relics.
Until the end of existence, they are for the faithful a basis for
cultivating merit
That never deteriorates, but ever increases; to you I pray.

Lord of the Teachings unrivaled in the three worlds,
Look to us with your wisdom eyes from your pure land.
Develop strong compassion toward me, your child, who prays to you.
In this life, bless me with the attainment of manifest enlightenment.

(*A Garland of Udumvara Flowers,* pp. 13b-14b)

TSANGMA SHANGTÖN

SHANGTÖN is the first Shangpa master for whom we have relatively reliable dates, 1234–1309. He lived during a period of immense transformation in Tibet, although we have no evidence that Shangtön knew or cared about his country's current events. The rulers of Mongolia were in the process of becoming emperors of the largest contiguous empire the world has ever known, and Tibet lay in their path. They invaded Tibet for the first time in 1206 and finally unified the country under their control in 1253, the first time since the fall of the Yarlung dynasty that Tibetans lived under a single government. There was a certain competition among Tibetan lamas for the Mongolian ruler's attention. Karma Pakshi, the second Karmapa, gave him empowerment in 1255; Drogön Pakpa, head of the Sakya monastic system, did so in 1260. Finally, it was the latter lama to whom the Mongol emperor entrusted the country; Drogön Pakpa returned to Tibet in 1265 as the first to rule Tibet from a religious throne.

This marriage of church and state was to have an enormous impact on all Tibetan monasteries, including those of the humble Shangpa lineage. (A census taken at the beginning of Mongol rule shows that in the Shangpa Monastery and its vicinity there lived 8,400 persons.[42]) Two minor effects of this change can be mentioned here. First, due to the instability of the system over time, power passed from one monastic system to another; monasteries once conceived as shelters from secular life became fortresses of the ruling elite or of those who aspired to take their place. One indication that Tibet's religious life changed from this point was the new administrative organization of its monasteries. Buddhist monastic life has its own rules, organization, and official roles, first established by the Buddha. However, this moment in Tibetan history saw a radical departure from Buddhist models and the adoption of a purely secular system, which was eventually copied by most if not all monasteries. Thirteen different official roles or functions, from treasurers and secretaries to cooks and attendants, were designated using a language and culture foreign to Buddhism. Those of us who speak Tibetan and are familiar with Tibetan monastic systems take these roles and functions as normal, yet they would have been as shocking to persons of Shangtön's day as if we entered a religious institution run like a business, with a chief executive officer, a board of directors, managers, and employees, all of whom were monks and nuns.[43] It was powerful, it was efficient, it was impressive, but was it Buddhism? While that question cannot be answered, we can affirm that it was far from the Shangpa lineage style. The Shangpa Kagyu as a series of institutions, if such a thing ever existed, was irrelevant to the Shangpa Instruction Lineage of teachings and was never a contender for Tibet's highest throne.

The second effect of the Tibetan marriage of church and state was the inevitable closing of doors of opportunity to women. I believe that Tibetan men did not first intentionally exclude women from Buddhist religious institutions, and the Shangpa lineage in particular should have been a woman-friendly environment. Yet I believe that power coming into the church's hands signaled the end to women's easy access to Buddhist teachings, if indeed such access existed before. We easily forget in the "enlightened" West how difficult was the relatively recent struggle for women's suffrage, how virulent and violent was men's reaction to the idea of women sharing the vote, let alone other forms of political power. Religion's doors are always open to one and all, as long as those doors do not lead to power; as soon as political power is involved, any flimsy excuse is good enough to exclude other individuals from meaningful participation in the exercise of that power, be it on the basis of gender, caste, race, language, culture, religion, or denomination within a specific religion. As is evident in the origins of the Shangpa lineage, there is no scriptural justification in tantric Buddhism for any exclusion or ignoring of women's spiritual needs. The enormous disparity in allocation of resources in building and education, still on shameless display in any native Tibetan Buddhist environment, is due, I suspect, to the marriage of Tibet's church and state, which began during this era.

As with other Shangpa masters, Shangtön's spiritual path first took him to many teachers, of practically all the major schools of his day, particularly the Path and Result lineage, although he also received teachings from the second Karmapa, Karma Pakshi (1204–1283). Jamgon Kongtrul mentions in the supplication below that Shangtön received Great Completion

(*Dzokchen*) teachings, assumed the postures and gazes of *Tögal* meditation, and immediately saw signs that indicated his realization had reached the third of four degrees in Great Completion, "the full measure of awareness." However, he did not continue with that meditation; he explains that he had little faith in the teacher from whom he had learned the techniques.

Shangtön lived the life of a renunciant; he owned only a meditation seat and one set of clothing. He firmly refused to accept any offerings for himself; he would use whatever he received to make offerings or to sponsor others' spiritual practice. Before Sangyé Tönpa died, he spoke with Shangtön and another of his accomplished disciples, named Zhonnu Drub. He remarked that since the latter had an active mind, he should go to help others. To Shangtön, already of a quiet nature, he advised meditation and more meditation. This Shangtön did—he stayed in closed retreat for many years until many disciples gathered to ask for empowerment and instruction. These he gave, then abruptly informed everyone that he had given his last teaching; he had nothing more to say, and they should leave. He continued to meditate in retreat until his death at the age of seventy-six.

He ordered the few close attendants and disciples who lived nearby to cremate his body after death and that no memorial of any kind should commemorate his life. He said he wanted to leave behind what Milarepa had: nothing. He told his close students to each take a piece of his bones with them after the cremation, presumably as a reminder of impermanence as well as a blessing, and to meditate in retreat. One of his disciples took a piece of Shangtön's skull to the Svayambunat Stupa on the outskirts of Katmandu, Nepal, where an accomplished master, impressed by its blessing, had it placed within the stupa.

Jamgon Kongtrul completed his text of the Shangpa lineage's preliminary practices with these words, drawn from the writing of two Shangpa masters—Shangtön's master, Sangyé Tönpa, and his master, Sangyé Nyentön. These words were undoubtedly precious to Shangtön and to all other meditators in the Shangpa tradition since his time.

> As the great Sangyé Nyentön said, the following is extremely important during both the preliminary and main practices:

> Among all essential meditation instructions, three reign supreme. [First,] develop a helpful and loving attitude by

undertaking all activity out of compassion. [Second,] concentrate continually and intensely on impermanence and death to the point that your preoccupations diminish and you feel you need nothing whatsoever. [Third,] pray wholeheartedly to your spiritual master so that extraordinary devotion wells up within you. Develop this unceasing devotion to your spiritual master to the point of sincerely crying.

These three points will cause spontaneous awareness of the illusory nature of phenomena; all appearances to seem unreal; spontaneous lucid dreams, during which you can act freely, replicate appearances, emanate forms, transform appearances, or actually discern a specific place; the arising of the clear, nondiscursive state of Great Seal during the day; and the spontaneous appearance of yourself as the deity or the arising of boundless radiant awareness during the night. All of these experiences will arise exactly as they are described [in meditation texts].

If you have not developed the three points mentioned above, it will be difficult for you to achieve the ultimate results of [tantric] meditation even by intense experiential cultivation over a long period of time. Therefore it is essential to cultivate them firmly and wholeheartedly.

In this and other teachings Sangyé Nyentön stressed these three points—compassion, impermanence, and devotion—and explained why it is indispensable to always keep them in mind. Further, he wrote:

Cultivate your spiritual life following these oral instructions:

An altruistic attitude and compassion produce all-embracing benefit for others.
Supplications make unbounded meditative experience and realization arise.
Single-minded directed intent results in rapid refinement of lucid dreams.
Intensive mantra practice leads to the attainment of boundless accomplishment.

Keeping tantric commitments attracts dakinis like clouds.
The feeling that you need nothing causes wealth to pour like rain.
Renunciation of jealousy makes persons of all social classes honor
    you.
Renunciation of self-grasping makes it impossible for obstacles to
    intrude.
Diligence in daily torma offerings purifies interruptions in their
    own ground.
Without grasping, you will not fall into mistaken paths.
Frank acknowledgment of evil acts purifies them all.
Cultivation of merit nurtures virtuous practice.
Effortlessness arises within exertion.
Not grasping when the five poisons arise liberates them.
The continual practice of not blocking appearances leads to
    enlightenment.
[Meditation] without anticipation or distraction produces
    awakening in months or years.
Limitless devotion overpowers other appearances with its intensity.
Non referential dedication increases merit immeasurably.
Renunciation of hope and fear leads to the quick attainment of
    the result.

Keep these words in your heart and put them into practice;
Before long you will accomplish the result.

Such was his advice.

The Collection of Short Sayings[44] states:

Misleading views cause the dissipation of all merit in this and
future lifetimes and impede the attainment of enlightenment:
train in pure vision!

Doubt impedes profound teaching and accomplishment:
develop certainty!

Varying spiritual masters, deities, and profound instructions
prevent rapid attainment of accomplishment: cultivate the
experience of whichever one inspires your certainty.

Inaction prevents the rapid purification of the two obscurations: exert yourself to cultivate merit and active virtuous practice.

Attachment to the reality [of phenomena] prevents the rapid completion of the cultivation of wisdom: know all phenomena to lack an intrinsic nature, like a magical illusion or a dream.

Self-interest prevents others' benefit: it is crucial to exert yourself in altruism and in prayers of aspiration. (*Shangpa Preliminary Practices*, pp. 7a-8a)

The Melody of Glory: A Supplication to the Learned and Accomplished Tsangma Shangtön by Jamgon Kongtrul

The flowers of your marks and signs of physical perfection exude the
   three trainings' fragrance.
The stamens of wisdom and love adorn your immaculate, handsome
   body.
To see you, to hear your voice, or to bring you to mind dispels all
   anxiety.
Shangtön, learned and accomplished lord of the teachings, to you
   I pray.

From the stem of your free and fully endowed human life, ethical
   conduct's leaves and petals flourish.
On the stable basis of your study and reflection, meditation's lotus
   blooms.
Your meditative experience and realization's delicious fruit has
   ripened.
Tsangma Shangtön, to you I pray.

In the region of Shang, to parents of the Ra clan,
You were born amid auspicious and virtuous portents.
With unlimited disengagement, devotion, and compassion,
You far surpassed childish behavior; to you I pray.

You grasped the victory banner of faultless ethical conduct
And guarded with your life even the minor points of training.
You were unrivaled in explanation, debate, and composition
And became widely educated; to you I pray.

You dedicated all your possessions to the Teachings.
Even as a joke, you would not disobey your spiritual masters.
You left aspirations for this life far behind
To devote yourself to single-minded meditation; to you I pray.

On your merely seeing the face of Rigong, Lord of the Teachings,
    Sangyé Tönpa,
Uncontrived devotion and sublime meditation welled up in you.
In one week, you achieved the qualities
Of the Six Doctrines; to you I pray.

"You are the first to drink the nectar of the single-disciple lineage,
The fortunate one foretold, first among my circle of disciples."
Thus you were made the unrivaled holy spiritual heir.
You became an indisputable learned and accomplished master;
    to you I pray.

"In this and future lives, you will perform infinite benefit for beings.
In Blissful, you will attain awakening's fourteenth stage.
Those who preserve your lineage will travel to the celestial realms."
This is the prophecy you received; to you I pray.

Vajra Sow granted you an introduction to the four empowerments.
When you received Atiyoga teaching, as soon as you had assumed
    the gazes,
You reached the full measure of awareness; infinite luminosity arose.
Appearances of delusion dissolved into the absolute expanse; to you
    I pray.

You liberated every hindrance and fault into great bliss.
You saw outer and inner appearing existence as infinite purity.
By Tara's blessing, your meditation and postmeditation merged into
    perfect continuity.

You truly gathered the dakinis; to you I pray.

You clearly displayed all the signs of nonreturn.
No insects disturbed your body, which had an immaculate glow.
Just to see your face changed the viewer's experience.
Great Compassion incarnate, to you I pray.

Your saliva could dispel any sickness or demon.
Any person who had faith and saw or heard you
Found that meditative states, such as illusion and clear light,
Would arise effortlessly; to you I pray.

You concealed your every quality.
Except for your cushion and one set of clothes,
You renounced all personal possessions
With perfect rejection of attachment; to you I pray.

After you had done great deeds for others, you displayed amazing
   miracles,
Such as welcoming dakinis whose numbers filled space.
You then departed for the pure lands
And left vast numbers of relics; to you I pray.

May the illustrious master's hook of compassion
Quickly draw us from the mire of existence.
May our plans in this life be accomplished according to the
   Teachings,
And may we later attain the state of enlightenment's three bodies.

(A Garland of Udumvara Flowers, pp. 14b-15b)

TANGTONG GYALPO

A MERE HALF-CENTURY separates the death of Tsangma Shangtön and the birth of Tangtong Gyalpo, but much changed in Tibet's spiritual landscape during that time. Despite politics' intrusion into spiritual life, the thirteenth century hosted an astounding group of masters whose writings we still treasure. Among them we find Sakya Pandita (1182–1251), Orgyen Rinchen-pal (1230–1309), Dolpo Sangyé (1292–1361), Rangjung Dorjé (1284–1339), and Longchenpa soon thereafter (1308–1363). Two notable Indian masters visited Tibet for a short time at the beginning of that period, Shakyashri (1204–1214) and Mitra-yogi (1198–1199). At the end of the thirteenth century, one innovation was to signal another major change in Tibet's religion: in 1288, Orgyen Rinchen-pal recognized Rangjung Dorjé as the reincarnation of his teacher (Karma Pakshi, the second Karmapa), and enthroned him, the first such recognition of a *tulku*, a reincarnate master.

The Shangpa tradition as well had not remained static during this period. Now that many teachers were endowed with the full lineage instructions, the lineage had spread more widely than ever before and grew into several distinct lines of transmission. One of these reached Tangtong Gyalpo through a relatively obscure lama called Jinpa Zangpo. His teacher, Namka Naljor, had another student whose fame is worldwide—Tsongka-pa (1357–1419), founder of the Gélugpa order. These two masters of the Shangpa teachings, Tangtong Gyalpo (1361–1485 or 1385–1464)[45] and Tsongka-pa, had an enduring impact on the Tibetan world.

Tangtong Gyalpo (also known as Tsöndru Zangpo) studied with five hundred lamas and is acclaimed as a master of both the Nyingma and Sakya lineages, besides our own. From a worldly perspective, he was a visionary, since "visionary experience" is our term for his frequent meetings with nonhuman buddhas, bodhisattvas, and dakinis. Yet Tangtong Gyalpo's life story is replete with such encounters, and a reader gets the impression that for him, the amazing didn't seem out of the ordinary.

He met Niguma on three occasions. The first time, Tangtong Gyalpo had just received the main lineage transmission from Jinpa Zangpo. Niguma appeared hovering on a cloud in space, then came to earth to give him empowerment and many teachings, to answer his questions, and to share a vajra feast. Based on that series of instructions, he wrote texts still used in Shangpa retreats, very original versions of Niguma's Six Doctrines and other meditations.

For their second meeting some years later, Niguma appeared as a singing fifteen-year-old girl with a large flock of sheep and goats. Tangtong Gyalpo asked her where she was from, what her name was, and why she was singing. She replied that she had neither homeland, family, nor name and that as a girl, she wasn't able to help sentient beings. She said she sang of sadness at the wheel of life, but no one listened to or understood her song; yet she claimed to have come to that place to make a spiritual connection with Tangtong Gyalpo. He asked her for teaching; she told him to wait there while she took her flock away and gathered offerings for a vajra feast. She returned in the middle of the night with many other young women, explaining that some of her companions had gone to India and Nepal to collect feast offerings (!); had he been waiting long? It was at this point that she revealed herself as Niguma and gave him further guidance.

Niguma's comment that it proved difficult to help others as a woman was a complaint that Tangtong Gyalpo had heard before; sometime after his first meeting with Niguma, Bodhisattva Great Compassion had appeared to him and predicted that he would meet a wisdom dakini. When Tangtong Gyalpo encountered a fifteen-year-old girl singing verses from a tantra, sitting with a skull cup full of alcohol, he suspected that she was the dakini. When he asked her for instruction, she related that she had traveled to all the places in central and western Tibet where many people gathered, with the intention to give her teachings to fortunate individuals, but that Tangtong Gyalpo was the only one who had recognized her. Although Tangtong Gyalpo had many such encounters with female teachers and dakinis, and had many realized female disciples, he seems to have been an exception in such impartiality.

Tangtong Gyalpo's third meeting with Niguma is only alluded to in the one biography I have read. Close to the end of his life, a disciple to whom Tangtong Gyalpo had given the traditional Shangpa teaching cycle gained control of his dreams and discovered that many other visualizations existed. He asked his teacher about these, who replied that they had been given directly by the dakini and that she had not allowed him to pass them on. One year later, the biography relates, Tangtong Gyalpo gave the same disciple the teachings; he explained that in the interim he received her permission. Like so many Shangpa masters, he had kept them to himself, once again in respect of Niguma's wish for secrecy.

These stories convey some of Tangtong Gyalpo's relationship to the Shangpa lineage, but his life's horizons extended far beyond Niguma's teaching. He constructed iron-link bridges throughout Tibet and is always pictured as a dark brown, long-haired yogi who holds a vase of immortality in his left hand and an iron chain in his right, reminders of his exceptionally long life and his work for the Tibetan people.[46] This yogi-engineer also constructed many stupas and temples on power points designated by such enlightened beings as Guru Rinpoché and Tara, and he is revered as the composer of the Tibetan opera Aché Lhamo, still performed regularly today. Many non-Tibetan Buddhists have a close connection to Tangtong Gyalpo, often without realizing it. The meditation on Bodhisattva Great Compassion that Kalu Rinpoché spread worldwide was originally taught by that bodhisattva to Tangtong Gyalpo in a vision.

Jamgon Kongtrul included only a few of Tangtong Gyalpo's songs in this collection, whereas the biography written by his nephew Lochen Gyurmé Déchen is replete with songs from this prolific master. The short supplication below gives an indication that this master's life was rich in teachings, meditation, experience, realization, and beneficial work for others throughout Buddhist Asia.

The Melody of Accomplishment:
A Supplication to the Great Accomplished Master Tangtong Gyalpo
by Jamgon Kongtrul

Great Compassion and powerful Horse Neck
Are inseparably united as Lake-Born Vajra Bearer [Guru Rinpoché],
Who displayed a miraculous emanation, refuge for beings of the
    degenerate age—
Venerable Tangtong Gyalpo, to you I pray.

Knower of all buddhas of the three times, Dolpo Sangyé,
Reincarnated in your form of an accomplished master, to guide
    difficult disciples.
Oldest child of all dakinis,
You were given five sublime names; to you I pray.

In Latö Jang, your vajra marks and signs of physical perfection
    manifested.
Encouraged by an exalted bodhisattva, you renounced home life and
    entered a monastery.
When your hair was cut, the sky filled with rainbow light and flowers.
Venerable Tsöndru Zangpo, to you I pray.

While studying Buddhist source texts, you lost yourself in meditative
    states.
Without training, you understood all teachings.
From the outset, you displayed boundless numbers of miracles.
Great self-manifest accomplished master, to you I pray.

You received unlimited numbers of teachings
From buddhas, bodhisattvas, yogis, yoginis,
Virtuous meditators, low-caste persons, and vagrants—
Five hundred authentic spiritual masters; to you I pray.

When you stayed in retreat at Tarpa Ling,
You truly saw the great Buddha Vajra Bearer,
Buddhas of the five families of enlightenment, the eight great
    bodhisattvas,
And the ten wrathful deities, with their goddesses.
You received the profound path and other deep teachings
To dispel the two obscurations' darkness; to you I pray.

Your compassion was universal; your wisdom embraced all subjects.
You mastered your own experience and the four enlightened
    activities.
Your realization liberated your stream of being and you perfected
    tantric discipline,
Overpowering the eight worldly concerns with your brilliance; to you
    I pray.

You made many aspirations in major sacred places
And you met past accomplished masters and deities' assemblies.
You enjoyed feast gatherings in charnel grounds
With spiritual heroes and dakinis; to you I pray.

"In the Snowy Land, humans, nonhuman spirits,
Wild animals, the sick, blind, deaf, destitute, and others
Who see you, hear you, or bring you to mind
Will temporarily have all their fears allayed
And will ultimately attain states of spiritual uplift and the certain
    fortune of awakening,
And the sacred Teachings will spread.
In particular, you must guide the barbarians of the border lands!"
With such words, All-Seeing One and Noble Tara
Repeatedly encouraged you; to you I pray.

The Honored One gave you unlimited teaching;
From Angiraja, you received instruction in transcendent knowledge.
The glorious Héruka and Yogini gave you empowerment
And entrusted their tantras to you; to you I pray.

In the great charnel ground of Blazing Skeletons,
The great illustrious master Virupa accepted you as his disciple.
He gave you the Path and Result transmission and sacred nectar
    substances,
Which prevented contamination; to you I pray.

The wisdom dakini Niguma met you three times
And gave you every empowerment and meditation instruction,
Engendering in you inconceivable miraculous powers and
    clairvoyance.
You committed her teachings to writing; to you I pray.

In Zangling, the accomplished master Shavari
Gave you his blessing and introduction to the nature of mind.
In Dola Mébar, venerable Brahmin Supreme Desire [Saraha] visibly
    entrusted you
With Great Black Protector as your guardian; to you I pray.

In the land of cannibal demons, at Copper-Colored Mountain's
    summit,
The spiritual master's three bodies of enlightenment, and Lord of
    Oddiyana [Guru Rinpoché] in particular,
Gave you boundless numbers of empowerments and teachings,
    including the Eight Great Sacred Circles,
And then bestowed prophecies; to you I pray.

Vajrasattva granted you instruction in Atiyoga.
Encouraged by the dakinis, you considered disciples in Tibet.
In lands of barbarians, your unlimited miracles
Tamed and converted them to Buddhism; to you I pray.

With miraculous powers,
You traveled to every major and minor land in the world,

Such as India, Nepal, Kashmir, Li, Oddiyana,
China, Mongolia, Dawa, Néling, Kalingka, and Priyangku.
You manifestly liberated fortunate individuals
And covered the earth with the Teachings.
Thus, with various skillful means, you ensured that you would
　　lead others
To spiritual maturity in the future; to you I pray.

You placed in the celestial states worthy disciples, regardless of
　　their age.
Even wild animals respectfully served you.
You tamed the eight classes of gods and demons, bound them
　　under oath,
And gained control of the four elements; to you I pray.

You spanned many rivers with iron bridges
And you erected an infinite number of the three sacred supports,
Such as the Auspicious, Many-Gated Stupa,
And many jeweled or cast sacred images; to you I pray.

You suppressed border conflicts and established geographical power
　　places.
You placed supreme sacred supports everywhere to control the four
　　elements.
Aspirations you made produced long-term shelter
To those fearful of sickness and famine; to you I pray.

Medicine Buddha gave you nectar that prevents death;
Buddha Infinite Life gave you longevity pills.
You rescued all beings from fear
Of sickness, demons, and untimely death; to you I pray.

When your body appeared in the border country of Kamataru,
An evil-acting king and his ministers
Tried but could not burn or drown you.
All were moved to faith and converted to Buddhism; to you I pray.

Among your disciples numbered six supreme children, eight close
  sublime sons,
Five wisdom dakinis, sixteen hidden dakinis,
Eighteen dakinis of the tantric commitments,
Thirty-seven male and female awareness holders,
Fifty-eight with karmic connections, five hundred nonreturners,
And one million eighty thousand persons who could help others.
You brought them to spiritual maturity, liberated them,
And compiled your instruction into eight sections.
Master empowered as [Buddha's] regent, to you I pray.

Your substantial body lived one hundred twenty-eight years.
On the Miracle Month's fourth day, it dissolved into a mass of light
  in space.
In answer to the plaintive songs of your heart disciples,
You displayed form bodies in the sky; to you I pray.

When they again prayed, your body, a cubit in height,
Appeared at your meditation place and dwelt in clear light for a week.
This amazing relic-support lasts forever without moving,
The place for gods and humans to make offerings; to you I pray.[47]

Afterward, in response to your fortunate disciples, near and far,
You continue to appear and to bless them.
Your enlightened activity for Tibet's happiness is uninterrupted;
Your kindness is inconceivable; to you I pray.

Powerful All-Seeing One, accomplished master, Lord of the Teachings,
Your compassion knows no weariness or fatigue.
For me and other unlucky persons of this final time,
Please show your face and give us your blessing!

Supreme accomplished master, may my accomplishment quickly
  become like yours—
Your life span, the extent of your disciples,
Your life of freedom, your aspirations, acts, and strength—
And may I liberate all beings whose numbers reach the bounds of space!

(*A Garland of Udumvara Flowers*, pp. 22b-24a)

KUNGA DROLCHOK

K UNGA DROLCHOK (1507–1566) was a master whose inclusive
vision of tantric Buddhist practice would later be called *rimé*,
nonsectarian. He began his religious career in the Sakya tradition and
showed a tremendous appetite and aptitude for all subjects of study. His
reincarnation, Taranata, called himself "the king of sloth" and credited
Kunga Drolchok's hard work in intense study for the brilliance he effortlessly displayed.

Kunga Drolchok received the Shangpa transmission at an early age and
met Niguma in a vision, yet he includes details of neither event in his
lengthy autobiography. He may likely have saved the stories for another,
more intimate recounting of his life, but the impression the book gives is
the same as that of the song Kongtrul included in the collection above:

> In the past, my karmic affinity was not insignificant.
> From a young age, I completely [realized phenomena to be] illusion's
>   display.
> Although I saw the mother dakini's lovely face,
> My mind wasn't satisfied; it was just illusion's own appearance.
>
> When I first saw the vase of my spiritual father Lekpa Gyaltsen's face,
> All my hesitations were freed by themselves.
> At that time, a single certainty without any doubts was born
> And it remains unchanged.

When he was twenty-seven, in the course of a wide-ranging and deep
education, Kunga Drolchok's life changed course; he decided to meditate
to the exclusion of all else. He doesn't explain what caused this dramatic
shift, but we can surmise it was due to meeting Niguma, for he states that
his spiritual life was to center upon the Shangpa teachings:

> From the time I reached my twenty-seventh year, I became moved
> by detachment and disillusionment and inspired to simplicity. I
> gradually lost interest in reading books and turned my attention to
> whatever flavor I had experienced in my education to that point,
> and particularly to Niguma's meditations. (*The Autobiography of
> Kunga Drolchok*, p. 60a)

As a meditator devoted to the Shangpa teachings, he reports quick mastery of Lucid Dream, then remarks, "I turned away from my attachment to books, sacred supports [statues and paintings], monasteries, monastic colleges, and monks and looked for deserted mountain retreats where I could live alone." (*Ibid.*)

It was after this change of heart that Kunga Drolchok met Gyagom Lekpa Gyaltsen, the lama he considered his principal master for the Shangpa teachings. It was in this teacher's presence that Kunga Drolchok promised to give the entire Shangpa transmission 108 times, a promise he kept. This activity of spreading Niguma's teachings far and wide probably made him the foremost Shangpa master of his day, although there were many others. Kunga Drolchok mentions that he received twenty-five different transmissions of the Shangpa instructions, presumably each from a different lineage holder. He states that twenty-four were variations of the main line of transmission that originated with Kyungpo Naljor; the single exception was the teachings that Tangtong Gyalpo received directly from Niguma.

Kunga Drolchok devoted much time and energy to meditation on Niguma's teachings and to their transmission, but he also continued to learn other traditions' meditations, specifically the Marpa Kagyu, Kalachakra, Orgyenpa's teachings, Dampa Sangyé's Pacification of Suffering, and Severance. He spent a period of time in what is now northern Nepal and other border regions. He met a large group of tantric yogis in the pilgrimage place Hundred Springs (Muktinat, Nepal) and traveled throughout areas of border tribes, where his only teachings consisted of the fundamentals of Buddhist practice, centered upon the recitation of the mantra *Om Mani Pémé Hung*. Perhaps Tangtong Gyalpo's example inspired this *mani* missionary work.

So strong was Kunga Drolchok's and his reincarnation's (Taranata's) influence on the Shangpa lineage that the name of their monastic seat,

Jonang, became synonymous in some people's minds with the Shangpa, although the Shangpa and Jonang's cohabitation lasted less than 150 years. Jonang Monastery was founded by Tukjé Tsöndru (1243–1313), who was principally a master of the Kalachakra Tantra. The monastery became a center for the practice of that tantra's meditations and for a philosophical school known for its central tenet, called variously "other-emptiness," "extrinsic emptiness," or "extraneous emptiness." In *Tibet Handbook*, Gyurmé Dorjé explains extrinsic emptiness as "the view that all the attributes of Buddhahood are extraneously empty of mundane impurities and defilements, but not intrinsically empty in a nihilistic sense, their experience thereby transcending all notions of existence and nonexistence." (p. 288) Although the Shangpa lineage masters have generally upheld this view since their sojourn in Jonang, there is no "official" connection between this monastery and the Shangpa lineage. Nevertheless, since the time of Kunga Drolchok and Taranata, many Shangpa lineage holders, including Jamgon Kongtrul, Kalu Rinpoché and Bokar Rinpoché, have also mastered the Jonang Kalachakra transmission.

One of Kunga Drolchok's lasting contributions to Tibetan spiritual life was his compendium *The Hundred Instructions*, a treasury of the meditation systems existent in his day. When, three hundred years later, Jamgon Kongtrul made an even larger collection he called *The Treasury of Profound Instructions*, he included Kunga Drolchok's work at the treasury's conclusion (Vol. 18, pp. 1-380), as a tribute to such impartial and universally beneficial work.

The Melody of Spiritual Maturity and Liberation: A Supplication to Noble Kunga Drolchok by Jamgon Kongtrul

Powerful accomplished master who preserved tantric conduct,
  foretold by the Buddha,
You spread the essential doctrine in the Himalayas
And displayed the form of Gentle Protector, Spiritual Hero of
  Accomplishment.
Venerable Kunga Drolchok, to you I pray.

When the emanated moon of your face appeared
On the Lowo Möntang Plain, it was as if a colorful and fragrant lotus
From the Three-Period City [of the gods]
Had bloomed, heralding spring; to you I pray.

When the touch of disturbed elements threatened the flower of your
  marks and signs of physical perfection,
You overcame all obstacles' attacks
And found the meaning of the Teachings within you
The moment you made contact with the dawn light of the Buddha's
  doctrine; to you I pray.

Endowed with both awareness and liberation,
You joyfully entered without hesitation the central region's lotus lake
  like a swan.
Although young in years, you bravely meditated
And gained supreme release from your mind's knots; to you I pray.

The strength of your previous training awakened and you effortlessly
　　learned the collections of teachings.
Melodious Goddess entered your throat, bringing you three forms of
　　erudition, such as eloquence.
At a young age, your clear-minded intellect
Captivated others' attention; to you I pray.

Your crown jewel [master] gave you prophecies and encouragement.
Four gems gave you meditation instruction's vital points.
Two scholars sliced through the net of your doubts.
You spontaneously accomplished your wishes; to you I pray.

Two who renounced action enriched your realization.
The lord of speech stimulated your interest in terms.
And in particular, Vajra Bearer incarnate, Lord Gyagom,
Entrusted you with his heart's treasury; to you I pray.

Outwardly, you were bound by faultless training in personal
　　liberation;
Inwardly, you had perfect control of the mind of awakening;
Secretly, you preserved Secret Mantra's tantric discipline.
Sublime leader, to you I pray.

Lord of Secrets and Slayer of Lord of Death dispelled your obstacles.
Male and female Vajra Creator of Delight, Binder of the Wheel,
Vajra Yogini, and other high deities
Granted their blessings and nurtured you; to you I pray.

Powerful one of the celestial realms, Noble Niguma,
Bestowed her Six Doctrines, Awakened Protector, and other
　　teachings.
You then realized clear light beyond center or limits.
You received the wonderful recent lineage; to you I pray.

In Sosa Park, you enjoyed a vajra feast with the great dakini,
Who foretold your awakening.
Your realization merging meditation and postmeditation experience
　　increased,

And the dakini protected you as her child; to you I pray.

Mitra-yogi gave you the three essential points;
Lekden Jé bestowed an empowerment with symbolic instruction.
Protectors such as Powerful Stealer of Strength and Son of the
    Renowned One
Acted as your servants; to you I pray.

Any appearance arose for you as the play of illusion.
Without dualistic clinging, your self-manifest, uncontrived mind, free
    from attachment,
Remained like the carefree behavior of a small child,
Yet all your acts were meaningful; to you I pray.

"To see me, hear me, bring me to mind, or be touched by me makes
    beings leave the miserable existences;
I am a person with whom any connection is significant!"
Such was the promise you made in your truthful vajra speech.
Lord protector of many beings, to you I pray.

You collected every stream of meditation teaching in the Himalayas
And you imparted Niguma's teachings more than one hundred times.
These deeds illustrate your altruistic acts that filled the bounds of
    space.
You then left for the celestial city; to you I pray.

You returned to Land of the Exalted, Tibet, Oddiyana, Damido,
And many other places, in many manifestations attuned to others'
    needs,
To purify the realms of your disciples,
And to attain unsurpassable awakening; to you I pray.

In all lifetimes, may you, Spiritual Hero of Accomplishment,
    accept me.
May the wheel of inexhaustible ornaments of my three mysteries
Display a cloud-ocean of infinite lifetimes of freedom,
To perform acts equal, noble master, to yours.

                  (*A Garland of Udumvara Flowers*, pp. 24b-25b)

KYENTSÉ WANGCHUK

JAMYANG KYENTSÉ WANGCHUK (1524–1567) was a scholar of the Sakya tradition, but neither his name, nor that of the teacher he mentions in his song (Lama Kartsi-wa) appears in the Shangpa lineages available to us. The only information I have found concerning his life was written by Jamgon Kongtrul in his account of the lives of the treasure-revealers (*tertön*).[48] Kongtrul reports that this master was a reincarnation of Tibet's eighth-century Buddhist king Trisong Détsen, specifically an embodiment of his qualities. He began his studies and meditation in the Path and Result tradition but later included a full range of Ancient Instruction Lineage and presumably Shangpa meditations in his spiritual practice. He led Zhalu Monastery, an institution founded in the eleventh century and made famous by such scholars as Butön Rinchen Drub. Kongtrul mentions that external circumstances prevented Kyentsé Wangchuk from revealing many treasures during his short life but that he managed to aid in the preservation and spread of both new and old tantric traditions.

It is somewhat a mystery why Kongtrul included this master's song in the collection; as far as I can discover, Kyentsé Wangchuk had no lasting influence on the Shangpa lineage.[49] What one may speculate is that Kyentsé Wangchuk was included for two reasons. First, he was a former incarnation of Jamyang Kyentsé Wangpo, one of Kongtrul's main teachers. Second, he represents a genuinely impartial figure during an earlier period of Tibetan history. In the following quote, his words are repeated in a modern publication as an example of a master of the new schools who accepted the Nyingma tradition:

I trained in the Sakya tradition,
Yet became skilled in Nyingma Secret Mantra.
I wonder: Is this not due to my karmic propensity?
Ah-Ho! I'm amazed!

I meditated upon the Path and Result Secret Mantra,
Yet my realization arose as Great Completion.
I wonder: Is this not due to my karmic propensity?
Ah-Ho! I'm amazed!

I supplicated to the Master of Yogis [probably Virupa]
Yet Lotus-Born from Oddiyana gave me his blessings.
I wonder: Is this not due to my karmic propensity?
Ah-Ho! I'm amazed!

(*Catalog of the Nyingma Tantras*, p. 35)

TARANATA

SHANGPA MEDITATORS recite lineage prayers that begin with Buddha Vajra Bearer, continue through an unbroken line of masters, and end with their personal spiritual master. Each of the names recited indicates an essential link in the chain of transmission, a realized master who received and realized Niguma's teachings and passed them to the next generation. Meditators who do not study the masters' life stories will probably become familiar with only four names: Kyungpo Naljor, Tangtong Gyalpo, Jamgon Kongtrul, and Taranata (1575–1634). Kyungpo Naljor was, of course, the source lama of the lineage; the other three composed most of the empowerments, rituals, liturgies, and commentaries used today in the Shangpa tradition. Of them, Taranata is clearly the dominant figure; Jamgon Kongtrul, who lived two centuries later, was an unabashed Taranata fan who took any opportunity he could to praise this lama who inspired him. This compendium of songs provides ample evidence of this: only the section on Kyungpo Naljor occupies more space, although other teachers, such as Tangtong Gyalpo, were as prolific as Taranata in songs of realization. Further, the lines Kongtrul wrote in the main text in Part 1 to introduce Taranata bear rereading:

> During this age of conflict, Taranata was a great Buddha Vajra
> Bearer whose renunciation and realization were indistinguishable
> from those of Land of the Exalted's accomplished masters.

In the Tibetan world, this was the highest possible praise. Each time the subject turned to Taranata, Kongtrul heaped on comparable superlatives to underline his undivided respect and devotion. In the compendium *Treasury of Profound Instructions*, Kongtrul includes works by Taranata in five of that compilation's eight categories. Among them, the two Shangpa volumes are almost entirely the work of Taranata and Jamgon Kongtrul;

Taranata wrote most of the longer empowerments, meditation texts, and commentaries, while Kongtrul produced simplified versions of the same material based on his hero's work.

Taranata, a self-recognized reincarnation of Kunga Drolchok, was an incredible prodigy. The account of his youth defies belief, so complex were the transmissions and empowerments that he granted from a very tender age. Readers have the impression that in him we meet an individual whose consciousness had changed bodies but whose mind didn't miss a beat from one lifetime to the next. He began to travel at an early age and continued to move around central Tibet for most of his life, thus the nickname he gave himself: Gyalkam-pa, the Wanderer. During his past life as Kunga Drolchok, his travels took him outside the perimeter of Tibet; Taranata stayed closer to home yet never rested for long in one place. His home base was Jonang Monastery; his main periods of residence there corresponded to his annual teaching sessions. At the age of forty, he designed and oversaw the construction of Takten Damchö Ling, a complex of temples and residences that reminds Bokar Rinpoché of buildings in the West. He reports that their layout resembles no other buildings he visited in Tibet.

Taranata was a wanderer and a meditator, but not a yogi. His travel destinations were more often monastic institutions than mountain caves. His countless teachings were given in retreat centers, monastic colleges, public gatherings, or private meetings indoors. While he often voiced cutting criticism of his contemporaries' spiritual practice, his main objection was that his contemporaries did not take Buddhist teachings to heart. According to him, some Buddhists weakened their faith with empty conformity to others' expectations or to social demands. Although he credited himself with acting only according to the spirit of Buddhism, he remained a creature of his day's culture and civilization, not a radical on the margins of society. This is another facet of his life that Jamgon Kongtrul imitated and emulated.

Taranata found time to write during his travels; his collected works span seventeen large volumes. Although the Shangpa lineage is indebted to his contribution, his writing on the Shangpa lineage fills only one volume. Like his predecessor, Kunga Drolchok, he met Niguma in a vision, but he also wrote of the experience outside his main autobiography and I have not yet found a detailed account of their meeting. In general, Taranata wrote on all things tantric; he explained in his autobiography that he considered that only tantra had sufficient power to deeply influence present-day individuals' habitual patterns. He also composed a number of important works on the history of Indian Buddhism. He met a number of Indian masters, themselves wanderers in Tibet, and he grilled them for information concerning their country's Buddhist history. None of his Indian teachers stayed with him for an extended period; perhaps they would have done so if they had foreseen how important his work would become—historians on both sides of the Himalayas still make reference to it, *Taranatha's History of Buddhism in India*, translated into English by Lama Chimpa and Alaka Chattopadhyaya.

Tibet has produced many enlightened masters over the centuries; some of them taught, some wrote, some served as administrators, some spent their lives meditating in perfect simplicity. Few, however, had what some might call genius. Taranata belongs to the category of genius. He transcended the bounds of erudition; he was more than a prolific writer, a dedicated meditator, or an astute social commentator. He thought for himself, spoke and wrote in a distinctive style, and acted according to his tantric conscience, thus making a name for himself as a nonconformist whose power as a teacher led to constant invitations to sit upon and teach from the highest thrones in the country. Taranata used his renown as a master of all schools of tantric Buddhism to encourage a nonsectarian and apolitical approach to Buddhism at a time of extreme upheaval in central Tibet, struggles that inevitably attracted the involvement of less inspired teachers.

As we will see, Taranata had no false modesty. It was he who wrote the first supplication to himself translated below, for use by his disciples, and this is not the only example of him using his ample eloquence to praise his own qualities. Jamgon Kongtrul wrote a supplementary supplication to Taranata and in fact seems to have composed the other supplications of the series to fit Taranata's work into the context of the Shangpa lineage. I see no evidence that Taranata himself intended his supplication as the exclusively "Shangpa" story of his life. He is the crown jewel of the Shangpa lineage, the master who gave form to the majority of its meditations, yet his life, inspiration, and influence (like those of Tangtong Gyalpo, Kyentsé Wangpo, and Jamgon Kongtrul) went far beyond the confines of the lineage.

The Wish-Fulfilling Tree of Faith:
The Illustrious, Holy Master's Life of Freedom
by Taranata

Most sublime exalted deity, lord of accomplishment, Gentle Melody;
Ever joyful sacred Teachings that reveal the essential meaning;
And congregation of those who perform its activity—
In supreme, inspired faith, to you I pay homage.

Boundless familiarity with the cultivation of merit and wisdom
Allowed you to display a miraculous birth
In the supreme circle of land, central Tibet,
Which resembles the gods' Hall of Excellent Teachings; I bow my
    head to you.

"Emanation of Jampé Dorjé,
He will be born with the name Dorjé in the clan of a translator."[50]
Just as foretold by Kunzang Drubpé Wangpo [Kunga Drolchok],
You were born as a supreme guide; I bow my head to you.

When harmed by the four elements' turmoil,
The protector of accomplishment,
Fiery Lord Protector, manifested
To dispel your outer and inner obstacles; I bow my head to you.

At that time, your circulating energy and mind entered the central
    channel

And you saw boundless numbers of victors and their spiritual heirs.
Your long-term connection with the Vajra Way fully awakened
And your inspiration in faith gathered strength; I bow my head to you.

Without your having been taught or encouraged by others,
Your compassionate commitment for all beings increased.
You gained inner knowledge of the Great Way's deities
And of awareness mantras' sacred Teachings; I bow my head to you.

You learned by yourself such subjects as the letters' shapes;
Single hearings of many subjects, such as the Buddha's past lives and
    legends,
Were enough for you to master them effortlessly,
Pleasing many persons around you; I bow my head to you.

At the age of seven, you composed many meditation texts for deities,
Such as Vajra Creator of Delight, Vajra Yogini,
Buddha Unmoving, Tara, and Gentle Melody.
Chief among brilliant ones, I bow my head to you.

Relying on the supremely learned master Jampa,
You trained in the Three Collections and their commentaries
And in the five subjects of Buddhist culture, including grammar and
    logic.
Incomparable lion of speech, I bow my head to you.

You approached the spiritual master named Kunga;
At that Lord of the Teachings' lotus feet, you gradually received the
    vows' three levels.
He completely filled your mind stream
With boundless numbers of tantric empowerments, transmissions,
    and pith instructions; I bow my head to you.

You completed the intensive meditations of an ocean of deities'
    sacred circles
And performed single-mindedly, day and night,
An ocean of Secret Mantra's phase of completion meditations
To become a guide on the path that pleases the victors; I bow my
    head to you.

You gained comprehension of the discourses' and tantras' precise
  intent
And became unrivaled throughout existence's three realms
In explanation, debate, and composition.
Ocean of qualities, I bow my head to you.

You mastered an ocean of tantras
And understood precisely and without confusion
The interpretations of a million learned and accomplished masters
From Land of the Exalted and the Himalayan Range's enclosure; I
  bow my head to you.

You manifestly attained the illusionlike meditative state
And defeated hindrances and obstacles
During nighttime's dreams.
You then actualized the profound meaning of emptiness; I bow my
  head to you.

Spiritual masters including Venerable Buddhagupta
Gave you the essential elixir
Of India's learned and accomplished masters' oral transmissions.
Chief of seas of extraordinary profound meaning, I bow my head to you.

You were directly linked during an infinite series of past lives
To the original protector, the supreme vajra master,
Who epitomized all lineages, your root spiritual master,
With whom you inseparably merged; I bow my head to you.

When he gave you the ultimate instructions,
You directly saw the primordial, abiding nature as intrinsic
  coemergence,
And all phenomena's essence as the body of ultimate enlightenment.
Lord protector of existence and quiescence, I bow my head to you.

You taught the infinitely vast and profound sacred Teachings
And attained the ultimate lineage, the single essence of all.
You perfected the phase of completion's deep wisdom.
Original king of great bliss, I bow my head to you.

You attained the signs of blessing from having inherited the lineage
Of Indian Buddhism's sixteen great chariots
And of the innumerable accomplished masters who steered them.
Spiritual master, king of the Teachings, I bow my head to you.

Following the Vajra Way's exalted path,
You actualized awakening's twelfth vajra stage
To become during this time of conflict
Lord Buddha Vajra Bearer's regent; I bow my head to you.

During your intensive meditation on the deity who nurtured you in
    all lifetimes,
Binder of the Wheel,
You saw signs that you embodied the Héruka.
Lord of infinite wonders, I bow my head to you.

When you received Tara's four empowerments,
An assembly of dakinis' blessings completely purified your body;
Everything took the appearance of volumes of tantra.
Chief of Secret Mantra's doctrine, I bow my head to you.

You saw the deity's sacred circle in space.
Aryadéva sliced through the net of your doubts;
Shantidéva taught you the meaning of *The Tantra of Matrix of
    Mystery.*
You attained the meditative state of the Teachings' river; I bow my
    head to you.

From the outset of settling in evenness on the Six Branches of
    Application,
You perfected the virtuous signs.
Many appearances manifested to indicate your control of vitality,
And you saw uncontrived wisdom; I bow my head to you.

While you settled in evenness on the meaning of Glorious Matrix of
    Mystery,
Gentle Melody's compassion blessed you to see all phenomena's true
    nature.

The king of wrathful deities, Slayer of Lord of Death,
Blessed you as a powerful master; I bow my head to you.

When you meditated on the extremely secret yoga's meaning,
Your body's vivid appearance as the deity became very stable.
You achieved a gathering with the three locations' messengers
And supreme coemergent bliss; I bow my head to you.

Because you were endowed with a pure heart,
Many masters of sublime accomplishment visited you in your dreams,
Such as Saraha, Shavari, Luyipa
Ghandhapa, Bardzin, and Shantigupta; I bow my head to you.

With these masters, you rid yourself of doubt.
When you then interpreted the tantras' meaning,
Infinite numbers of spiritual heroes and dakinis used symbols
To introduce you to the profound meaning; I bow my head to you.

From Joyful Heaven, the one named Shakya visited you;
Invincible Protector [Bodhisattva Loving-Kindness] manifestly gave
     you his blessing
And you gained signs of it.
Continual wealth of the Teachings, I bow my head to you.

You received full authorization for the sacred Teachings
From supreme masters, such as Lotus-Born,
Daö Zhonnu [Gampopa], and the one endowed with the four
     reliances [Dolpo Sangyé].
Master accepted by supreme spiritual guides, I bow my head to you.

Perfect in study and reflection; joyful in single-minded meditation,
You have filled the entire world with your cycle of teachings.
Incomparably wonderful, precious spiritual master,
With supreme respect, I bow my head to you.

I, Taranata, wrote this supplication in response to my disciples' request.

The Flower of Faith: A Supplementary Supplication
to the Precious Noble Master's Life of Freedom
by Jamgon Kongtrul

Father of all victors, you are all victors' spiritual heir,
You have renounced existence and quiescence; you are the chief of
    existence and peace.
Glorious Binder of the Wheel in the form of a spiritual master,
Venerable Drolwé Gönpo [Taranata], to you I pray.

In a past life as the main athlete in the king's palace at Sravasti,
You had boundless strength.
In the presence of Buddha All-Seeing, you developed the
    determination to awaken
And definitely attained a wondrous state; I bow my head to you.

Thereafter, you always accompanied buddhas
And displayed bodhisattvas' special conduct.
With infinite miracles, you brought your disciples' innate enlightenment
To full maturity; I bow my head to you.

In the midst of five hundred bodhisattvas around Buddha
    Shakyamuni,
You appeared as an extremely brilliant individual.
You donned the armor of perseverance in every way
Within the doctrine of the essential, definitive meaning; I bow my
    head to you.

In various forms—as an accomplished master, awareness holder,
Seer, scholar, ruler, government official, Brahmin,
Householder, and ordinary person—you preserved the Buddha's
    doctrine
And emptied the depths of the wheel of life; I bow my head to you.

In the eastern pure land, Free from Affliction,
In Transcendent Buddha Chambhaka's presence, you were a
    universal monarch.

You displayed eight forms simultaneously,
Such as one on a mountain peak; I bow my head to you.

Likewise, in other worlds and in this land of Tibet,
You displayed many emanations simultaneously.
The leader among them was the spiritual hero from Oddiyana,
    Vishnu-raja,
The basis of your manifestations; I bow my head to you.

The Héruka entrusted you with his secret treasury;
Shakyamuni empowered you as lord of all his Teachings.
The eight great bodhisattvas blessed you as the source
Of every discourse and tantra; I bow my head to you.

All-Seeing One praised you as a bodhisattva who would guide beings;
Bodhisattva Essence of the Sky gave you modes of higher training;
Noble Tara always showed you her face and bestowed prophecies—
Your wisdom greatly increased; I bow my head to you.

Padmakara placed you in the sacred circle of blood-drinkers;
Yeshé Tsogyal gave you empowerment through profound symbols;
Dombi Héruka authorized you as chief
Of the three locations' dakinis; I bow my head to you.

Chandragomin introduced you to meditative states;
Aryadéva washed away your pain during an illness;
Melodious Goddess bestowed mastery of speech.
Master of wide, inconceivable wisdom, I bow my head to you.

When you prayed to the eighty accomplished masters, translators,
    and congregation of meditators,
They gave you teachings.
Abhaya had you enter an infinitely large configuration
Of the tantras; I bow my head to you.

Guhya-jnana granted you the four secret empowerments;
The dakinis gave you supreme, victorious medicine.

In Dévikotri, the dakini's instruction
Made the harvest of the Six Doctrines ripen; I bow my head to you.

Luyipa introduced you to great bliss.
In the three circles, you enjoyed vajra feasts.
You received the prophecy that, on the path of great passion, all who
    saw, heard, remembered, or were touched by you
Would gain complete liberation; I bow my head to you.

You traveled through miraculous powers
To Oddiyana, Copper-Colored Mountain, and Shambhala,
Where you drank the oral transmission's nectar
From Indrabhuti, Lotus-Born, and the great lineage-bearing
    monarch; I bow my head to you.

Vajra Sow, Wheel of Time, and Matrix of Mystery
Granted you the empowerment of great light
And reassured you, "Your commentaries on the tantras' meaning are
    excellent!"
Lord of Secrets, Vajra Teachings, I bow my head to you.

Gentle Splendor [in the form of] Dark-Red Fearsome Vajra
Bestowed empowerment and prophesied that you would overcome
    demons.
The eight accomplished spiritual masters' blessings
Allowed you to plumb the Teachings' depth; I bow my head to you.

In the descent of wisdom, you saw appearances, sound, and thoughts
    as infinite pure appearances.
Your vajra songs made the assembly of karmically connected persons
Gain realization and liberation simulataneously
When their wisdom awakened; I bow my head to you.

When you did major work, such as empowerments, offering-practice
    rituals, or turning the wheel of the Teachings,
Rainbow lights appeared, rains of flowers fell,
Dakinis sang symbolic songs, perfumes pervaded the area,

And you displayed miraculous manifestations and transformations;
   I bow my head to you.

You reversed the historical tradition's decline and dispelled delusion.
By introducing previously unknown new chariots of the doctrine,
You restored the supreme Vajra Way's essential, definitive meaning
From its foundation; I bow my head to you.

The omniscient Lord of the Teachings revealed Blissful Pure Land,
Giving you dominion over the spiritual kingdom of nonreturn.
The great Butön gave you the crown of the teachings.
Lord of the Buddha's doctrine, I bow my head to you.

When you reached the bounds of accomplishment,
Spiritual masters, impartial scholars, and accomplished masters
   pronounced auspicious, joyful blessings of "Excellent!"
And in an imposing lion's roar,
They said, "After three lifetimes, you will attain enlightenment!"; I
   bow my head to you.

Powerful protectors who had seen Buddha's face
Served as your servants and offered you their life-essence mantras.
Male and female Mahakala and their entourage
Did whatever you asked; I bow my head to you.

During this lifetime, the view guided your acts;
In the next life, in Damido, you will actually spread
Such teachings as *The Discourse That Gathers All Intentions*,
   Vajrasattva's Magical Net, and Atiyoga's mind class
As leader of Lotus Skull-Garlanded Adept's enlightened activity; I
   bow my head to you.

Encouraged by Vajra Sow, Tara, Holder of Conduct, and Lotus Bliss,
Spiritual heroes and dakinis presented you with full offerings
Of song, dance, parasols, hand drums, bells, and nectar for
   maintaining bliss,
And you departed to infinite pure lands; I bow my head to you.

Demons' abodes shook;
Infinite worlds attained meditative states, such as wondrous omens.
You were consort of the awareness woman, and your virtuous signs of
    accomplishment
Pervaded everywhere; I bow my head to you.

In Oddiyana, you appear as King of Diligence;
In Damido, as Blissful Protector;
In the pure lands of Lapis Light and Blissful,
As a lord bodhisattva on awakening's tenth stage; I bow my head to
    you.

In essence, you are coemergent Binder of the Net;
In the experience of ordinary persons, in a world called Luminous,
You will attain enlightenment as Transcendent Buddha Circle of
    Space.
To these and your other inconceivable miraculous appearances, I bow
    my head.

Like Abhayakara-gupta in Land of the Exalted,
There will never be another like you.
You definitely attained the state of the sixth Buddha's regent.
Unsurpassable Héruka, illustrious lord, spiritual master,
To you I respectfully bow and present clouds of wonderful offerings.
I acknowledge all my faults and rejoice in others' virtues.
I pray that you turn the wheel of the Teachings and always remain in
    this world.
I dedicate all my virtue to the attainment of your state.

May I become similar in every way
To the enlightened body, speech, mind, noble qualities, and activity
    of Kunga Nyingpo's life of freedom.
May I spread to the ten directions your excellent speech of total
    victory
And bind all beings in the dakinis' net.

In this life, the next, and the intermediate state between,
May I not be separated from you even in a dream, Taranata.

May I attain your secret treasury, accomplish impartial tantric
  conduct,
And attain enlightenment in the play of union's great bliss.

May I always do what pleases you, noble master;
May your blessings enter my stream of being;
And, inseparable from you,
May my infinite enlightened activity fill the world with glorious,
  auspicious illumination.

I composed this supplement to the supplication to [Taranata's] life of
freedom, *The Wish-Fulfilling Tree of Faith*, because previous holy individuals' works were either too extensive or too short, or the stream of their
reading transmission is no longer extant. Therefore, for myself and others,
I, Karma Ngawang Yönten Gyatso, wrote this supplication of faith at
Palpung Monastery's secluded retreat center. May excellent virtue increase!

TARANATA, THE SEQUEL

BUDDHISTS WHO ENTER the main Shangpa tradition find themselves most often guided in their meditations by Taranata's words.
Many of the lineage's other texts written by Jamgon Kongtrul contain high
praises of this sixteenth-seventeenth-century master. Shangpa adepts
remember the anniversary of Taranata's death, the twenty-sixth day of the
second lunar month, with offerings to his memory on a par with those
made on the fourteenth day of the ninth lunar month, Kyungpo Naljor's
death anniversary. In fact, Jamgon Kongtrul had his three-year retreat center celebrate the memory of Taranata for three days each year, the only
master to be so extravagantly honored. To most modern Shangpa meditators, this might seem like a normal lineage love-fest, and to a point they
would be correct in that assumption. Yet there is much more to Taranata's
story and his place in Tibetan history, information that casts a different
light on Tibet, Taranata, and Jamgon Kongtrul.

Taranata was an immense figure during his day, a great lama given ample
recognition from a very early age. In a country intent upon Buddhist
scholasticism and meditation, he fulfilled the aspirations of his people for
a realized and articulate spiritual leader. Although he was bluntly outspo-
ken in his opinions, he used his acidic tongue to point out the folly of
those whose Buddhism was halfhearted, compromised by worldly ambi-
tions. He was well positioned by his status as a reincarnate lama, by his
brilliance, and by his role as head of the Jonang school of monasteries to
become powerful politically, but this was against his reading of Buddha's
word.

He seems the perfect lama. Nevertheless, after his death he became the
perfect villain, portrayed as a terrible shadow that fell upon Tibet and
threatened the entire country's spiritual life. Few individuals in Tibetan history have been as reviled and suppressed as Taranata. This obviously bears
some explanation.

Taranata's ill-starred life span corresponded to a critical period in Tibet's political history. Each of the major schools of Tibetan Buddhism has enjoyed a period of political power; Taranata was born ten years after the Karma Kagyus continued their ascendancy in spite of a change in Tibet's leadership. The Karmapas and Zhamarpas had gained prominence under the Rinpung administration (1478–1565) and then rode on the coattails of a lay political leader, Karma Tséten Dorjé (d. 1599), of a new ruling clan that made Zhigatsé (in Tsang, western Tibet) the capital of Tibet. During Taranata's lifetime, the son, grandson, and great-grandson of this family lived short and eventful lives and succeeded one another on the unlucky throne. Taranata and the Jonang monasteries, centered in the Zhigatsé area, were supported by that ruling family; Taranata ministered to one of the kings (Karma Puntsok Namgyal, d. 1621), a ruler he respected, as he lay dying from poison.

Eight years after Taranata's death, the dynasty fell, to be replaced by that of the Fifth Dalai Lama. Soon after the defeat, imprisonment, and execution of the Tsang king (the great-grandson, Karma Tenkyong, 1604/06–1642), the Jonang monastic system was dismantled and its pieces dissolved into the Gélugpa school. It is said that even the paintings on the walls were reworked, the past hierarchs' hats changed to yellow, more in keeping with the new landlords' team colors.

The motives for this suppression were undoubtedly political—this seemed to put the finishing touches on a victory that in fact marked the last major transfer of power in Tibet until the modern day. It was politics as usual, the way the game was played in Tibet. Nevertheless, this change marked the end of a period of lay rule and return to an oligarchy, rule from a religious throne. Of course, no one ignored that the sponsors of the change were once again the Mongolians, yet what home rule they allowed the Tibetans now belonged to the church-state. We can only imagine that if the Mongolians had chosen lay persons to be their agents on Tibet's throne, the Jonang would have been allowed to continue to exist. However, when power returned to lamas' hands, it is possible that other lamas and monasteries were seen as potential rivals even after any secular competition had been crushed. Further, if a secular ruler decided to suppress what he saw as a troublesome religious institution, it is likely that the justification offered would have been couched in secular terms, such as, "This institution, which has sacrificed its stated mission of religious training for political intrigues, threatens the stability of the country."

In Tibet's new political world, this was insufficient grounds for action: a "spiritual" justification had to be given for the extinguishing of Jonang institutions. Our spiritual ancestor, the recently deceased Taranata, provided a suitable target. Two charges were leveled against him. First, he was deemed a corrupt monk. As evidence, his own very explicit account of his sexual encounters was read in public.[51] Had he been alive, he might have retorted, the tantras' chapters and verses in hand, that his chosen spiritual path was that of the highest level of Buddhism. He preferred to view the lower paths of Buddhism from the perspective of the higher, rather than the other way around. His reading of the three vows corresponded to that of many accomplished tantric masters of India and Tibet. The Tibetan debate concerning the proper integration of Buddhism's three levels of vows began many centuries before him and continues to the present day, but this marked a low point in the conversation. Taranata's views were branded unreasonable and dangerous; the system of monasteries he had led was deemed contaminated.

The new central government did not stop there. A second charge was leveled against Taranata and the Jonang system, that of heresy. What was the view so wicked and inimical to warrant the closure of a monastic system? Precisely the one mentioned earlier in relation to Kunga Drolchok—extraneous emptiness. To repeat Gyurmé Dorjé's words, it is "the view that all the attributes of Buddhahood are extraneously empty of mundane impurities and defilements, but not intrinsically empty in a nihilistic sense, their experience thereby transcending all notions of existence and nonexistence." To put it in slightly easier language, proponents of extraneous emptiness contend that our innate enlightenment, buddha nature, is not merely empty but constitutes an infinite mine of enlightenment's inconceivable and indescribable qualities, which cannot be identified as existent or nonexistent. What is truly empty is that which veils our enlightened nature—the "mundane impurities and defilements," such as karma, negative states of mind, and habitual patterns.

Kalu Rinpoché used to characterize this debate, which has kept lamps burning during long Tibetan nights for many centuries before and after the Jonang, as an argument over whether a glass is half empty or half full. However, the early seventeenth century was no place for such an open-minded attitude. The new government declared Taranata and the Jonang system guilty of heresy. As punishment, they impounded the wood blocks used to print the heretical works. Thus, *Taranata's Collected Works* remained in prison for two centuries.⁵² Thankfully, the extraneous-emptiness repression restricted itself to the Jonang, as much of the greatest writing Tibet had produced (such as Longchenpa's works, to name but one among many) would have been incarcerated with those of Taranata had the repression been countrywide.

The justification given for the end of the Jonang centered on Taranata, his corrupt views and conduct. As absurd as the charges were in the Tibetan context—many of Tibet's greatest masters were contentedly guilty of the same "crimes"—they were enough to justify the action taken against the Jonang and to blacken Taranata's reputation in many circles. Certainly, the removal of his written works from circulation ensured that the only account of his life and thought available to the public was the official version.

Woven into this tale of the transformation of Taranata into Tibet's public enemy number one, we can find easily discern dark family hatreds. Who gained by Taranata's fall? The new ruler of Tibet, the Fifth Dalai Lama (1617–1682), was none other than Taranata's nephew. In Tibet's past, maternal uncles have a way of appearing as the bad guys. For example, although scholars have not yet decided why some government ministers under the early kings were called *zhang-lön*, the *zhang* in their title could refer to their family relation as maternal uncles, *ah-zhang* in Tibetan. (*Lön* is a contraction of *lönpo*, government minister.) At the time of Guru Rinpoché's visit to Tibet, many of the "evil government ministers" are referred to as *zhang-lön*. Although it seems that the title predated Tibet's formal relations with China, the ties between the Chinese and Tibetan royal families were referred to as those of nephew-uncle, again the maternal uncle (*ah-zhang*) rather than the paternal one (*ah-ku*). Even today, I have Tibetan friends who refer to Chairman Mao as "ah-zhang," not from fidelity to the Party but with all the wry humor of an oppressed people whose seeming embrace of Mao and his political offspring as family members reserves for them the implied role of family villains. No Tibetan needs to have that reference interpreted.

Taranata, then, was the Fifth Dalai Lama's maternal uncle. Although their lives overlapped, the defining acts of their relationship occurred after Taranata had left for the pure lands. The nephew's dismantling of his uncle's reputation and life work led to a popular Tibetan proverb, "A goat's horns can grow to poke out the goat's own eyes; a nephew can grow to undermine his own uncle." For Tibetans, this is a rare example of the nephew and not the maternal uncle cast in an unfavorable light.

With this background, we can reexamine the modern Shangpa lineage. We find a lineage dominated by the writings and the spirit of a man whose name invokes in some circles the cringing or awe-filled fascination we reserve for twisted, wicked genius. We also can now understand that Kongtrul's repeated testimonials to his idol's greatness amount to public declarations of his opinion on a number of difficult subjects. For example, at the beginning of the *Songs*, we read Kongtrul's two-line supplication to Taranata:

Noble Taranata, Héruka,
Illustrious Lord of Secrets, to you I pray.

Tibetans informed of their country's history read this as a declaration of faith in Taranata as a tantric adept. "Héruka" is a word that designates a wrathful tantric deity; "Lord of Secrets" is a name of Bodhisattva Vajra-in-Hand, who received, compiled, and guarded Buddha's tantras. Kongtrul could be read here as flatly stating his opinion of one of the two charges against Taranata, that he was a corrupt monk. He goes beyond how some modern persons integrate the questionable behavior of those they admire: "Taranata was a brilliant scholar who had a weakness for sex." Kongtrul does not equivocate:

You received the prophecy that, on the path of great passion, all who saw,
    heard, remembered, or were touched by you
Would gain complete liberation.

And, as the supplication draws to the close, he makes this aspiration:

In this life, the next, and the intermediate state between,
May I not be separated from you even in a dream, Taranata.
May I attain your secret treasury, accomplish impartial tantric conduct,
And attain enlightenment in the play of union's great bliss.

Tibetan readers do not have to have either of these lines decoded: the subject in both these passages is sex. For Kongtrul, Taranata personified a wrathful tantric deity, a bodhisattva. This is a call to 100 percent pure vision, repeated throughout the Shangpa lineage's texts. Kongtrul never addresses the subject explicitly, but his words made his attitude crystal clear for any informed Tibetan reader.

Elsewhere, Kongtrul uses Taranata as one of his main authorities, whom he quotes liberally throughout his *Encyclopedia of Buddhism*, alongside his other favorite past masters, the Third Karmapa Rangjung Dorjé and Longchenpa. These two lamas also wrote widely from the perspective of extraneous emptiness, the other black mark against Taranata's name. Again, Kongtrul made no secret of his devotion to Taranata's philosophical views; he wrote repeatedly of the primacy of extraneous emptiness, that it represents the crown of Buddha's teachings. It was not Kongtrul's style to engage in a historical debate, to write of the stories that everyone knew but dared not speak. He rewrote history somewhat quietly and subversively, without debating with or attempting to preach to the unconverted.

His inclusion of Taranata's work throughout his *Treasury of Profound Instructions* provides another example of his devotion. At every juncture in *The Treasury*, we find empowerments, meditations, and major commentaries by Taranata, even rituals for the bodhisattva vows and a presentation of the bodhisattva path from the pre-Gélugpa school, Buddha's Word as Instruction Lineage. Even our "Seven Points of Mind Training" lineage passes through Taranata; Kongtrul mentions him by his monastic name, Kunga Nyingpo, in his commentary to that meditation.

Kongtrul had a wealth of other texts to choose from, but he consistently chose those by Taranata. In fact, Taranata's rehabilitation constitutes one of the major themes of Jamgon Kongtrul's life and work. We will see in the life of Losal Tenkyong an event that contributed to Taranata's resurrection during Kongtrul's lifetime.

THE PATH NOT TAKEN
BY THE SHANGPA LINEAGE

F ROM THE STORIES of Shangpa masters to this point, it is clear that
they spurned any form of worldly ambition for themselves and for
their lineage of teachings. With Kunga Drolchok and Taranata, both of
whom met Niguma in visions, the lineage became associated with the
Jonang monasteries and their patrons, the royal family of Tsang, then
rulers of Tibet. Both these masters' spiritual lives far exceeded the bounds
of the Shangpa lineage—within Taranata's *Collected Works*, for example,
we find his first texts on Shangpa meditations in volume eleven. Those
few works are of vital importance to us still; they number among the core
textbooks in Shangpa meditation training, yet they represent a small fraction of Taranata's literary output. In reflecting on his own life, Taranata
attributed his lifelong inspiration to repeated encouragement and guidance in visions of Guru Rinpoché and Dolpo Sangyé. Nevertheless, for
the Shangpa lineage, the fact that Niguma had appeared to these Jonang
masters was sufficient evidence that the principal lineage passed through
them.

The Jonang monasteries' fate, obliteration from the map of Tibetan
institutions, meant that the Shangpa transmission was again homeless, a
guest in other schools' monasteries and retreat centers. This was not a new
experience for the lineage, but the fact that none of Taranata's books could
be reprinted was undoubtedly a hardship. Further, for many in Tibet,
Taranata's name had become associated primarily with corruption and was
the focus of official state censorship of the most stringent kind. The
Shangpa lineage entered a period of marginal existence, although its lineage holders during this dark period include such illuminated masters as the
Nyingma lama Rikzin Tséwang Norbu (1698–1755) and his disciple, the
seventh Drukchen Rinpoché, head of the Drukpa Kargyu school, Kagyu
Trinlé Shingta (1718–1766). I have not seen accounts of these masters'

teaching of the Shangpa lineage, but it is easy to imagine that the climate for passing on Taranata's works in public was inauspicious.

Had the Mongolians not put the Dalai Lamas on Tibet's throne, the Shangpa lineage's cohabitation with the Jonang monasteries might have changed its character to that of a worldly, earthbound school. We can compare its marginal existence to that of the Gélug tradition, which grew exponentially after assuming power. Consider this: A census report by Dési Sangyé Gyatso, the Fifth Dalai Lama's regent, in 1694 (thirteen years after the Fifth Dalai Lama's death), reveals that there were 1,807 monasteries of all schools in Tibet, of which 534 were Gélugpa. Those monasteries housed 97,538 monks and nuns, of whom less than a third, 26,789, were Gélugpa.

Forty years later, in 1733, another census reveals an astounding change. Monasteries under the Dalai Lama numbered 3,150 institutions housing 342,560 monks and nuns; institutions affiliated with the Panchen Lama numbered 327, with 13,670 ordained members.[53]

It would be tempting to think of this more than tenfold increase in the Gélug school's monastic population in terms of a religious revival on a grand scale, but these were not times of love and light. Those who had reviled Taranata undoubtedly witnessed with horror the Sixth Dalai Lama's joyful libertine lifestyle, which could have seemed to them to have more in common with the evil uncle than the good nephew. Relations with the Mongol powers behind the throne soured and Tibet saw a period of sad destruction. Beginning in 1717, accounts with the Nyingma monasteries were settled—many monasteries of that school, including Dorjé Trakgön and Minling, were destroyed and many lamas were executed, including the Dotrak Tulku Péma Trinlé (1614–1717) and two wonderful lamas of Minling Monastery, Péma Gyurmé Gyatso (1686–1718) and Lochen Dharmashri (1654–1718).

The only coherent explanation for the Gélug school's rapid development during this dark time is the building of the national government's administrative structure and its need for workers, bureaucrats, and administrators. This marriage of church and state had its effects on the Buddhist life of these institutions. As with the previous Sakya administration, the monasteries' inner organization now conformed to secular codes; Buddha's rules and regulations for the life of his monks and nuns were confined to history. Lozang Trinlé, a historian and Gélug reincarnate master, comments, "The customs of law according to the regulations of Buddhism's own traditions became mere words written in history books." (*Ibid.*, pp. 592-593) Buddhist monks ruled Tibet according to secular laws and government policies, which defined much of monastic life. This was not a "Gélug problem" per se—any school that assumed power probably would have developed in much the same way. Had things turned out differently, it could have been the Shangpa lineage that became bloated with the demands of running a country.

As it was, the Shangpa tradition avoided both worldly loss and gain. It had no viable institutions of its own, thus its masters did not become targets for violent repression after the Jonang monasteries were dissolved into the Gélugpa system. On the other hand, the Shangpa connection to Taranata protected the tradition from the curse of success, Tibetan style, with its deadly mixture of politics and religion. My phrase, "deadly mixture of politics and religion" reflects Shangpa lineage values; others in Tibet's Buddhist landscape openly and vigorously support the marriage of church and state. The question is still hotly debated. The Shangpa lineage texts themselves give no party line to follow on the subject, but it is difficult to imagine that their attitude would be any different from that of Paltrul Rinpoché who wrote these lines in *The Words of My Perfect Teacher*:

> Nowadays we think we can practice Dharma alongside our worldly activities, without the slightest need for determination or for hardship, all the while enjoying comfort, well-being and popularity. "Other people manage to do it," we insist, and say admiringly, "Now, that's a good lama, he knows how to combine Dharma and worldly life."
>
> But how could there be a way to marry Dharma with worldly life? Those who claim to be doing so are likely to be leading a good worldly life, but you may be sure that they are not practicing pure Dharma. To claim that you can practice Dharma and worldly life at the same time is like saying that you can sew with a double-pointed needle, put fire and water in the same container or ride two horses in opposite directions. All these things are simply impossible.
>
> Could an ordinary person ever surpass Buddha Shakyamuni? Yet even he found no way of practicing Dharma and worldly life side by side. Could Milarepa really have been too hopeless to know how to combine the two? (pp. 242-243)

The lineage that Niguma and Sukasiddhi nurtured never evinced any signs of an agenda other than meditation and realization. These dakinis' spiritual heirs convincingly turned deaf ears to calls for investment in land and large buildings. Niguma blessed Kunga Drolchok and Taranata with teachings that renewed the lineage, but the eventual tragedy of the slander of Taranata's name and the suppression of his work was a catastrophe for Tibetan Buddhism in general, not for the Shangpa lineage, which had nothing to lose. If the Shangpa teachings, revitalized by Taranata, disappeared from public view because of a generalized repression, wasn't that entirely in character for a lineage that had been passed from one master to one disciple during its first seven generations? Capturing and maintaining a market share in Tibet's spiritual bazaar was never a concern of the Shangpa lineage. The eminent Western translator Matthew Kapstein proposes this view:

> The history of the *Shangs-pa bKa'-brgyud* like that of several of the other schools must take into account two separate aspects of the one tradition; namely its existence as a sect, and as a lineage. By *sect*, I mean a religious order that is distinguished from others by virtue of its institutional independence; that is, its unique character is embodied outwardly in the form of an independent hierarchy and administration, independent properties and a recognizable membership of some sort. A lineage on the other hand is a continuous succession of spiritual teachers who have transmitted a given body of knowledge over a period of generations but who need not be affiliated with a common sect. Such a distinction is particularly useful when considering a school such as the Shangs-pa; for the sect and the lineage have not shared a similar fate: while the one waned, the other actually flourished. (The Shangs-pa bKa'-brgyud: An Unknown Tradition of Tibetan Buddhism, in *Tibetan Studies in Honour of Hugh Richardson*, p. 139)

I have dwelled on the history of this period for two reasons. First, the story has rarely been addressed in Western publications; I have given its bare outline with the intention to point out that there is a complex and intriguing story here. Second, the story's resolution in the modern era, through the life and work of Jamgon Kongtrul, speaks volumes concerning the Shangpa lineage agenda, past, present, and future.

LOCHEN GYURMÉ DÉCHEN

Lochen Gyurmé Déchen (1540–1615) figures in the Shangpa lineage that runs parallel to the main lineage through a line of Sakya masters. We remember Gyurmé Déchen as a scholar of Sanskrit (Lochen, the prefix to his personal name, means "great translator"), as the nephew of Tangtong Gyalpo (as he was born almost 180 years after his uncle, he was likely at least a great-grandnephew), and as Tangtong Gyalpo's biographer. In the two Shangpa volumes within *The Treasury of Profound Instructions*, Jamgon Kongtrul included a pair of short texts by Gyurmé Déchen on Transference of Consciousness. This, however, represents a small fraction of his literary output in the Shangpa lineage. Gyurmé Déchen and his disciple Ngawang Chödrak (1572–1641) produced a number of Shangpa textbooks more in keeping with the character of the Sakya lineage than with the main Shangpa tradition, which produced spare books on meditation instruction rather than wordy presentations of the path. Gyurmé Déchen's work will perhaps become appreciated now that the Shangpa lineage has reached persons less familiar with this material, Tantric Buddhism 101. In the past, Gyurmé Déchen's work met with an ambivalent response in the Shangpa tradition. Kongtrul owned a copy of the books but did not sponsor their reprinting. That event had to wait until the late 1980s, when Kalu Rinpoché received the old books he had left behind in Tibet, a collection that had once belonged to Kongtrul. Kalu Rinpoché had the texts recopied and printed in India.

LOSAL TENKYONG

THE NAME LOSAL TENKYONG (1805–c.1865) does not appear in Shangpa lineage prayers, but Kongtrul had an important reason for including him in this collection. Losal Tenkyong was the head of the west Tibet Zhalu Monastery, made famous by Butön, the fourteenth-century scholar. As a resident reincarnate lama of western Tibet close to Zhigatsé and Jonang, Losal Tenkyong was able to secure the unsealing of Taranata's banned books for his eastern Tibetan friends, Kongtrul and Kyentsé. It is for this act that he is most often cited in modern histories of Tibet's spiritual life, as he thus aided Kyentsé and Kongtrul, who reprinted Taranata's works throughout his five treasuries. E. Gene Smith reports the following:

> A close associate of Kong sprul [Kongtrul] and Mkhyen brtse [Kyentsé] in revitalizing the Gzhan stong [extraneous emptiness] theories was the Zhwa lu Ri sbug sprul sku, Blo bsal bstan skyong [Zhalu Ripuk Tulku, Losal Tenkyong]. This Kalachakra master from Gtsang [Tsang] was ultimately successful in persuading the administrator of Bkra shis lhun po [Tashi Lhunpo] to allow him to survey the extant blocks at Dga' ldan Phun tshogs gling [Gaden Puntsok Ling], Taranatha's monastery, and Ngam rings [Ngam Ring], the provincial capital of the La stod Byang pa [Latö Jang-pa] myriarchs. The majority of the blocks stored in the printeries of these two establishments had been sealed by the Fifth Dalai Lama who went so far as to forbid even the copying of existent prints. The liberal Bkra shis Lhun po [Tashi Lhunpo] administrator agreed with Blo gsal bstan skyongs [Losal Tenkyong] that the Jo nang pa works should be again be printed; consequently, a number of impressions were made from the ancient blocks. (*Among Tibetan Texts*, p. 250, square brackets added)

Losal Tenkyong's good relationship with Tashi Lhunpo—he took full monastic ordination there from the Panchen Lama at the age of twenty-one—probably aided in his later efforts to retrieve the texts mentioned. In a note [*Ibid.*, p. 333, n. 847], Smith dates Losal Tenkyong's completion of his "survey of the sealed blocks" in 1873, but a recent Tibetan source, *Concise Biographies of Himalayan Master-Scholars*, situates this work in Losal Tenkyong's fifty-fifth year (probably 1859) and mentions that he suffered a stroke in 1860 that kept him bedridden for the remainder of his life (pp. 681-682). The author guesses that 1865 is the likely year of his death. This earlier date for Losal Tenkyong's work would be more consistent with Kongtrul's work as well.

Losal Tenkyong was a major master of Kyentsé Wangpo and passed on to him a large body of teaching, including the Shangpa transmission. In *The Treasury of Profound Instructions*' two Shangpa volumes, Jamgon Kongtrul included two major works by Losal Tenkyong of vital importance to the Shangpa lineage, the empowerments for all meditations related to the phase of completion, such as Niguma's Six Doctrines. This inclusion was undoubtedly in honor of his liberation of Taranata's work, which allowed Kongtrul to further the rehabilitation of that master's memory.

JAMYANG KYENTSÉ WANGPO

T HERE IS LITTLE DEBATE concerning the identity of the greatest master of the last century: then and now, meditation masters, scholars, and ordinary practitioners concur that it was Kyentsé Wangpo. We have only to read Kongtrul's introduction to Kyentsé's songs he chose to include in this collection to hear his informed opinion, loud and clear:

> During the extreme degeneration that marks this time of conflict, this master's life is as rare and as very significant as [the blossoming of] an *udumvara* flower. A wondrous, supreme manifestation of enlightenment, masterful lord of the seven transmissions, his outstanding, unparalleled life of freedom made him renowned throughout the horizon of the Himalayas by the name of Jamyang Kyentsé Wangpo.

Kongtrul repeats such praises in many of his writings and throughout the biography of his master and friend, written a few years after Kyentsé's death.

Jamyang Kyentsé Wangpo (1820–1892) was born in eastern Tibet as a Sakya reincarnate master, but his influence covered the Himalayan region and permeated every lineage. He received every lineage's teachings, understood them, reflected upon them, practiced them, gained visions and other signs of accomplishment, and passed them on better and more vital than he had found them. The wealth of over a thousand years of Tibetan spiritual life passed through his hands. In an acknowledgment of that, which is surprising given the context, Kongtrul here mentions part of Kyentsé's activity that had no relation to the Shangpa teachings: He informs us that Kyentsé is the "masterful lord of the seven transmissions," the seven ways treasure revealers can receive the instructions of Guru Rinpoché: the Canon, earth treasures, re-revealed treasures, mind treasures, recollected treasures, pure vision treasures, and direct oral instruction treasures.

In relation to the Shangpa lineage, the names of three of Kyentsé's many past lives are now familiar to us: Tangtong Gyalpo, Jamyang Kyentsé Wangchuk, and Taranata.[54] When Kyentsé was twenty-four, he visited Zhang-zhung Monastery, which housed a statue of its founder, Kyungpo Naljor. Above the statue, he saw an umbrella of blue light in which many empty forms of the tantric deities vividly appeared. They dissolved into the statue, which then spoke symbolic words to Kyentsé: "Evam-maya-ho!" Light from the statue's heart flowed to Kyentsé and awakened his karmic connection with the Shangpa teachings. As Kongtrul recounts the story (in *The Biography of Jamyang Kyentsé Wangpo*, p. 83a), this seems to have been the crucial moment in Kyentsé's relationship with the Shangpa instructions, although at the age of fifteen, he met Tangtong Gyalpo in a dream and then immediately upon waking. On that occasion, he received a significant treasure transmission and instruction in Niguma's Six Doctrines and Great Seal Amulet Box. (*Ibid.,* pp. 83a, 112b)

Kyentsé seems to have had an unlimited number of visions. One that unites three names from this collection arose within his experience of clear light. He saw a place that he thought was like India, wide and even, with grass, trees, and lakes embellished with many white and red flowers, a delightful and attractive environment. There, Kyentsé was joined by four of his friends and masters, each astride a different animal, each in the guise of a Héruka, a tantric practitioner. Kyentsé himself rode a golden tortoise; Losal Tenkyong, a white lioness; Gyalsé Zhenpen Tayé (b. 1800), an ash-white elephant; Chokgyur Déchen Lingpa (1829–1870), a fierce tigress; and Jamgon Kongtrul, a turquoise dragon. The many spiritual heroes and dakinis who surrounded them wore silk, jewels, and bone ornaments and carried various sacred objects. They sang and danced together for a long time in intense happiness. Kongtrul remarks that since the animals upon which the lamas rode were related to their respective qualities and activities, he found the vision very meaningful. He captured the vision in a painting and offered it to Kyentsé, who was delighted, consecrated it, and displayed it close by over a long period.[55]

Finally, we note with interest Kongtrul's selection of songs for Kyentsé. The first, a song that describes Tangtong Gyalpo's inner state, is related to the Shangpa tradition by the subject alone, not by the content. The second, a song related to the experiences of the Six Doctrines and Great Seal, seems to have more to do with Naropa's Six Doctrines than Niguma's. The last song contains these lines:

> In the voice of the *kati* crystal channel,
> I sing the song of rainbow drops.
> All marks of aggregates' and sense elements' solidity
> Dissolve within the exhaustion of phenomena beyond the mind's
>   domain.

This verse uses terminology unique to Great Completion's Tögal meditation, again outside the Shangpa lineage's scope. In the supplication to Kyentsé Wangpo that follows, which Kongtrul wrote and included in the collection of supplications to Shangpa lineage masters, he breathes not a word in reference to the Shangpa lineage. We can only speculate concerning Kongtrul's reasons for this. He and Kyentsé were both committed to an ecumenical approach to tantric Buddhism, as were most of the past Shangpa masters. Perhaps he felt it was more important to honor the Buddha in Kyentsé than to use the supplication for the lineage's publicity purposes. Perhaps he felt the best service he could render the Shangpa lineage was to make bridges between it—a marginal, homeless lineage—and mainstream Tibetan Buddhism. Perhaps he wished to remain faithful to the Shangpa spirit, which never followed such common, loyalty-inculcating practices as elaborate visualizations of masters, deities, dakinis, protectors, and so on, gathered in a "lineage tree." The Shangpa teacher-student relationship is based entirely in the present, one on one, and does not make reference in visualization for refuge to any other figure, be it as an enlightened human or a deity. It is possible that all these considerations motivated Kongtrul to refrain from a lineage-centered approach to these final songs and supplications, for in the supplication he composed to himself, Kongtrul refers to himself as a Karma Kagyu, not Shangpa Kagyu, master.

The Melody of the Auspicious Coil:
A Supplication to the All-Knowing Jamyang Kyentsé Wangpo
by Jamgon Kongtrul

You know the nature and the details of every subject;
Your universal compassion considers beings as your children;
King of the Teachings, you empty the depths of the wheel of life—
Venerable Kyentsé Wangpo, to you I pray.

Sole father of the victors, noble Bodhisattva Gentle Splendor
Fills the absolute expanse with manifestations to guide others in
  fitting ways.
Among them, you intentionally took rebirth as a glorious lord protec-
  tor and refuge
For Buddhism and beings of this degenerate time; to you I pray.

In lower Do-Kham, in the medicinal province of the four kinds of
  magnificence and the ten virtues [of land], [56]
At the place that is the manifestation of enlightened activity to guide
  beings,
You displayed enlightenment's manifest body within a pure family
After you saw the five sublime visions;[57] to you I pray.

Supreme guides who attained wisdom
Foretold in unison that you were a holy individual.
You transcended common behavior;

All gods and humans praised you as beings' lord protector; to you
  I pray.

You traveled over greater Tibet's central and western regions
And relied on over one hundred tutors, pleasing them in three ways.[58]
Without fatigue or regret, you searched for the sacred Teachings
With boundless determination; to you I pray.

When you meditated in the great Sakya [Kunga Nyingpo's] cave,
Exalted deities' forms dissolved into your heart,
Liberating the eight great treasures of your confidence
And perfecting the two forms of wisdom's great display; to you I pray.

You excelled in Buddhist culture's five main and secondary subjects,
Such as grammar, logic, art, medicine, astrology, and poetic
  embellishments.
Your fame as a scholar
Filled the Himalayan region; to you I pray.

By merely seeing their texts, you plumbed the depths of discipline,
  knowledge, the Middle Way,
Transcendent knowledge, and Secret Mantra's tantras.
You gained a flawless memory and overtly displayed
The form of Stable Wheel [Manjushri]; to you I pray.

Your vision saw profound and vast subjects without the slightest
  impurity.
You engaged in teaching, debate, and composition without hesitation
  or impediment.
You exhausted delusion's impurities in any act or conduct,
Inspiring confidence in gods and humanity; to you I pray.

You concealed your inner qualities, an ocean of treasures;
To others' most minor noble quality, you offered praise and homage.
For the doctrine and beings' benefit, you parted with cherished
  possessions
As if they were as worthless as grass; to you I pray.

You mastered an ocean of recollection, meditative states, and
   clairvoyance
And became worthy of offerings from the three worlds' beings,
Yet you never became arrogant—
You gladly undertook great hardships for the sake of one word of the
   Teachings; to you I pray.

You set aside mundane activity, such as preserving or protecting false
   teachings,
And you lived without fixation.
Like a fearless lion, you engaged in ever excellent conduct
Unrivaled in this world; to you I pray.

Every stream of the eight great chariots' historical traditions of
   meditation—
Their source texts, guidance, and pith instructions—swirled into your
   mind's ocean.
Their techniques for spiritual maturity and liberation passed through
   you
To revitalize the doctrine; to you I pray.

You gave your disciples appropriate antidotes impartially
From among the great chariots of Shakyamuni's entire doctrine.
Without bias, you became the crown jewel
Of every school of philosophy; to you I pray.

Your enlightened activity was done only for others' good.
Any connection with you was meaningful; you displayed many
   wonderful signs.
You produced an inconceivably great cultivation of merit—
Lord of awakening's tenth stage, to you I pray.

The master from Oddiyana and his consort,
Venerable Vimalamitra, religious kings, their ancestors and
   descendants, [Guru] Chöwang, omniscient [Longchenpa],
And other spiritual masters from many lineages and the exalted
   deities
Granted you their blessings and accomplishment; to you I pray.

In particular, master Manjushri-mitra
Gave you the discourses' and tantras' secret treasury.
He blessed you as enlightenment's wisdom body inseparable from
    him,
Fully awakening your wisdom's realization; to you I pray.

The very loving uncle and nephew, along with their [Sakya] lineage,
Bestowed empowerment and entrusted you with their tantras.
Many other learned and accomplished masters from India and Tibet
    repeatedly taught you
In waking life, dreams, and meditative experience; to you I pray.

When you entered Matrix of Mystery's configuration, the sublime
    teacher So gave you the wisdom empowerment,
Purifying your residual psychophysical aggregates and sense elements
    with its power;
You were transformed into Vajrasattva's three mysteries;
Supreme master of all families of enlightenment, to you I pray.

The victors' mother, Vajra Queen, accepted you as her disciple
And appearing existence arose as the circle of infinite purity.
You clearly saw your vajra body's sacred configuration.
Supreme son of accomplishment, to you I pray.

You gathered with outer, inner, and secret dakinis;
The three blazing fires' wisdom greatly increased.
You perfected auspicious connections with the three forms of
    conduct.
Master of tantric adepts, to you I pray.

Your karmic connections from many past lifetimes awakened—
A million rivers of rare volumes of the discourses' and tantras'
    canonical transmission,
Sublime sacred supports, and sacred substances
Swirled into the seas of your life of freedom; to you I pray.

You were endowed with the Six Lineages,[59]
Treasures discovered in the earth, the mind, pure vision, an aural

lineage, recollection, and retrieval of reconcealed treasures.
You thus gained dominion of the seven precious transmissions.
Leader of the Teachings, to you I pray.

You mastered your own experience and awed others with your
  brilliance.
You effortlessly accomplished the four kinds of enlightened activity.
Dakinis, guardians, and forceful arrogant spirits
Did as you commanded; to you I pray.

Your innumerable vast and profound teachings
Brought millions of fortunate persons to spiritual maturity and libera-
  tion.
You lived an inconceivable, exalted life of freedom.
Paragon of compassion, to you I pray.

By the force of my single-minded prayers of undivided respect,
From this lifetime forward until I reach awakening,
May I not be separate from you, sublime, illustrious master;
May you accept me and may I realize your life of freedom.

May I rely upon you in the three ways to please you;
May I attain your enlightened mind's essence and reach the end of my
  experiential cultivation.
After I complete the noble qualities of awakening's paths and stages,
May I accomplish powerful Buddha Vajra Bearer's state.

May obstacles not arise in my spiritual practice consistent with the
  Teachings;
And with the mastery that I attain in the doctrine of scripture and
  realization,
May I spread the powerful Sage's doctrine throughout the world
To become, like you, a sovereign of the Teachings.

(*A Garland of Udumvara Flowers,* pp. 27a-28b)

JAMGON KONGTRUL

JAMGON KONGTRUL'S LIFE (1813–1899) and work embraced the entire range of Tibetan nontheistic spirituality, Bön and Buddhist. To characterize him as an exclusively Shangpa lama, Kagyu lama, or Nyingma lama is to diminish him. His enlightening influence was felt in all traditions of Tibetan meditation and religious practice. He had a tremendous impact on the Shangpa lineage, but it would be wise to keep in mind the words of his close disciple Tashi Chöpel, who accurately resumes his teacher's wide-ranging life:

> This noble master strove to study every subject. He began with an education in reading and writing within the context of study of the common arts and sciences, and he continued to pursue a higher education [within Buddhism]. There was nothing he did not learn: from the Three Collections of Buddha's teaching to the extraordinary Vajra Way, his studies included even the most minor empowerments, transmissions, meditation instructions, styles of explanation, and practical procedures of the four classes of tantra. The complete record of his education extends to two volumes. An examination of it gives the impression that he spent his entire life studying.
>
> The extent of his bestowal of empowerments, reading transmissions, and instructions from the Canon and Treasures of the Later and Original Schools gives the impression that he spent his entire life teaching.
>
> [This master] was unlike those who finish their study and reflection with a rough understanding [of the subjects]. They then wish to write and compose, and call the few words they write with a competitive spirit and desire for fame *My Collected Works*. Unlike them, this master's work furthered the continuity of the Buddha's

entire doctrine when it was about to expire. The extent of his teaching, principally contained in his wonderful *Five Treasuries*, fills ninety volumes.[60] When we consider this aspect of his life of freedom, we have the impression that he spent his entire life writing.

An examination of how he performed the intensive practices of an ocean of meditations from the Later and Original Schools' discourses and tantras gives the impression that he spent his entire life [meditating] within a strictly sealed meditation room.

Only awakened persons can understand this master's life of freedom; [to persons like us] it is inconceivable. This account is not a dishonest exaggeration written in memory of my own master; it is an account reflecting the whole truth. Its accuracy will be clearly evident to the wise. (*The Last Days*, pp. 6a-b)

If we look back to Jamgon Kongtrul's past lives, it is easy to understand why his life led him to the Shangpa lineage—he is the reincarnation of Kyungpo Naljor, Kunga Drolchok, and Taranata, three pillars of the tradition. The Shangpa lineage was not the sole beneficiary of his brilliant energy, but he definitely revitalized it at every level. Kongtrul's name can be found at every junction in our contact with the Shangpa teachings. What Taranata left unfinished or overly complex, Kongtrul completed or simplified—empowerments, meditation texts, commentaries, and supplementary texts, such as this collection of songs and the supplications.

His influence was also felt in training meditators in the Shangpa lineage: when he established a three-year retreat at his home, the program was heavily weighted toward the Shangpa tradition. The first year and a half was devoted to the full range of Shangpa meditations, the next half-year to the Jonang meditations on the Kalachakra Tantra's phases of creation and completion, and the third year to Great Completion meditation. Practically, this meant that the first two years of Jamgon Kongtrul's three-year retreat program immersed meditators in Taranata's work. In a fortunate confluence of events, Taranata's work had been liberated by Losal Tenkyong in 1859; the first three-year retreat Kongtrul led began the following year.

Kalu Rinpoché related the following account of Kongtrul's original impulse to found a meditation center, here retold by Lama Drubgyu Tenzin of Canada:

One time, Jamgon Kongtrul the Great, already an important lama of Palpung Monastery, had entered a strictly sealed retreat. During the course of this retreat he heard that the principal holder of the Shangpa Instruction Lineage, one Lama Norbu (Zhenpen Özer) was to visit Palpung. Kongtrul was already familiar with the Shangpa tradition and had profound respect for these teachings. He had also heard that Lama Norbu was an extraordinary individual. He felt the opportunity to receive the transmission directly from this, the actual lineage holder, was an extremely rare one, and so made the decision to break his retreat in order to meet this person.

Hearing of the arrival of Lama Norbu, Kongtrul left his retreat and made his way to the visitor's apartments to pay his respects, and investigate the possibility of receiving transmission from this lama. Upon arriving in Lama Norbu's room, Kongtrul found he was completely ignored. Although one of the principal lamas of the monastery, it was as though he didn't exist! To Jamgon Kongtrul's great consternation, as long as he remained, no sign was given that he was even present.

Very disturbed by this turn of events, Kongtrul returned to his own rooms. He reflected on his misfortune, and wondered what former negative actions he must have committed to so rupture his connection to the Shangpa tradition and its lineage holder. At no point did he entertain any thought critical of Lama Norbu; rather he examined himself again and again to discern his own faults. So concerned was he that he did not sleep that night but passed the whole of it reflecting on his own shortcomings, performing confession and purification, and reciting the mantra of Vajrasattva.

As dawn was approaching an idea entered into Kongtrul's mind. Perhaps by offering to establish a retreat center expressly dedicated to the propagation of the teachings of the Shangpa tradition he would be able to make atonement and so establish a fruitful personal connection with these teachings! The more he considered this idea, the more convinced he became of its appropriateness.

First thing in the morning, Kongtrul once again made his way to the rooms of Lama Norbu with this idea foremost in his mind. As he was entering the room, before he could say a word, Lama Norbu addressed him saying, "That is an excellent idea! I don't

have the time at the moment to give you all the transmissions, but
you should go ahead with this plan and I will return as soon as
possible to give you the full transmission of the Shangpa cycle of
teachings."

Although this story does not appear in Kongtrul's autobiography, he
reports having met this lama for the first time in 1840 (at the age of twenty-
seven) and was given just a few instructions on that occasion. He received
the full transmission of the Shangpa Instruction Lineage from Lama
Norbu in 1843. The first three-year, three-fortnight retreat at Tsadra
Rinchen Drak began in 1860; Kongtrul was forty-seven years old.

The Shangpa tradition had not had such a training center for hundreds
of years, if ever. Lineage holders before Kongtrul were accomplished masters, but no record remains of them showing any interest in creating institutions or programs; after the suppression of the Jonang monasteries, the
lineage had been homeless. (Lama Norbu, Kongtrul's main Shangpa connection, was a reincarnation of Mokchok Rinchen Tsöndru; his lama was
a reincarnation of Kyergang Chökyi Sengé. True to their roots, they spent
their lives gaining a high level of realization.) With Kongtrul, the Shangpa
lineage found a home, his own, at Tsadra Rinchen Drak. This center in
turn gave birth to another three-year retreat center, at Satsa Monastery;
after the reincarnate master of that institution completed a three-year
retreat under Jamgon Kongtrul's guidance, he founded a similar retreat at
his own monastery. That retreat, like the retreat at Tsadra, still functions
today.

We might try to imagine Jamgon Kongtrul's world at that time. He had
received the Shangpa transmission from an accomplished master and had
promised to revive the lineage by creating a retreat institution. In a land
where monastic communities could number in the thousands—how large
was the retreat center that Kongtrul built, how many Shangpa lamas would
he train in each retreat? The answer: four. Not four thousand, four hundred, forty, or fourteen. Four. In all, eight persons lived in his small community: a vajra master (Kongtrul's teaching assistant), five retreatants (of
whom one did not meditate on the Shangpa doctrines but was responsible for the protector temple), a cook, and a woodsman.

This, then, was Kongtrul's grand vision for the continuation of the
Shangpa lineage: four lamas every three and a half years, at most.
Kongtrul's lack of worldly ambition bears some serious reflection; his sim-

plicity and evident disinterest in large institutions seem totally in keeping with the character of Niguma's lineage. No Shangpa text that I have seen gives directives to lineage holders to restrain their institution-building impulses, yet Kongtrul's minimalism is consistent with Shangpa masters before or since. What made the Shangpa tradition different from its better-known sister traditions was only its outer poverty and humility, not deficiencies in the lineage, its masters' realization, or the effectiveness of its instructions.

Another contribution Kongtrul made to the Shangpa tradition was to include its main empowerments, practice texts, and commentaries and this collection of songs in two volumes (numbers eleven and twelve) of his *Treasury of Profound Instructions*, an eighteen-volume compendium of the main instructions of Tibet's eight lineages of meditation practice. This had two effects: first, it ensured that many copies of the essential Shangpa teachings spread far and wide in Tibet, some copies of which left to India and Nepal with the refugees. Second, it placed the Shangpa teachings on the same stage as other better-known cycles of instruction. After lamas of any school received the treasury's empowerments and transmission, as many prayed to have the fortune to do, they needed to familiarize themselves with the Shangpa tradition to understand and experience what they had received before they passed it on to another generation. Kongtrul thus made a lasting place for the Shangpa tradition, where its true value could be appreciated.

In the following supplication, written to himself, Kongtrul follows a pattern he set when writing the supplication to Kyentsé Wangpo: although he included the prayers in a collection of supplications to the Shangpa masters, he makes not a single mention of the Shangpa lineage. In fact, he introduces himself as a leader of the Karma Kagyu. The Shangpa tradition did not have walls without or within to restrict it.

For the most complete picture of Jamgon Kongtrul's life and past lives, please read Richard Barron's excellent translation *The Autobiography of Jamgon Kongtrul*. This monumental work, impeccably done, is worth the effort: readers learn both of Kongtrul and his times and of the sources of modern-day tantric Buddhism.

The Melody of Ever Excellent:
A Supplication to the Illustrious Spiritual Master [Jamgon Kongtrul]
by Jamgon Kongtrul

Supreme illuminator of the Karma Kagyu doctrine,
Lord of speech, wide sea of noble qualities,
The waves of your virtuous and excellent enlightened activity are all-
pervasive.
Venerable, illustrious, excellent master, to you I pray.

You studied, reflected, and meditated upon Buddhist culture's ten
facets,
Those that stem [errors], those that nurture others, and
supplementary forms of knowledge.
Your intellect, free from attachment or impediment,
Endowed you with infinite analytic comprehension; to you I pray.

Spiritually nurtured by Great Powerful Lotus [Guru Rinpoché] and
others,
You upheld the compassionate awareness-mantras of Lord of the
Dance.
Master of enlightened activity's display to guide beings,
Sublime, illustrious master, to you I pray.

You were freed [born] within the Garuda clan of accomplished
	masters;
Karmic connections you made during previous lifetimes' training
	awoke to virtuous Teachings.
You collected within yourself the conducive circumstances for the two
	cycles [of training].
Wonderful, exemplary master, to you I pray.

You renounced harming others, along with its basis, and restrained
	your mind.
You dedicated yourself to training for others' benefit, including its
	basis.
You meditated on every form of tantric meditation's two phases—
Vajra holder endowed with the three levels of vows, to you I pray.

You relied on many tutors, outstanding scholars, and accomplished
	masters.
With diligence and superior motivation, you plunged into the seas of
	discourses and tantras.
With excellent gifts—jewels of source texts, meditation instruction,
	and pith instructions—
You dispelled your fortunate disciple's poverty; to you I pray.

The accomplished leaders who reveal treasures
According to the vajra commands of Oddiyana's omniscient master
Foretold you to be an emanation of Buddha Illuminator, Bérotsana,
And installed you [as a treasure revealer]; to you I pray.

Sublime visionaries—Victor [the Fourteenth] Karmapa and his
	spiritual heirs, Chokgyur Déchen Lingpa,
And Jamyang Kyentsé Wangpo—
Proclaimed you to be a manifestation of Taranata and Gyurmé Dorjé[61]
And honored you as a supreme teacher; to you I pray.

You preserved impartial pure vision toward the Victor's doctrine
And superior motivation to work impartially for others' good.
In your conduct of integrating whatever arose into your
	spiritual path,

You replicated holy persons' lives of freedom; to you I pray.

In the secluded retreat at Tsadra Rinchen Drak,
You planted the victory banner of single-minded meditation.
You performed the activity of teaching and composing the
    transmissions you received,
Thus spontaneously accomplishing both goals; to you I pray.

As directed clearly by the vajra scriptures,
You made sacred images of the Héruka's body, speech, and mind
To create benefit for others
For as long as the doctrine lasts; to you I pray.

By the force of my devotion and by infallible interdependent
    connections,
May I never be separated from you, illustrious, sublime spiritual
    master.
May we meet in the celestial realms' grand city
And reach Vajrasattva's supreme domain!

May your three mysteries remain as firm as vajras
And may you always make the vast and profound teachings resound,
Bringing us all to the destination of all excellent paths.
May our wishes meet with brilliant, glorious, virtuous, and
    spontaneous success!

When an individual untouched by even the faintest fraction of praise-
worthy noble qualities writes such praises to himself, this amounts to the
despicable custom of fools. However, so as not to refuse the urgent request
of the diligent meditator and holy spiritual master Péma Norbu, I, a man
with three concerns,[62] Yönten Gyatso, wrote this by my own hand. May
the doctrine's excellent virtue increase!

(*A Garland of Udumvara Flowers*, pp. 28b-29b)

Péma Norbu, the lama mentioned here as the one who asked Kongtrul to compose this supplication, graduated from the first three-year retreat at Tsadra. A reincarnate lama, he married and returned to his homeland and his medical practice. His third child was recognized as a reincarnation of Jamgon Kongtrul and became known to us as Kalu Rinpoché.

KALU RINPOCHÉ

Aᴛ ᴛʜᴇ ᴛᴜʀɴ ᴏꜰ ᴛʜᴇ twentieth century, in 1901, a Pan-American
Exhibition was held in Buffalo, New York. One of the exhibits
was an outdoor display of electric lights. It is said that people were captivated and in tears. They were looking at unbelievable, unexpected magic
and at the future, which had just taken on a new dimension. That is how
many people felt on meeting Kalu Rinpoché (1905–1989). And, yes, some
of them cried. For many of us, in disparate countries and cultures throughout the world, meeting Rinpoché did in fact deeply change the course of
our lives.

For all his impact, Rinpoché was not an imposing presence. He caused
barely a ripple when he entered a room. He was a quiet and very private
person, as we might expect from a person who spent most of his life in
retreat, either as a student or a teacher.

As extraordinary as Kalu Rinpoché seemed to us, he was in part a prod-
uct of his background as surely as the magic of electric light depends on
the convergence of many causes and conditions.

Rinpoché's father was a reincarnate lama and disciple of Jamgon
Kongtrul. He attended Jamgon Kongtrul's first three-year retreat at Tsadra,
alongside a future Shangpa lineage holder, Tashi Özer (1836–1910). The
picture Rinpoché painted of his father makes me think of Chögyam
Trungpa Rinpoché—a realized master with an impressive daily intake of
alcohol and with a number of children by a variety of women. I used to
cringe when people came to Kalu Rinpoché to complain about Trungpa
Rinpoché's behavior. Although their lifestyles were dissimilar, Rinpoché
loved his father and was devoted to him as a realized master; he had learned
at a young age to look beyond the guise of conventional or unconventional conduct.

Kalu Rinpoché was a reincarnation of Jamgon Kongtrul but was twice
saved from enthronement and all the leaden responsibilities it entailed in

old Tibet. The first time, his father refused to give his young son to the monks (from Dzokchen Monastery), who arrived at the door with offerings for the family and an invitation to the child to return to the monastery with them. The second time (later in Rinpoche's life, after his twelve-year period of retreat), it was Karmapa who predicted that although Kalu Rinpoché was Jamgon Kongtrul's rebirth, to enthrone him would limit his activity and shorten his life. Thus, Kalu Rinpoché was a nobody in terms of Tibetan Buddhist hierarchy, yet his lack of confinement to a specific institution allowed him to live his own life to the fullest. He valued his independence and wished the same for anyone close to him. His whole life long, he never rested on his laurels; instead, he always changed, gave himself new challenges, and called himself into question.

He grew up in far eastern Tibet (Kham), much closer to China than to Lhasa. His valley (close to Ganzé in eastern Tibet) is gentle and fertile, with a mighty river cutting through it. The people of his region speak a dialect distinct from that of central Tibetans; people a couple of valleys away on either side of his homeland speak and dress differently. The road through his village is a main highway linking China and Lhasa; to this day, pilgrims prostrate along it, on their way to the holy places of central Tibet. Kalu Rinpoché's background was not monocultural or monolingual, and his spiritual journey would force him to leave his homeland repeatedly. When he walked to Palpung Monastery at the age of fifteen to enter three-year retreat, he found that his language was unintelligible to the residents of his new home. He undoubtedly learned the Dergé area dialect and, later, central Tibetan, although it must be admitted that his accent when speaking his version of Lhasa Tibetan remained atrocious his whole life. These experiences, of contact with foreigners and of being a foreigner—he spent relatively few years in his homeland—served him well later in life, when he traveled the world and managed to make us feel as if he understood us completely, despite significant age and culture gaps.

Kalu Rinpoché was head of the Shangpa lineage, recognized as such by his teacher Norbu Döndrub, who dreamed of Six-Armed Protector welcoming the new lineage holder on the eve of Kalu Rinpoché's arrival at Palpung Monastery. Norbu Döndrub was the retreat master at Tsadra; he spent most of his life in seclusion. He inherited the lineage from two of Jamgon Kongtrul's disciples, Tashi Özer and Tashi Chöpel, whose final years were spent in complete renunciation. Kalu Rinpoché related that in the home the two lamas shared at Palpung, they would keep only the food they would eat that day, to better recall the imminence of death and the futility of storing food and possessions for an imaginary future. Thus, when Kalu Rinpoché inherited the Shangpa lineage, it was these examples he received, not land, buildings, riches, or followers.

Rinpoché spent his early life mastering the entire range of Buddhist meditation techniques; he sought instruction from masters of all schools. He was fiercely impartial and ecumenical, never missing an opportunity to cut through sectarian bias. Uncomfortable with a label often given him as a "Kagyu" lama as this came to be understood, he would sometimes say that he was a human department store of Buddhist meditation—you could find anything you want. Or he might say, "Yes, I'm a Kagyu lama. A Nyingma Kagyu lama, a Kadampa Kagyu lama, a Lamdré Kagyu lama, a Kagyu Kagyu lama, a Shangpa Kagyu lama," and so on. This was difficult to translate, as Rinpoché used "Kagyu" here in its literal sense, "Oral Instruction Lineage," and applied it to names most people in his audience were unaware of, the eight Tibetan schools of tantric meditation.[63] Nevertheless, it is worth repeating in this context, as Rinpoché would have resisted the label "Shangpa Kagyu lineage holder" as much as any other. He was fond of saying that there is no such thing as a "Nyingma Buddha" or a "Kagyu Buddha" or any buddha limited to a single school of Buddhism. Or to Buddhism. Rinpoché gave Bön empowerments on occasion and made a point at every new city to proclaim his faith in all spiritual traditions, both theistic and nontheistic, as paths to the same goal and as evidence of Buddha's enlightened activity.

I hope this information helps explain why, as head of the Shangpa lineage, Kalu Rinpoché did next to nothing to give the lineage public exposure. For all the public meditation centers he founded worldwide, he never established a "Shangpa Kagyu" center. For all the public talks he gave, he rarely mentioned the Shangpa lineage. Even at his home monastery in India, visitors to the old temple are greeted by statues of Buddha Boundless Light, Bodhisattva All-Seeing One, and Guru Rinpoché; the wall paintings behind his seat in the new temple are of Guru Rinpoché and his twenty-five disciples. The new temple was built not for a Shangpa conclave but to host Rinpoché's six-month transmission of Guru Rinpoché's treasure texts.

What Kalu Rinpoché did do for the Shangpa lineage was to establish three-year retreat centers where the entirety of the Shangpa meditations were passed on to new generations, which included Tibetans from all regions, as well as many Bhutanese, Sikkimese, Nepali, and Chinese meditators. From 1976, their numbers were joined by Westerners, black and white and other, men and women, ordained persons and lay persons, homosexual and heterosexual, or all or none of the above. To us all, Rinpoché was categorical: what he wanted was that his retreat teach us to become independent, that we finish with enough tools and experience in meditation not to have to depend on anyone, that we could take our meditation to its limits on our own. He did not have to add, "as I did after my retreat." Rinpoché continued his training after his three-year retreat and then spent twelve years wandering throughout the mountainous region between his homeland and Dergé, sometimes living in a tent, sometimes in caves, most often under assumed names.

Kalu Rinpoché did not encourage us to exit at the end of our retreat with the idea that we should spread the Shangpa teachings. Not one hour of his three-year retreat program was spent on teacher training; he was equally eloquent in his exclusion of study apart from a handful of meditation texts, of which this collection of songs figured prominently. Even then, he asked us to restrict our reading, even of helpful, recommended books, to three pages a day, maximum.

I believe Rinpoché's intention was to employ the Shangpa lineage only as a set of teachings that could lead individuals to enlightenment and to preserve it as a zone free from institutions, possessions, hierarchy, and politics. It is my impression that Bokar Rinpoché, Kalu Rinpoché's perfect disciple and spiritual heir, has maintained his master's style. As head of the Shangpa lineage, he does little to promote it and has yet to found a three-year retreat center for its meditations. Instead, the retreat center at his monastery is focused on the Karma Oral Instruction Lineage cycle of meditations.

The Melody of Spontaneously Accomplished Enlightened Activity: The Illustrious Spiritual Master's Supplication to His Own Life of Liberation by Kalu Rinpoché

Imbued with the glory of merit and wisdom's cultivation from
    countless eons past,
You master the phases of creation and completion and the mind of
    awakening.

You enjoy the splendor of having reached the goal for yourself and
    others—
Rangjung Kunchab, at your feet I bow.

After he attained the state of accomplishment based on the Shangpa
    Doctrines,
The illustrious and excellent reincarnate master took rebirth
    intentionally
As the tantric practitioner Lekshé Drayang.
You clearly saw him and his wife as your parents; to you I pray.

After your parents' diligent meditation during a tenth lunar-day
    festival of offering,
They dreamed that the noble master Jamgon Kongtrul
Said, "I must borrow this space" and dissolved into them.
The male and female masters from Oddiyana visibly appeared
And you entered the womb; to you I pray.

During your mother's pregnancy, her health was excellent
And she saw continual, amazing signs concerning her future child.
Within a rain of flowers on the roof and a tent of rainbow light,
Your body was born straight; to you I pray.

At birth, you had a glowing smile
And you spoke—your parents were overjoyed.
Everyone showered you with praises
And you became known as an amazing manifestation of
    enlightenment; to you I pray.

During your childhood, your virtuous habits awoke.
You were naturally intent upon renouncing this life
To live in isolated caves in the mountains,
Caring only for meditation; to you I pray.

Due to your past habits' innate power,
You felt compassion toward sentient beings' suffering in destitution or
    harmful circumstances

And devotion toward the spiritual masters with whom you had a
  connection through empowerments and teachings that brought
  you to spiritual maturity and liberation.
Your compassion and devotion moved you to tears; to you I pray.

At thirteen, you renounced home life and entered the doctrine.
At fifteen, in the midst of an assembly during the summer rains' retreat,
You fearlessly and confidently explained the three levels of vows
With a clear intellect and captivating mental power; to you I pray.

At sixteen, you entered a three-year meditation retreat
At the large retreat center founded by Kyungpo incarnate,
Lama Jamgon Kongtrul, whose life was foretold by the Transcendent
  Victor.
You were imbued with limitless faith and diligence; to you I pray.

During that time, in the presence of the noble spiritual master
  Norbu Döndrub,
Who reached the limits of meditative experience and realization,
You received infinite numbers of instructions for spiritual maturity,
  liberation, and support, from both New and Ancient traditions,
And especially the great accomplished master Kyungpo's Golden
  Doctrines,
As if the contents from one vase were poured into another; to you
  I pray.

You relied on many other learned and accomplished masters,
And you applied yourself diligently to listening, reflection, and
  meditation
On their infinite cycles of instruction in discourses, tantras, and the
  profound teachings from New and Ancient traditions.
You became a heart disciple of them all; to you I pray.

In your dreams, you met noble Lama Jamgon Kongtrul,
Who bestowed upon you the full four empowerments—
You became Lotus-Born Master and brought gods and demons
  under your control.
The *tenma* goddesses offered you their songs; to you I pray.

During your familiarization practice of the deity, you tamed *gyalgong*
    and *damsi* spirits.
Tara foretold that you would emerge victorious over obstructors'
    attacks.
You met assemblies of buddhas, bodhisattvas, and exalted elders
And made positive aspirations; to you I pray.

From the age of twenty-five, you abandoned home life
And wandered as a renunciant, content with whatever came your way.
You dedicated to the Teachings all offerings made to you in faith or
    for the dead.
King of renunciants, to you I pray.

In harmony with all, you had no attachment to anyone.
You cared equally with compassion for friends, foes, and neutral
    persons.
Unattached to sensual pleasures, you enjoyed them as vajra feast
    offerings.
King of tantric adepts, to you I pray.

You renounced harmful acts and their basis and restrained your own
    mind.
You were forever diligent in helping others, motivated by the mind
    of awakening.
You perfected your integration of tantric meditation's two phases.
Vajra holder endowed with the threefold discipline, to you I pray.

Many holy masters said you were definitely a reincarnation
Of such masters as Lodrö Tayé
And Jamgon Benza Ratna.
Transcendent victors' holy heir, to you I pray.

With myriad skillful means, such as recitation of profound formulas
    and names of buddhas,
And sacred substances, as described in the Canon and Treasures,
You placed many millions of beings, such as fish, flies, and ants,
On the path to freedom; to you I pray.

Your excellent aspiration to teach, spread, uphold, and preserve
The Victor's doctrine in general and the Shangpa lineage in particular
Revived the doctrine's spread and prolonged the life of the profound
    teachings.
Incomparable supreme guide, to you I pray.

To sublime learned and accomplished spiritual masters of every
    lineage—
Kardo, Lhatsun, Tokmé, and Lord Mokchok—
And to many great individuals, such as Bokar Tulku,
You entrusted the Shangpa Lineage; to you I pray.

In places such as glorious Jonang and Zhang-zhung,
You restored the doctrine and continued its activity.
In the presence of sacred images in central and western Tibet, you
    made a full measure of offerings with faith and positive aspirations.
You made your free and bountiful human life meaningful; to you
    I pray.

Armies of barbarians overran the Himalayan region;
By the strength of previous aspirations, you traveled to Land of the
    Exalted.
In every area, you taught and spread the Teachings.
Teacher of the excellent path to freedom, to you I pray.

You respectfully approached the sixteenth holder of the black crown,
Rangjung Rikpé Dorjé,
Who accepted you with great love as his disciple
And entrusted you with the lineage of accomplishment's doctrine; to
    you I pray.

You accepted as your disciples the Victor's sons, who took rebirth
    intentionally—
Zhamar, Situ, Jamgon, and Gyaltsab Rinpochés.
You granted them pith instructions of the four doctrines' lineage,
As if you poured the contents from one vase into another; to you
    I pray.

The sublime leader of the Victor's entire doctrine in the Himalayan
  region,
Tenzin Gyatso, gave you profound and secret instructions.
Doing as he commanded, you imparted to many holy persons
Empowerments, instruction, and profound guidance; to you I pray.

Moreover, to many incarnate masters and great individuals,
You offered instructions that led to spiritual maturity and liberation.
You created a prodigious wave of activity to serve the doctrine
  impartially.
Sun of the Victor's Teaching, to you I pray.

You offered unlimited respectful service to the doctrine of scripture
  and realization.
At major sacred sites, you made a full measure of offerings and
  positive aspirations.
You founded retreat centers for hundreds of members of the Spiritual
  Community.
Lamp of the doctrine, to you I pray.

Everywhere around Land of Jambu and in adjacent lands,
Among fortunate disciples of different races and languages,
You arrived like a swan landing upon a lake of lotus flowers.
You brought individuals to spiritual maturity and liberation; to you
  I pray.

You flew to all major continents through the sky's expanse,
And led men and women of different races and languages
To the realm of Bodhisattva Great Compassion's disciples.
Unmistaken guide on the excellent path, to you I pray.

You sent disciples, holders of the doctrine, in one hundred directions,
To raise the great banner of the ten virtues' ethical conduct to its
  highest point.
You spread spiritual cultivation and purification throughout the
  world.
Sun of the Victor's doctrine, to you I pray.

At seventy-eight years of age, you traveled throughout the world
   in every direction,
Across oceans, to major and minor continents,
To lands including thirty-five large countries,
Traveling paths traced in space; to you I pray.

You established beings within the Three Buddhist Ways, according
   to their needs.
In particular, you founded many large retreat centers.
You spread the doctrine of the six-syllable mantra throughout
   the world.
Any connection with you was meaningful; to you I pray.

Especially in the regions of Tibet and China,
You brought back to life the dying embers of the discourses' and
   tantras' doctrine.
With a prodigious wave of activity, you spread happiness throughout
   those lands.
Creator of a festival of benefit and happiness, to you I pray.

At seventy-nine years of age, in the midst of the Kagyu lineage's
   spiritual heirs
And thousands of faithful disciples from throughout the world,
You bestowed the inner tantras of the great *Treasury of Precious
   Rediscovered Teachings,*
Opening the door to spiritual maturity and liberation; to you I pray.

In brief, you merged your mind with those of your incomparable,
   sublime masters
And fulfilled their intentions,
Never wavering from the phases of creation and completion and the
   mind of awakening.
Holy heir of the Victor, to you I pray.

By this supplication's blessing,
May I enjoy the glory of both goals, for others and for myself.
May I take miraculous rebirth in the pure land of Blissful
And become a guide and leader for every sentient being.

Writing praises to oneself is the despicable practice of fools, yet many holy, great individuals, including Kardo Rinpoché, who have vast spiritual insight and have trained in pure vision, insisted that I compose this supplication. In response, I, Karma Rangjung Kunchab, wrote this, in a state of devotion and positive intention, inseparable from past spiritual masters' great wisdom.

BOKAR RINPOCHÉ[64]

by Lama Tcheuky Sengé (François Jacquemart)

B OKAR RINPOCHÉ was born on October 15, 1940, in a small village of herders on the high, dry steppes of western Tibet.

At the age of four, he was recognized as the reincarnation of Karma Shérab Özer.

Karma Shérab Özer (1890–1939) was a monk born in Kham, who at a certain moment in his life decided to undertake a pilgrimage to Lhasa. He used the opportunity to visit the Fifteenth Karmapa at his monastery, Tsurpu, not far from the Tibetan capital. Without originally intending to do so, he stayed there for several years, living in a cave close to the monastery, and became a close disciple of Karmapa. Later, he decided to continue his route westward, to make a pilgrimage to the holiest mountain in the Land of Snows, Mount Kailash. It was a journey of several months. A fortnight before arriving at his destination, he stopped at a cave that seemed to him very conducive to meditation, Cave of the Celestial Palace, close to a peak called Bokar (or Burkar), which means "White Hill." He began the practice of one thousand *nyung-né* (a day of complete fasting, alternating with a day of partial fasting).

His residence in the cave lasted three years. Once finished, he had no special wish to stay in that region, to which only a detour on a pilgrimage route had led him. Nevertheless, the local people had developed so much faith and devotion toward him that they pleaded that he remain among them and found a monastery. To sway the venerated hermit, they asked the Fifteenth Karmapa to support their request, which he gladly did. Karma Shérab Özer could do nothing but accept the will of the head of the lineage: he stayed in the region and, having become responsible for the community, founded Bokar Monastery or Bokar Gonpa. He thus became the first Rinpoché of the White Hill, the first Bokar Rinpoché.

After his death, it was thanks to indications given by the young Sixteenth

Karmapa that the young Bokar Tulku was found, a few days' walk from the monastery. The new Bokar Rinpoché was enthroned and began a traditional training at Bokar Gonpa. At the age of thirteen, he left for Tsurpu Monastery to continue his studies under the Karmapa's guidance. He stayed three years, then returned to his home monastery.

When he reached his twentieth year, Bokar Rinpoché traveled again to Tsurpu to participate in the traditional three-year retreat. Yet he had not counted on the unfolding of dramatic events. The year was 1959; Chinese troops had just invaded Tibet. He found himself caught in the tumult of Lhasa newly occupied by the Red Army; it was with difficulty that he was able to flee and return to Bokar Gonpa.

The young Rinpoché knew immediately that hell was about to engulf Tibet and that escape was imperative, even if his own region was momentarily safe. Inviting those who wished to join him, he set out for exile with a group of about seventy-five persons, accompanied by yaks, goats, and sheep. In the dead of winter, battered by snowstorms, chased by Chinese, crossing passes over sixteen thousand feet high, it took fifteen days of walking and enormous hardship to cross the border and to find sanctuary in Nepal, in the province of Mustang. Shortly thereafter, the Chinese razed Bokar Monastery.

Bokar Rinpoché stayed a while in Nepal, then journeyed to Rumtek in Sikkim (then an independent country) with the intention to live near Karmapa, who had established his residence-in-exile there. Bokar Rinpoché's wishes were only partially granted: although he was reunited with Karmapa, he found himself unable to remain with him for long. The illness of one of his elderly attendants obliged him to return to Darjeeling and to make a home for himself there.

This event marked a turning point in his life. Not knowing where to live, he was permitted to pitch a tent in the courtyard of Bhutia Bustee Temple, which happened to be the home of another lama in exile: Kalu Rinpoché. Thus fate formed the connection that would make the reincarnate lama from Bokar the closest disciple of Kham's great master. Further, this connection created a link for Bokar Rinpoché with the Shangpa lineage, since his training to that point had introduced him only to the teachings of the Karma Kagyu lineage.

A few years after of Bokar Rinpoché's arrival in Darjeeling, Kalu Rinpoché received a gift of land at Sonada, a village about nine miles away. Kalu Rinpoché soon planned to build a monastery there, as well as a three-year retreat center. Bokar Rinpoché, who had long deeply wished to accomplish such a retreat, was overjoyed at the plans and helped enthusiastically with the building work, which was done with whatever was at hand since money was scarce. The work was finished in three months and the retreat began. The program was devoted to the Shangpa lineage practices; Kalu Rinpoché himself transmitted to his disciples the empowerments and instructions. This was how during three years (1964–1967) Bokar Rinpoché joyfully absorbed the new lineage now available to him.

During the second retreat at Sonada, Bokar Rinpoché continued to live in the retreat center but did not participate in the full program of meditation. While he was free to come and go as he pleased, Kalu Rinpoché conferred on him the responsibility of guiding the new retreatants, the role of retreat master (*drubpön*). Later, however, he joined the third retreat (1971–1974) as a full participant, happy that Kalu Rinpoché had accepted his request that the retreat be focused on the Karma Kagyu lineage, which fulfilled his aspiration that had been frustrated a few years earlier by the Chinese army's occupation of Lhasa. The training he received in this retreat allowed him to later accept Karmapa's invitation to be the master of Rumtek's retreat center.

In all, Bokar Rinpoché stayed with Kalu Rinpoché for twenty-five years and accompanied him until his final breath. Here is his personal assessment of that relationship:

> To be honest, in the beginning I saw him as a good lama, whom I respected and in whom I had confidence, but I didn't have any special feelings of devotion or faith toward him. Then gradually over the years, I glimpsed his vast qualities. In fact, they were so deep that they were impossible for me to grasp right away. Yet the more I discovered them, the more my faith and devotion grew until I became convinced that Kalu Rinpoché was one with Buddha Vajra Bearer, which is to say that he had realized the nature of all things, the body of ultimate enlightenment.

On completion of his retreats at Sonada, Bokar Rinpoché planned to withdraw into a hermitage, but Kalu Rinpoché dissuaded him. He advised his disciple to continue living in a monastic setting.

In 1984, while visiting Mirik, a village near Sonada that seemed promising to him, Bokar Rinpoché had the idea of founding a small retreat center there dedicated to Kalachakra. Kalu Rinpoché approved the project and even helped with money needed for the buildings. Nevertheless, what began as a modest place for meditation practice has become over the years a burgeoning monastery. It now includes a monastic community of close to two hundred monks, a number of buildings, and a large retreat center where Karma Kagyu meditations are taught. Bokar Rinpoché plans to soon add a second retreat center dedicated to Niguma's lineage.

When we examine Bokar Rinpoché's present activity, we see clearly that his foremost focus is to assure the pure transmission of Buddhism, to give each the best that he or she can receive. He does this in the context of his monastery in India and in his monastery in Tibet, where he was able to rebuild the buildings and where a community has regrouped. He does it not only in his guidance of Mirik's retreat center, but also in such centers at Sonada and Lhawa (close to Gangtok). He does it in organizing annual seminaries for his foreign disciples, for whom he oversees a gradual and sustained training. And he does it in giving special care and attention to the education of the young Kalu Rinpoché, who is always close to him in Mirik.

No better words can be found to describe Bokar Rinpoché than those of Kalu Rinpoché. During his last visit to France, he inaugurated the Temple of a Thousand Buddhas in Bourgogne on August 30, 1987. He introduced Bokar Rinpoché, who accompanied him, to the public with these words:

> It's likely that you don't know exactly who Bokar Rinpoché is.
>
> In western Tibet there was a monastery known as Bokar Monastery, where once lived a very great lama, Karma Shérab Özer. Bokar Rinpoché is that lama's reincarnation. When tragedy erupted in Tibet, he went into exile in India, where he met me in Darjeeling. Since then he has always stayed close to me.
>
> In the beginning under my guidance, he completed impeccably the four preliminary practices. His knowledge of the Teachings was excellent.
>
> Later, we were able to establish a retreat center in Sonada; Bokar Rinpoché participated in the first three-year, three-month retreat, dedicated to the Shangpa lineage practices. Since I had transmitted every necessary empowerment and instruction, at the end of the retreat I had him become Sonada Monastery's retreat master.

He later accomplished the third retreat at Sonada, dedicated to the Karma Kagyu lineage, during which he practiced Naropa's Six Doctrines.

When a retreat center was founded at Rumtek, seat of His Holiness Karmapa, that lama as well conferred upon him the responsibility of retreat master.

Bokar Rinpoché is an extraordinary lama, perfectly accomplished both in the realm of scholarship and in the realm of meditation.

Naropa gave a prophecy to his disciple Marpa that, in his lineage, each disciple would surpass the master who preceded him. Thus, Milarepa, Marpa's direct disciple, surpassed his teacher. Likewise, Bokar Rinpoché will succeed me and be greater than I.

CONCLUSION

I FIRST MET His Holiness the Dalai Lama in Dharamsala, India, when I accompanied Bokar Rinpoché and a group of lamas who had completed a three-year retreat at Kalu Rinpoché's monastery in India. What did His Holiness want to talk about with these Shangpa lamas? He never asked about buildings or gatherings of students; what he wanted to know was, "How is your meditation on Fierce Inner Heat? Who is proficient in Lucid Dream?" I was surprised and delighted. I had expected a more mundane meeting, an occasion for monastic small talk or institutional shoptalk, but His Holiness spoke the Shangpa language.

Throughout this section on the lives of the Shangpa masters, I have dwelled at length on the subject of this lineage as an unstructured, decentralized, unorganized school. Just as a pickpocket who meets a saint sees only her pockets, when persons from organized religions (even Tibetan schools) meet Niguma, Sukasiddhi, and their spiritual children, they search for institutional structures.

I do not suggest that Shangpa lamas have rules that prohibit public teaching and empire building, yet my reading of the historical evidence is that they have not done so to date. Nondual, timeless wisdom does not change, but conditions can and do; it is entirely possible that a Shangpa master will one day give the lineage a public presence. At the moment, however, we meet the Shangpa lineage as it has been for many centuries. It presents us with a stark choice: there is only one reason to involve ourselves with it—to travel the path to enlightenment. It has no institutions, it asks no school loyalty, it provides no support, it makes no demands, it boasts no glorious past, it lays no plans for the future, and it has no impressive present, except for the simple meeting of you and your spiritual master. It's a do-nothing lineage.

Even in the enlightened Buddhist West, it is very easy to enlist people and resources in support of building projects, such as for temples or stupas—the cultivation of merit—but difficult to ask for the same invest-ment of time, money, and energy for the cultivation of wisdom, which is immaterial and insubstantial. Many seem very eager to be of help to won-derful lamas, but far less willing to help themselves attain enlightenment. Kyungpo Naljor claimed that his lineage would prove helpful whenever we meet it, at the outset of our spiritual path, at its mid-point, or as we near its destination. His lineage, now epitomized by Bokar Rinpoché, remains alive and available to Buddhists intent on buddhahood.

Jamgon Kongtrul ended his book of supplications to the Shangpa mas-ters with a supplication to all spiritual masters and with a prayer for the book itself. I include here a translation of those verses to end this book.

The Melody of Complete Success:
A General Supplication to All Spiritual Masters
by Jamgon Kongtrul

Illustrious spiritual masters, each of you Buddha incarnate,
In your great, universal compassion, come here,
Sit on a lotus and moon seat in the sky before me,
And consider me, your faithful, devoted child.

In bodies numbering the atoms in all realms, all sentient beings
    with me
Respectfully bow and pay homage to you, in body, voice, and mind.
In melodies that have oceans of musical aspects,
I praise your every form and pray to you.
To you I offer my bodies and possessions, real or imagined,
In a cloud-bank ocean of Bodhisattva Ever Excellent's offerings.
I regretfully acknowledge and vow not to repeat the bad karma,
    obscurations, faults, and downfalls—
Both natural and in relation to vows—that I have accumulated since
    time immemorial.
I sincerely rejoice in all virtues, both contaminated and
    uncontaminated,
That exist in the wheel of life and in states of transcendence.
I request you to turn the wheel of the Three Ways' Teachings,
In styles suited to the capacity of each of us, for as long as realms of
    beings exist.
I ask that your enlightened forms remain forever, as firm as vajras,
Within your unceasing, universal compassion.
I dedicate all I have done that is good in the past, present, and future,
    including this, my prayer,
That my parents and I, sentient beings whose numbers fill all space,
May quickly accomplish the body, speech, mind,
Noble qualities, and enlightened activity of the holy, illustrious
    spiritual masters.

Spiritual masters, may you nurture me with your compassion!
May I not have a moment's disrespect or misguided view!

In serving you in many ways, may I reach perfection in the three
  manners of pleasing you,
That my mind be merged as one with yours.

Noble masters, in all my lifetimes,
May I not be separated from you even for an instant.
May I see whatever you do as perfect and accept whatever you say
  as true.
May I become inseparable from my spiritual master's three mysteries.

By the force of this prayer I make in heartfelt faith,
May I alone replicate in my own life
Every life of freedom of the holy masters,
From Buddha Vajra Bearer until my root teacher.

Concluding Prayers and Colophon to
A Garland of Udumvara Flowers
by Jamgon Kongtrul

The half-burned wood of this ordinary person's speech
Has no brilliant glow of blessing,
Yet may the virtue of having written this book with devotion alone
Make me inseparable from the spiritual masters.

No noble qualities inhabit my being,
Yet a qualified spiritual master has accepted and nurtured me,
And I have received the blessings of a lineage of instruction such as
   this.

With the power of superior intention and the wish to help Buddhism
   and beings,
A fortunate person with three concerns,
Ngawang Yönten Gyatso, wrote this text
On the hillside of Tsadra Rinchen Drak,
On the occasion of the Victor's descent from the heavens [the twenty-
   second day of the ninth lunar month].

May this series of lute strings' songs,
A sea of supplications in complex melodies,
Be heard by the beings of the three worlds,
And may they raise their voices in unison with mine.

May virtue and excellence increase!

GLOSSARY

T HE FOLLOWING LISTS—of personal names; names of buddhas, deities, meditation practices, and lineages; and place names—are included to help those who might need to navigate the swelling seas of books on the subjects of Tibetan and Buddhist culture. Beside the name as it appears in the book, you will find in brackets the name as it appeared in the Tibetan text, rendered in the Wylie system. (Names mentioned in the foreword, preface, and additional material appear here in their most common rendering.)

As long as a commonly accepted transliteration scheme from Tibetan (Lhasa dialect pronunciation? Khampa dialect? Amdo?) to English (American? British? Australian?) eludes us, these lists will remain a feature of books translated from Tibetan. As for Wylie itself, even that useful tool comes in more than one version: readers may have noticed that E. Gene Smith writes "Bka' brgyud" while Matthew Kapstein prefers "bKa'-brgyud." The lists below feature another option, without hyphens or capital letters: Kagyu would be written bka' brgyud.

Personal Names

Abhaya (*a bha ya*)

Abhayakara-gupta (*'jigs 'byung sbas pa*)

Accomplishment of Bliss (*bde ba'i dngos grub*) also known as Sukasiddhi

Advayavajra (*gnyis med rdo rje*) also known as Métripa

Amogha (*a mo gha*)

Amoghani-vajra (*a mo gha ni benzra*)

Angiraja (*yan lag 'byung*)

Aryadéva (*arya de wa, 'phags pa'i lha*)

Atayavajra (*a ta ya benzra*)

Atisha (*jo bo rje*)

Bal (*'bal*)

Bardzin (*'bar 'dzin*)

Ba Tsultrim Lodrö (*rba tshul khrims blo gros*)

Beautiful Goddess of Illusion (*sgyu ma lha mdzes*)

Bépé Naljor (*sbas pa'i rnal 'byor*),
also known as Sangyé Nyentön

Bérotsana (*bee ro tsa na*)

Black One of the Charnel Ground
(*dur khrod nag po*)

Bokar Rinpoché (*'bo dkar rin po che*)

Brahmin Supreme Desire (*bram ze
mchog sred*), also known as
Saraha

Buddhagupta (*sangs rgyas sbas pa*)

Burgom Nakpo (*bur sgom nag po*)

Butön Rinchen Drub (*bu ston rin
chen grub*)

Chandragomin (*tsan dra go mi*)

Chégom (*lce sgom*)

Chögyam Trungpa Rinpoché (*chos
rgya drung pa rin po che*)

Chöjé Tönpa (*chos rje ston pa*), also
known as Sangyé Tönpa

Chökyi Sengé (*chos kyi seng ge*)

Chökyi Shérab (*chos kyi shes rab*),
also known as Sangyé Nyentön

Chokgyur Déchen Lingpa (*mchog
gyur bde chen gling pa*)

Dakgom Tsultrim Nyingpo (*dvags
sgom tshul khrims snying po*)

Daö Zhonnu (*zla 'od gzhon nu*),
also known as Gampopa

Déleg-pal (*bde legs dpal*)

Dési Sangyé Gyatso (*sde srid sangs
rgyas rgya mtsho*)

Dha Bodhisattva (*dha byang chub
sems dpa'*)

Dharma Prajna (*dharma
pradzanya*), Sanskrit for Chökyi
Shérab

Dharma Singha (*dharma singha*),
Sanskrit for Chökyi Sengé

Dilgo Kyentsé Rinpoché (*dil mgo
mkhyen brtse rin po che*)

Doctor from Dakpo (*dvags po lha
rje*), also known as Gampopa

Dolpo Sangyé (*dol po sangs rgyas*)

Dombhipa (*drom bhi pa*)

Dombi Héruka (*drom bhi he ru ka*)

Dorjé Denpa (*rdo rje gdan pa*)

Dorjé Gyal (*rdo rje rgyal*)

Dotrak Tulku Péma Trinlé (*rdo brag
sprul sku padma phrin las*)

Draktong-pa (*brag stong pa*)

Dring Yeshé Yönten (*'bring ye shes
yön gtan*)

Drogön Pakpa (*'gro mgon 'phags
pa*), also known as Pakpa Lodrö
Gyaltsen

Drokmi (*'brog mi*)

Drolwé Gönpo (*sgrol ba'i mgon po*),
also known as Taranata

Dromtön (*'brom ston*)

Drongbu Tsengö (*'brong bu tsan
rgod*)

Dro Shérab Drakpa (*'bro shes rab
grags pa*)

Drukchen Rinpoché (*'brug chen rin
po che*)

Drum Yeshé Gyaltsen (*'brum ye shes
rgyal mtshan*)

Dungkar Lozang Trinlé (*dung dkar
blo bzang phrin las*)

Fifth Dalai Lama (*rgyal dbang lnga
pa*)

Gampopa (*sgam po pa*)

Gangadhari (*gangga dha ri*)

Ghandhapa (*dril bu pa*)

Gö Lotsawa (*'gos lo tsa ba*)

Gonya Tokden (*sgo nya rtogs ldan*)

Goza Tashi Kyi (*mgo bza' bkra shis
skyid*)

Guhya-jnana (*gsang ba ye shes*)

Guna-akara (*gu na a ka ra*)

Gunaprabha (*yon gtan 'od*)

Guru Chöwang (*gu ru chos dbang*)

Guru Rinpoché (*gu ru rin po che*)

Gyagom Lekpa Gyaltsen (*rgya sgom legs pa rgyal mtshan*)

Gyalkam-pa (*rgyal khams pa*), also known as Taranata

Gyalsé Zhenpen Tayé (*rgyal sras gzhan phan mtha' yas*)

Gyaltsab (*rgyal tsab*)

Gyi Jo Dawé Özer (*gyi jo zla ba'i 'od zer*)

Gyurmé Déchen (*lo chen 'gyur med bde chen*), also known as Lochen Gyurmé Déchen

Gyurmé Dorjé (*'gyur med rdo rje*)

Harikéla (*ha ri ke la*)

Indrabodhi (*indra bo dhi*)

Jakchen Gyaltsen Büm (*'jag chen rgyal mtshan 'bum*)

Jamgon Benza Ratna (*'jam mgon benzra ratna*)

Jamgon Kongtrul (*'jam mgon kong sprul*)

Jamgon Rinpoché (*'jam mgon rin po che*)

Jampa (*byams pa*)

Jampé Dorjé (*'jam pa'i rdo rje*)

Jamyang Kyentsé Wangchuk (*'jam dbyangs mkhyen brtse dbang phyug*), also known as Kyentsé Wangchuk

Jamyang Kyentsé Wangpo (*'jam dbyangs mkhyen brtse dbang po*)

Jinpa Zangpo (*sbyin pa bzang po*)

Jnana Sagara (*pradzanya sa ga ra*)

Jungné Sengé (*'byung gnas seng ge*)

Kagyu Trinlé Shingta (*bka' brgyud phrin las shing rta*)

Kanakashri (*ka na ka shri*)

Kalu Rinpoché (*ka lu rin po che*)

Kampala (*kam pa la*)

Kardo Rinpoché (*mkhar rdo rin po che*)

Karma Ngawang Yönten Gyatso (*karma ngag dbang yon gtan rgya mtsho*), also known as Jamgon Kongtrul

Karmapa (*karma pa*)

Karma Pakshi (*karma pakshi*)

Karma Puntsok Namgyal (*karma phun tshogs rnam rgyal*)

Karma Rangjung Kunchab (*karma rang 'byung kun khyab*), also known as Kalu Rinpoché

Karma Shérab Özer (*karma shes rab 'od zer*)

Karma Tenkyong (*karma bstan skyong*)

Karma Tséten Dorjé (*karma tshe brtan rdo rje*)

Kartsi-wa (*dkar rtsi ba*)

Khampa Aseng (*khams pa a seng*)

Könkar (*dkon mkhar*), also known as Latö Könkar

Kön Konchok Gyalpo (*'khon dkon cog rgyal po*)

Kor Nirupa (*skor ni ru pa*)

Krishnacharya (*nag po spyod pa*)

Kuklung-pa (*lkugs lung pa*)

Kukuripa (*ku ku ri pa*)

Kunga (*kun dga'*)

Kunga Drolchok (*kun dga' grol mchog*)

Kunga Nyingpo (*kun dga' snying po*), also known as Taranata or Sakya Kunga Nyingpo

Kunga Ö (*kun dga' 'od*)

Kunzang Drupé Wangpo (*kun bzang grub pa'i dbang po*), also known as Kunga Drolchok

Kusulu (*ku su lu*)

Kyentsé Wangchuk (*mkhyen btse dbang phyug*)

Kyentsé Wangpo (*mkhyen brtse dbang po*), also known as Jamyang Kyentsé Wangpo

Kyergang-pa (*skyer sgang pa*), also known as Chökyi Sengé

Kyungpo Naljor (*khyung po rnal 'byor*)

Kyungyal Takyé (*khyung rgyal stag skyes*)

Lachen Gongpa Rabsal (*bla chen dgongs pa rab gsal*)

Lalitavajra (*rol pa'i rdo rje*)

Lama Norbu (*bla ma nor bu*), also known as Zhenpen Özer

Langri Öden (*glang ri 'od ldan*)

Langri Tangpa (*glang ri thang pa*)

Latö Gönpo (*la stod mgon po*), also known as Latö-pa

Latö Könkar (*la stod dkon mkhar*)

Latö Marpo (*la stod dmar po*)

Latö-pa (*la stod pa*)

Lekden Jé (*legs ldan 'byed*)

Lekshé Drayang (*legs bshad sgra dbyangs*)

Lhatsun (*lha btsun*)

Lochen Dharmashri (*lo chen dharma shri*)

Lochen Gyurmé Dorjé (*lo chen 'gyur med rdo rje*)

Lodrö Tayé (*blo gros mtha' yas*), also known as Jamgon Kongtrul

Longchenpa (*klong chen pa*)

Lord of Oddiyana (*o rgyan rje*), also known as Guru Rinpoché

Losal Gyatso-dé (*blo gsal rgya mtsho sde*), also known as Kunga Drolchok

Losal Tenkyong (*blo gsal bstan skyong*)

Lotön Dorjé Wangchuk (*lo ston rdo rje dbang phyug*)

Lotus-Born Master (*padma*), also known as Guru Rinpoché

Lumé Tsultrim Shérab (*klu mes tshul khrims shes rab*)

Luyipa (*lo hi pa*)

Machik Lapdrön (*ma gcig lab sgron*)

Madhyantika (*nyi ma'i gung*)

Mahavajra (*ma ha benza*)

Mandarava (*manda ra ba*)

Manjushri-mitra ('*jam dpal bshes gnyen*)

Marpa (*mar pa*)

Métri-gupta (*mee tri gupta*), also known as Métripa

Métripa (*mee tri pa*)

Méutön Drimé (*rme'u ston dri med*)

Milarepa (*mi la ras pa*)

Mitrayogi (*mi tra dzo gi*)

Mokchok-pa (*rmog lcogs pa*), also known as Rinchen Tsöndru

Mokchok-pa Kunga Ö (*rmog lcogs pa kun dga' 'od*), also known as Kunga Ö

Nagarjuna (*klu sgrub*)

Namgyal-wa (*rnam rgyal ba*)

Namka Naljor (*nam mkha' rnal 'byor*)

Naropa (*na ro pa*)

Narotapa (*na ro ta pa*), also known as Naropa

Ngawang Chödrak (*ngag dbang chos grags*)

Ngomshö Lachö (*ngom shod lha mchod*)

Ngultön Rinwang (*dngul ston rin dbang*)

Niguma (*ni gu ma*)

Norbu Döndrub (*nor bu don grub*)

Nyémo Zhuyé (*snye mo zhu yas*)

Nyentön-pa (*gnyan ston pa*), also
known as Sangyé Nyentön

Nyima Namgyal (*nyi ma rnam
rgyal*)

Ogyé (*'o brgyad*)

Öntön (*dbon ston*), also known as
Kyergang-pa

Orgyen Rinchen-pal (*o rgyan rin
chen dpal*)

Padampa Sangyé (*pha dam pa sangs
rgyas*)

Padmakara (*padma ka ra*)

Pakmo Drupa (*phag mo gru pa*)

Pakpa Lodrö Gyaltsen (*'phags pa blo
gros rgyal mtshan*)

Paltrul Rinpoché (*dpal sprul rin po
che*)

Pamting-pa (*pham mthing pa*)

Péma (*padma*) refers in this text to
Tai Situpa

Péma Gyurmé Gyatso (*padma 'gyur
med rgya mtsho*)

Péma Norbu (*padma nor bu*)

Prajna-varma (*shes rab go cha*)

Prince Sakara (*rgyal bu sa ka ra*)

Punyakara-gupta (*bsod nams 'byung
gnas*), also known as Dorjé Denpa

Queen of Accomplishment (*grub
pa'i rgyal mo*)

Rahula (*ra hu la; sgra gcan 'dzin*)

Rahula-gupta (*ra hu la gupta*), also
known as Rahula

Rahula-gupta-vajra (*sgra gcan 'dzin
sbas pa'i rdo rje*), also known as
Rahula

Rakshi Tsultrim Jungné (*rag shi
tshul khrims 'byung gnas*)

Ra Lotsawa Dorjé Drakpa (*rva lo
tsa ba rdo rje grags pa*)

Rangjung Dorjé (*rang 'byung rdo rje*)

Rangjung Kunchab (*rang 'byung
kun khyab*), also known as Kalu
Rinpoché

Rangjung Rikpé Dorjé (*rang 'byung
rig pa'i rdo rje*)

Ratnadévi (*rin chen lha mo*)

Ratnakara-shanti (*rin 'byung zhi ba*)

Ratna Virya (*ratna bi rya*) Sanskrit
for Rinchen Tsöndru

Réchungpa (*ras chung pa*)

Rikzin Tséwang Norbu (*rig 'dzin
tshe dbang nor bu*)

Rinchen Dorjé (*rin chen rdo rje*)

Rinchen Losal Tenkyong (*rin chen
blo gsal bstan skyong*), also known
as Losal Tenkyong

Rinchen Tashi (*rin chen bkra shis*)

Rinchen Tsöndru (*rin chen brtson
'grus*)

Rinchen Zangpo (*rin chen bzang
po*)

Ritrö-pa (*ri khrod pa*)

Rongpo Géshé Könchok Gyal (*rong
po dge bshe dkon mchog rgyal*)

Rongzom Chökyi Zangpo (*rong
zom chos kyi bzang po*)

Sakya Pandita (*sakya pan chen*)

Samantabhadri (*kun tu bzang mo*)

Samding Zhonnu Drup (*bsam lding
gzhon nu grub*)

Sangyé Nyentön (*sangs rgyas gnyan
ston*)

Sangyé Tönpa (*sangs rgyas ston pa*)

Saraha (*mda' bsnun*)

Shakyamuni (*shakya thub pa*)

Shakyashri (*shakya shri*)

Shangkar Rinchen Gyaltsen (*shangs
dkar rin chen rgyal mtshan*)

Shangpa Dugu-pa (*shangs pa gdu gu
pa*), also known as Kyungpo
Naljor

Shantidéva (*zhi ba lha*)
Shantigupta (*zhi ba sbas*)
Shantivarma (*zhi ba'i go cha*)
Shavari (*sha ba ri, ri khrod mgon*)
Shérab Répa (*shes rab ras pa*)
Shérab Sengé (*shes rab seng ge*)
Shri Jnana (*dpal ldan ye shes sde*)
Shrijnana (*dpal gyi ye shes*), also
    known as Niguma
Shrimati (*dpal gyi blo gros*)
Shuddhodana (*zas gtsang ma*)
Siddharta (*don grub*)
Situ (*si tu*)
Spiritual Hero of Accomplishment
    (*grub pa'i dpa' bo*), also known as
    Kunga Drolchok
Sukasiddhi (*su kha siddhi*)
Sukavajra (*bde ba'i rdo rje*)
Sumati (*su ma ti*)
Sumati-kirti (*su ma ti kirti*)
Sumpa Yeshé Lodrö (*sum pa ye shes
    blo gros*)
Tangtong Gyalpo (*thang stong rgyal
    po*)
Taranata (*ta ra na tha*)
Tashi Chöpel (*bkra shis chos 'phel*)
Tashi Özer (*bkra shis 'od zer*)
Tatagata Raksheeta (*ta tha ga ta
    rakshi ta*)
Tenpé Gyaltsen Palzangpo (*bstan
    pa'i rgyal mtshan dpal bzang po*),
    also known as Kyentsé
    Wangchuk
Tenzin Gyatso (*bstan 'dzin rgya
    mtsho*)
Tilopa (*te lo pa; til li*)
Tokmé (*thog med*)
Trisong Détsen (*khri srong lde btsan*)
Tsagom Penpuk-pa (*tsha sgom spen
    phug pa*)

Tsangma Shangtön (*gtsang ma
    shang ston*)
Tsöndru Sengé (*brtson 'grus seng ge*),
    also known as Sangyé Tönpa
Tsöndru Zangpo (*brtson 'grus bzang
    po*), also known as Tangtong
    Gyalpo
Tsongka-pa (*tsong kha pa*)
Tsultrim Gönpo (*tshul khrims mgon
    po*)
Tukjé Tsöndru (*thugs rje brtson 'grus*)
Tutob (*mthu stobs*)
Upa Dékar-wa (*u pa de dkar ba*)
Vairochana Raksheeta (*bee ro tsa na
    rakshi ta*)
Vimalamitra (*dri med bshes gnyen*)
Virupa (*vir wa pa*)
Virya Singha (*bi rya sing ha*)
    Sanskrit for Tsöndru Sengé
Wearer of Bone Ornaments (*rus
    pa'i rgyan can*), also known as
    Niguma
Yeshé Tsogyal (*ye shes mtsho rgyal*)
Yöngom (*yon sgom*)
Yönten Gyatso Lodrö Tayé (*yon
    gtan rgya mtsho blo gros mtha'
    yas*), also known as Jamgon
    Kongtrul
Yorpo Gyamo (*gyor po rgya mo*)
Zangyul-pa (*bzang yul pa*)
Zhamarpa (*zhva dmar pa*)
Zhangom Chöseng (*zhang sgom
    chos seng*)
Zhang Tsöndru Drakpa (*zhang brt-
    son 'grus grags pa*)
Zhenpen Özer (*gzhan phan 'od zer*)
Zhonnu Drub (*gzhon nu grub*)
Zhonnu Sengé (*gzhon nu seng ge*)

Names of Buddhas, Deities, Meditations, and Traditions

Activity Dakini (*las kyi mkha' 'gro*)

All Seeing (*kun gzigs*)

All Seeing One (*spyan ras gzigs, Avalokiteshvara*)

Ancient Instruction Lineage (*rnying ma*)

Atiyoga (*shin tu rnal 'byor*)

Awakened Protector (*ye shes mgon po*), also known as Six-Armed Protector

Babrom Kagyu (*'bab rom bka' brgyud*)

Binder of the Wheel (*'khor lo sdom pa*), also known as Wheel of Supreme Bliss

Blissful Protector (*bde ba'i mgon po*)

Body of Manifest Enlightenment (*sprul pa'i sku, nirmanakaya*)

Body of Perfect Rapture (*longs spyod rdzogs pa'i sku, sambhogakaya*)

Body of Ultimate Enlightenment (*chos kyi sku, dharmakaya*)

Boundless Light (*'od dpag med, Amitabha*)

Brahma (*tshangs pa*)

Buddha's Word as Instruction Lineage (*bka' gdams pa*)

Central Channel's Nectar (*dbu ma'i bdud rtsi*)

Chambhaka (*tsam bha ka*)

Circle of Emanation at the Navel (*lte ba'i sprul 'khor*)

Circle of Space (*nam mkha'i thig le*)

Clear Light (*'od gsal*)

Dakpo Kagyu (*dvags po bka' brgyud*)

Damsi (*dam sri*)

Dark-Red Fearsome Vajra (*dmar nag rdo rje 'jigs byed*)

Deathless Mind (*sems 'chi med*)

Drigung Kagyu (*'bri gung bka' brgyud*)

Drukpa Kagyu (*'brug pa bka' brgyud*)

Eight Great Sacred Circles (*sgrub chen brgyad*)

Essence of the Sky (*nam mkha'i snying po*)

Ever-Excellent Radiant Awareness, King of Luminosity (*kun bzang rig snang 'od kyi rgyal po*)

Familiarization and Accomplishment (*bsnyen sgrub*)

Fearsome Vajra (*rdo rje 'jigs byed, Vajra Bhairava*)

Fierce Inner Heat (*gtum mo*)

Fiery Lord Protector (*'bar ba'i mgon po*)

Five Golden Doctrines (*gser chos lnga*)

Five Tantras' Deities (*rgyud sde lha lnga*)

Five Topknots (*zur phud lnga*)

Four Classes of Great Kings (*rgyal chen rigs bzhi*)

Four Seats (*gdan bzhi*)

Garuda (*khyung*)

Gentle Melody (*'jam dbyangs, Manjughosha*)

Gentle Splendor (*'jam dpal, Manjushri*), also known as Gentle Melody

Glorious Lotus (*padma'i dpal*)

Glory of Immaculate Space (*dri med nam mkha'*)

Great Compassion (*thugs rje chen po*)

Great Completion (*rdzogs pa chen po*)

Great Mother (*yum chen mo*, also known as *Prajnaparamita*)

Great Powerful Lotus (*padma dbang chen*), also known as Guru Rinpoché

Great Seal (*phyag rgya chen po*, *Mahamudra*)

Great Seal Amulet Box (*phyag chen ga'u ma*)

Gyalgong (*rgyal 'gong*)

Héruka (*khrag 'thung*)

Holder of Conduct (*spyod 'chang*)

Horse Neck (*rta mgrin, Hayagriva*)

Illuminator (*rnam par snang mdzad, Vairochana*)

Illusory Body (*sgyu lus*)

Immortal Body (*lus 'chi med*)

Immutable (*mi 'khrugs pa*)

Infallible Mind (*sems phyugs med*)

Infinite Life (*tshe dpag med, Amitayus*)

Integrated Practice of the Four Deities (*lha bzhi dril sgrub*)

Intermediate State (*bar do*)

Invincible Protector (*mi pham mgon po*), also known as Loving-Kindness

Jewel Dakini (*rin chen mkha' 'gro*)

Kalachakra (*dus kyi 'khor lo*)

Karma Kagyu (*karma bka' brgyud*)

King of Diligence (*birya ra dza*)

Kshétrapala (*kshé tra pa la*)

Lake-Born Vajra Bearer (*mtsho skyes rdo rje 'chang*)

Liberation from the Four Faults (*skyon bzhi rang grol*)

Limitless Light (*snang ba mtha' yas*)

Lion-Faced Dakini (*seng ge'i gdong can*)

Lord of Death (*'chi bdag*)

Lord of Secrets (*gsang ba'i bdag po*)

Lord of the Dance (*gar gyi dbang phyug*)

Lotus Bliss (*padma bde*)

Lotus Dakini (*pad ma mkha' 'gro*)

Lotus Skull-Garlanded Adept (*padma thod phreng rtsal*)

Loving-Kindness (*byams pa, Maitreya*)

Lucid Dream (*rmi lam*)

Mahakala (*nag po chen po*)

Mahamaya (*sgyu 'phrul chen mo*)

Marpa Instruction Lineage (*mar pa bka' brgyud*)

Marwa Kagyu (*smar ba bka' brgyud*)

Matrix of Mystery (*gsang ba 'dus pa, Guhyasamaja*)

Medicine Buddha (*sman bla*)

Melodious Goddess (*dbyangs can ma, Sarasvati*)

Oral Instruction Lineage (*bka' brgyud*)

Pacification of Suffering (*zhi byed*)

Pakdrub Kagyu (*phag grub bka' brgyud*)

Path and Result (*lam 'bras*)

Pékar (*dpe dkar*)

Phase of Completion (*rdzogs rim*)

Phase of Creation (*bskyed rim*)

Powerful Stealer of Strength (*stobs 'phrog dbang po*)

Purifying Ah of Inner Space (*a'i stong ra*)

Selfless One (*bdag med ma*)

Severance (*chö*)

Shampo (*sham po*)

Shangpa Instruction Lineage (*shangs pa bka' brgyud*)

Shukseb Kagyu (*shug gseb bka' brgyud*)

Six Applications Lineage (*sbyor ba yan lag drug*)

Six-Armed Awakened Protector (*yes shes mgon po phyag drug pa*)

Six-Armed Protector (*phyag drug pa*)

Six Doctrines (*chos drug*)

Slayer of Lord of Death (*gshin rje'i gshed, Yamantaka*)

Son of the Renowned One (*rnam thos sras, Vaishravana*)

Stable Wheel (*btan pa'i 'khor lo*), also known as Gentle Melody

Supreme Bliss (*bde mchog*), also known as Wheel of Supreme Bliss

Swift Awakened Protector (*myur mdzad ye shes mgon po*), also known as Six-Armed Protector

Taklung Kagyu (*stag lung bka' brgyud*)

Tanglha (*thang lha*)

Tara (*sgrol ma*)

Tenma (*bstan ma*)

Three Aspects of the Unborn (*skyes med rnam gsum*)

Three Modes of Natural Repose (*rang babs rnam gsum*)

Three Paths of Integration (*lam khyer rnam gsum*)

Tögal (*thod rgal*)

Transference of Consciousness ('*pho ba*)

Tropu Kagyu (*khro phu bka' brgyud*)

Tsalpa Kagyu (*tshal pa bka' brgyud*)

Unheated (*ma dros pa*)

Union with the Spiritual Master's Mind (*bla ma'i rnal 'byor*)

Universal Compassion (*snying rje mkha' khyab*)

Unmoving (*mi gyo ba*)

Vajra Bearer (*rdo rje 'chang, Vajradhara*)

Vajra Creator of Delight (*dgyes pa rdo rje, Hévajra*)

Vajra Dakini (*rdo rje mkha' 'gro*)

Vajra Queen (*rdo rje btsun mo*)

Vajrasattva (*rdo rje sems dpa'*)

Vajra Sow (*rdo rje phag mo, Vajravarahi*)

Vajra Yogini (*rdo rje rnal 'byor ma*)

Varuna (*wa ru na*)

Vase Breathing (*bum pa can*)

Vase of Ambrosia (*bdud rtsi bum pa*)

Vishnu (*khyab 'jug*)

Vishnu-raja (*bi ka ra dza*)

Wheel of Supreme Bliss ('*khor lo bde mchog, Chakrasamvara*)

Wheel of Time (*dus kyi 'khor lo*), also known as Kalachakra

Wisdom Star-Gate (*ye shes skar khung*)

Yazang Kagyu (*gya' bzang bka' brgyud*)

Yelpuk Kagyu (*yel phug bka' brgyud*)

Place Names

Bhiraji (*bhi ra dzi*) (India)

Black Mountain (*ri nag po*) (India)

Blazing Skeletons (*keng rus me 'bar*)

Blissful (*bde ba can*) (pure land)

Brahmaputra River (*lo hit*)

China (*ma ha tsi na, rgya [nag]*)

Cool Grove (*gsil ba'i tshal*) (India)

Cool Province (*bsil ldan ljongs*)

Copper Colored Mountain (*zang mdog dpal gyi ri bo*) (pure land)

Daklha-Gampo Monastery (*dvags lha sgam po*)

Dakpo (*dvags po*)

Damido (*'gro lding*)

Daryul Draknak (*dar yul brag nag*)

Dawa (*zla ba*)

Dergé (*sde dge*)

Dévikotri (*de bi ko tri*)

Dingma (*sdings ma*)

Do-Kham (*mdo khams*)

Dola Mébar (*rdo la me 'bar*)

Dorjé Trakgön Monastery (*rdo rje brag dgon*)

Dzokchen Monastery (*rdzogs chen*)

Élabhisha (*e la bhi sha*) (India)

Free from Affliction (*mya ngan bral ba*) (pure land)

Gangkar (*gangs dkar*)

Gangkar Da (*gangs dkar mda'*)

Ganzé (*dkar mdzes*)

Gégyé Jéma Ling Temple (*dgé rgyas bye ma gling*)

Glorious Mountain (*dpal gyi ri*) (India)

Gulang (*gu lang*)

Gyalzang (*rgyal bzang*)

Gyédé Tang (*rgyas sde thang*)

Hall of Excellent Teachings (*chos bzang lha'i mdun sa*)

Heart of Great Awakening (*snying po byang chub chen po*) alternate version of *byang chub snying po*, name of Bodhgaya, India

Heaven of the Thirty-Three (*sum cu rtsa gsum*)

Highest Pure Land (*'og min*)

Hundred Springs (*chu mig rgya rtsa*) (Nepal)

Jalandhara (*dza lan dha ra*) (India)

Jokang (*jo khang*)

Jonang Monastery (*jo nang*)

Joyful Heaven (*dga' ldan*)

Joyous (*mngon dga'*) (pure land)

Kachung Temple (*ka chung lha khang*)

Kalingka (*ka ling ka*)

Kamataru (*ka ma ta ru*)

Kamsum Zangkang Ling Temple (*khams gsum zings khang gling*)

Karek (*mkha' reg*)

Kashmir (*kha che'i yul*) (India)

Kyergang (*skyer sgang*)

Land of Jambu (*dzam bu gling*)

Land of the Exalted (*'phags yul*) (India)

Lapis Light (*bee dur ya snang ba*) (pure land)

Latö Balung (*la stod sba lung*)

Latö Jang (*la stod byang*)

Lhapu (*lha phu*)

Lhasa (*lha sa*)

Li (*li*)

Lowo (*glo bo*)

Lowo Möntang Plain (*glo bo smon thang*)

Lubuk (*klu sbugs*)

Luminous (*'od ldan*) (pure land)

Magadha (*ma ga*) (India)

Malabar (*ma la bar*) (India)

Mangyul (*mang yul*)

Medicinal Sandalwood Grove (*tsan-dan sman gyi nags tshal*) (India)

Minling Monastery (*smin gling*)

Mirik (*mi rigs*) (India)

Mokchok (*rmog lcogs*)

Mokchok Cliff (*rmog lcogs kyi brag*)

Mongolia (*hor* or *sog*)

Morchak-déu (*mor chag de'u*)

Mount Kailash (*gangs te se*)

Mount Malaya (*ri ma la ya*) (India)

Nalanda Monastery (*na lenda*) (India)

Néling (*nas gling*)
Nésar (*gnas gsar*)
Nyémo (*gnye mo*)
Oddiyana (*o rgyan yul*) (India)
Palpung Monastery (*dpal spung*)
Penpo (*'phan po*)
Penyul Jokpo (*'phan yul 'jog po*)
Potala (*po ta la*)
Priyangku (*pri yang ku*)
Radiant (*'od phro can*) (pure land)
Radreng Monastery (*rva sgreng*)
Ramoché (*rva mo ché*)
Rigong (*ri gong*)
Rinpung (*rin spung*)
Sakya Monastery (*sa skya*)
Samding (*bsam sdings*)
Samten Cliff (*bsam gtan brag*)
Samyé Monastery (*bsam yas*)
Satsa Monastery (*sa tsatsha*)
Shambhala (*sham bha la*)
Shang (*shangs*)
Shang-pu (*shangs phu*)
Shri Jala Sarvata (*shri dza la sarva ta*)
Sosa Park (*so sa gling*) (India)
Sravasti (*mnyam ldan*) (India)
Strewn Flowers (*me tog bkram pa*) (pure land)

Takten Damchö Ling (*rtag brtan dam chos gling*)
Tarpa Ling (*thar pa gling*)
Tashi Lhunpo (*bkra shis lhun po*)
Three-Period City (*skabs gsum grong*)
Tradruk (*khra 'brug*)
Tsadra Rinchen Drak (*tsa 'dra rin chen brag*)
Tsang (*gtsang*)
Tsurpu Monastery (*mtshur phu*)
Vajra Seat (*rdo rje gdan*) (India)
Vikramashila Monastery (India)
Willow Leaf (*lcang lo can*), alakavati) (pure land)
Yardrok Taklung (*yar 'brog stag lung*)
Yarlung (*yar lung*)
Yoru (*gyo ru*)
Zangling (*zangs gling*)
Zhalu Monastery (*zhva lu*)
Zhang-zhang (*zhang zhang*) alternate (incorrect?) spelling for Zhang-zhong
Zhang-zhong (*zhang zhong*)
Zhigatsé (*gzhis ka rtse*)

BIBLIOGRAPHY

Publications in Tibetan:

The Collection of Shangpa Masters' Biographies (*shangs pa bka' brgyud bla rabs kyi rnam thar*). Lhasa: Tibetan Shin-ha Bookstore, 1996. This is a different version from that contained in the following collection.

The Collection of Shangpa Masters' Biographies: A Garland of Gold (*shangs pa gser phreng*). Volume 1 of *The Collection of Shangpa Kagyu Texts*; Sonada, India: Samdrup Darjyé Ling Monastery. (n.d.) This collection is a reprint of the Palpung Monastery edition of the Shangpa masters' life stories, sponsored by Kalu Rinpoché.

Chöying Tobden Dorjé. *The Treasury of Discourses and Tantras* (*mdo rgyud rin po che'i mdzod*). Lama Tarchin Rinpoché's private collection.

Dungkar Lozang Trinlé. *The Collected Works of Dungkar Lozang Trinlé* (*dung dkar blo bzang 'phrin las kyi gsung rtsom phyogs bsgrigs*). Beijing: China's Tibetan Cultural Press, 1997.

Kunga Drolchok. *The Autobiography of Kunga Drolchok* (*zhen pa rang grol gyi lhug par brjod pa'i gtam skal bzang dad pa'i shing rta 'dren byed*). New Delhi: Tibet House, 1982.

Jamgon Kongtrul. *The Biography of Jamyang Kyentsé Wangpo* (*rje btsun bla ma thams cad mkhyen cing gzigs pa 'jam dbyangs mkhyen brtse'i dbang po kun dga' bstan pa'i rgyal mtshan dpal bzang po'i rnam thar mdor bsdus pa ngo mtshar au dumba ra'i dga' 'tshal*). *The Collected Works of Jamgon Kongtrul*, vol. 10, pp. 1-236. Katmandu: Shechen Publications, 2002.

————. *A Catalog of Shangpa Texts: The Beryl Key* (*dpal ldan shangs pa bka' brgyud kyi gser chos rin po che'i mdzod yongs su phye ba'i dkar chag bedurya'i lde'u mig*) *The Collected Works of Jamgon Kongtrul*, Vol. 6, pp. 619-670. Katmandu: Shechen Publications, 2002.

————. *The Flower of Faith* (*rje btsun rin po che'i rnam thar gsol 'debs kha skong dad pa'i me tog). The Treasury of Profound Instructions*, vol. 12, pp. 453-456. Katmandu: Shechen Publications, 1999.

―――. *A Garland of Udumvara Flowers: Supplications to the Lives of a Wonderful Lineage of Jewels, the Masters of the Glorious Shangpa Instruction Lineage (dpal ldan shangs pa bka' brgyud kyi ngo mtshar rin chen brgyud pa'i rnam thar gsol 'ba 'debs pa u dumba ra'i phreng ba). The Treasury of Profound Instructions*, vol. 12, pp. 389-448. Katmandu: Shechen Publications, 1999.

―――. *The History of the Sources of the Profound Treasures and Treasure Revealers (zab mo'i gter dang gter ston grub thob ji ltar byon pa'i lo rgyus mdor bsdus bkod pa rin chen bedurya'i phreng ba). The Treasury of Rediscovered Teachings*, vol. 1, pp. 291-760. Paro, Bhutan: Ngodup and Sherab Drimay, 1976.

―――. *An Impartial History of the Sources of Spiritual Instruction (ris med chos kyi 'byung gnas mdo tsam smos pa blo gsal mgrin pa'i mdzes rgyan). The Collected Works of Jamgon Kongtrul*, Vol. 5, pp. 859-890. Katmandu: Shechen Publications, 2002.

―――. *A Sea of Blessing: Songs of the Shangpa Masters (dpal ldan shangs pa bka' brgyud kyi do ha rdo rje'i tshig rkang dang mgur dbyangs phyogs gcig tu bsgrigs pa thos pa don ldan byin rlabs rgya mtsho). The Treasury of Profound Instructions*, vol. 12, pp. 463-560. Katmandu: Shechen Publications, 1999.

―――. *Shangpa Preliminary Practices (ye shes mkha' 'dro ni gu las brgyud pa'i zab lam gser chos lnga'i sngon rjes ngag 'don rdo rje'i tshig rkang byin rlabs 'od 'bar). The Treasury of Profound Instructions*, Vol. 11, pp. 29-44. Katmandu: Shechen Publications, 1999.

Koshul Drakpa Jungné and Gyalwa Lozang Kédrup. *The Compendium of Names of Himalayan Scholars and Adepts (gangs can mkhas grub rim byon ming mdzod)*. Xining?: Ching-Hai People's Press, 1992.

Lochen Gyurmé Déchen. *The Biography of Tangtong Gyalpo (thang rgyal rnam thar)*. Chengdu: Sichuan People's Press, 1982.

Minyak Gönpo. *Concise Biographies of Himalayan Master-Scholars*. Chinghai: China's Tibetan Cultural Press, 1996.

Taranata. *The Autobiography of Taranata (rgyal khams pa ta ra na thas bdag nyid kyi rnam thar nges par brjod pa'i deb gter shin tu zhib mo ma bcos lhug pa'i rtogs brjod)*. Paro, Bhutan: Ngodrup and Sherab Drimay, 1978.

―――. *A Mine of Jewels, The Amazing and Excellent Lives of the Sevenfold Transmission Lineage Masters (bka' babs bdun ldan gyi brgyud pa'i rnam thar ngo mtshar rmad du byung ba rin po che'i khungs lta bu'i gtam). The Collected*

Works of Taranata, vol. ?, pp. 551-690. Leh: C. Namgyal and Tsewang Taru, 1985.

————. *A Supplement to the History of the Lineages (khrid brgya'i brgyud pa'i lo rgyus kha skong).* The Treasury of Profound Instructions, vol. 18, pp. 99-116. Katmandu: Shechen Publications, 1999.

————. *The Tree of Faith (dpal ldan bla ma dam pa'i rnam par thar pa dad pa'i ljon shing).* The Treasury of Profound Instructions, vol. 11, pp. 449-452. Katmandu: Shechen Publications, 1999.

Tashi Chöpel. *The Last Days of the Life of Jamgon Kongtrul (rje kun gzigs 'jam mgon ngag gi dbang phyug yon tan rgya mtsho'i zhabs kyi 'das rjes kyi rnam par thar pa ngo mtshar nor bu'i snang ba).* The Collected Works of Jamgon Kongtrul, vol. 10, pp. 739-784. Katmandu: Shechen Publications, 2002.

Tübten Chödar. *Catalog of the Nyingma Tantras (rnying ma rgyud 'bum gyi dkar chag gsal ba'i me long).* Beijing: People's Press, 2000.

Tübten Puntsok. *The Ruby Key: A General History of Tibet (bod kyi lo rgyus spyi don padma ra' ga'i lde mig).* Chengdu, China: Sichuan People's Press, 1996.

Publications in English:

Barron, Richard, translator. *The Autobiography of Jamgon Kongtrul.* Ithaca, N.Y.: Snow Lion Publications, 2003.

Chang, Garma C. C., translator. *The Hundred Thousand Songs of Milarepa.* Boston: Shambhala Publications, 1999.

Chattopadhyaya, Alaka. *Atisha and Tibet.* Delhi: Motilal Banarsidass, 1999.

Dorje, Gyurme. *Tibet Handbook.* 2d ed. Bath, England: Footprint Handbooks, 1999.

Gö Lotsawa Zhonnu Pal. *The Blue Annals.* Translated by George N. Roerich. New Dehli: Motilal Banarsidass, 1978.

Harding, Sarah, translator. *Machik's Complete Explanation.* Ithaca, N.Y.: Snow Lion Publications, 2003.

Kapstein, Matthew. "The Shangs-pa bKa'-brgyud: An Unknown Tradition of Tibetan Buddhism," in *Tibetan Studies in Honour of Hugh Richardson: Proceedings of the International Seminar on Tibetan Studies.* Edited by Michael Aris and Aung San Suu Kyi. Warminster, England: Aris and Phillips, 1980.

Kongtrul, Jamgon. *Jamgon Kongtrul's Retreat Manual.* Translated by Ngawang Zangpo. Ithaca, N.Y.: Snow Lion Publications: 1994.

Lama Kunga Rinpoché and Brian Cutillo, translators. *Drinking the Mountain Stream.* Boston: Wisdom Publications, 1995.

Nalanda Translation Committee. *The Rain of Wisdom.* Boston: Shambhala Publications, 1989.

Patrul Rinpoché. *The Words of My Perfect Teacher.* Translated by Padmakara Translation Group. San Francisco: HarperCollins, 1994.

Ray, Reginald A. *Indestructible Truth: The Living Spirituality of Tibetan Buddhism.* Boston: Shambhala Publications, 2000.

Ricard, Matthieu, translator. *The Life of Shabkar.* Albany: State University of New York Press, 1994.

Smith, E. Gene. *Among Tibetan Texts.* Boston: Wisdom Publications, 2001.

Stearns, Cyrus. *The Buddha from Dolpo.* Albany: State University of New York Press, 1999.

Taranata. *Taranatha's History of Buddhism in India.* Translated by Lama Chimpa and Alaka Chattopadhyaya. Delhi: Motilal Banarsidass, 1997.

Tsang Nyön Heruka. *The Life of Marpa the Translator.* Translated by Nalanda Translation Committee. Boston: Shambhala, 1999.

Zangpo, Ngawang. *Sacred Ground.* Ithaca, N.Y.: Snow Lion Publications, 2001.

NOTES

1 An edited version of this article appeared as "The Shangs pa Bka' brgyud Tradition," Chapter 4 in E. Gene Smith, *Among Tibetan Texts* (pp. 53-57).

2 Matthew Kapstein, "The Shangs-pa bKa'-brgyud: An Unknown Tradition of Tibetan Buddhism," in *Tibetan Studies in Honour of Hugh Richardson*, p. 140.

3 The Shangpa tradition has a series of source texts in verse, called vajra verses. Kongtrul included only this one in his collection, although he gives it prominent mention in the book's subtitle: "*Collection of Vajra Verses and Melodious Songs of Realization.*"

4 Throughout this text, where the gender of a spiritual master, deity, protector, buddha, or bodhisattva is not specified, masculine pronouns are used in the absence of a gender-neutral alternative in English. Personal pronouns of either gender (or of *any* person, singular or plural) rarely appear in the original Tibetan text.

5 These last two lines, like a number of pairs of lines in this song, juxtapose opposites. "The path of the messenger" refers to the practice that corresponds to the third empowerment, that of wisdom engendered by an embodiment of transcendent knowledge. Métripa's practice of this incurred his expulsion from the monastery. To "focus on the tip of the nose" can refer to tranquillity meditation at the outset of the Buddhist path.

6 The sound Iti (*eetee*), which closes many songs in this collection, is used to indicate that the words must not be altered. According to Steven Rhodes, this word in Sanskrit closes a quote.

7 According to Bokar Rinpoché, *brjod med* in the text should be read as *brjed med*.

8 The Lhasa edition of *The Collection of Shangpa Masters' Biographies* (p. 39) has *dman ma* (old), not *smas ma* (wounded).

9 The first name here, Dorjé Denpa, is the common Tibetan name for this master; Punyakara-gupta is his monastic name in Sanskrit. Although Tibetans commonly translate Indian names into Tibetan (for example, "Nagarjuna" is usually referred to as "Ludrub"), Dorjé Denpa is alone among Kyungpo Naljor's main teachers to be most often referred to with a Tibetan name, a convention I have followed in this book.

10 According to Bokar Rinpoché, these are the four main philosophical systems— Vaibashika, Discourse, Mind Only, and Middle Way.

11 The three versions of this song available to us—*A Sea of Blessing*, p. 10b.; *The Collection of Shangpa Masters' Biographies* (Sonada edition), pp. 77-78; *The Collection of Shangpa Masters' Biographies* (Lhasa edition), p. 14)—diverge considerably in these last four verses. This passage from a modern Tibetan history has informed my reading of them:

[Kyungpo Naljor] lived for one hundred and fifty years and taught Buddhism widely. To summarize his style of teaching, he gathered all subjects into three graded paths—explanation, debate, and meditative practice.

The graded path of explanation employs the discourses and their treatises and the tantras and their commentaries to correctly present the Way of Characteristics' four great philosophical systems and the Vajra Way's four great classes of tantra.

In the graded path of debate, it could be said that he had studied such texts as *The Seven Treatises on Valid Cognition* in the custom of dialecticians of later times, yet he mainly employed earlier forms of valid cognition—to use the four proofs to define the three characteristics and, within valid cognition, to differentiate among direct perception, logical inference, and belief to reply fully to objections.

The graded path of meditative practice comprises the entire range of experiential cultivation in the Way of the Transcendent Perfections, which employs the causes [of awakening as the path] and the Vajra Way, which employs the result [of awakening as the path]. [Kyungpo Naljor] would teach these by means of pith instructions that encapsulated how to engage in experiential cultivation using the common and special vital points of the subject of awakening's thirty-seven aspects.

[Kyungpo Naljor] was exceedingly kind in thus improving Tibetan methods of education and reflection. (*The Ruby Key: A General History of Tibet*, vol. I, pp. 468-469).

This passage would seem to support Matthew Kapstein's statement, "In brief it is clear that the original *Shangs-pa* teaching was not merely a vast collection of miscellaneous doctrines, but was also a complete system embracing all major aspects of Buddhist study and practice." ("The Shangs-pa bKa'-brgyud", p. 140.)

The passage from *The Ruby Key* echoes a passage from Kongtrul's *A Catalog of Shangpa Texts: The Beryl Key*, pp. 5b-6a.

12 According to Bokar Rinpoché, the three rains are of physical comfort, verbal power, mental realization; the three gatherings are of humans, wealth, and food.

13 The names of Kyungpo Naljor's six heart sons and their respective specialties in meditation are listed in the supplication to Kyungpo Naljor by Jamgon Kongtrul, on page 254.

14 There would seem to be a line missing in the original text at this point.

15 According to Bokar Rinpoché, the three characteristics are to hold a lineage, to have experience in meditative practice, and to maintain an altruistic, loving attitude.

16 According to Bokar Rinpoché, the three facets of spontaneous presence are the basis, path, and result.

17 According to Bokar Rinpoché, *yid shes* in the text should be read *ye shes* (wisdom).

18 "Supplementary confusion" is a common term used in the Six Doctrines to refer to dreams, which add experiences of confusion at night to add to our full share during the day.

19 The text's *nang* has been read as *rang* (intrinsic).

20 According to Bokar Rinpoché, the five supreme branches refer to stages of the phase of creation.

21 An *udumvara* flower appears only during a buddha's life.

22 According to Bokar Rinpoché, the three syllables referred to here are *Om Ah Hung*.

23 This is a play on the word "garuda" (*kyungpo* in Tibetan), which is both a bird's name and Kyungpo Naljor's clan name.

24 According to Bokar Rinpoché, Péma (Lotus) refers here to Tai Situpa.

25 I find it impossible to improve upon the translatation of this song by Richard Barron (Chökyi Nyima), and I appreciate his kind permission to include it here.

26 According to Lama Gyaltsen, Kalu Rinpoché's longtime attendant, Kalu Rinpoché used many names to conceal his identity to visitors while he lived in retreat in the mountains. Lodrö was among those names.

27 Lama Tcheuky Sengé and I were residents of this three-year retreat in 1982 when Bokar Rinpoché visited and sang this song, marking our first meeting with him.

28 Niguma's mother's name and her birth name are missing from the Tibetan woodblock edition, which is in error. I found the correct version in a handwritten copy in the University of Honolulu library.

29 Madhyantika means "midday" in Sanskrit; here it refers to the foremost of a group of Ananda's followers, who attained the state of foe-destroyer (arhat) at midday. A short account of Madhyantika's blessing of Kashmir can be found in *Taranatha's History of Buddhism in India*, Chapter 3, pp. 29-33.

30 See Sarah Harding's translation of Machik Lapdrön's life and teachings, *Machik's Complete Explanation* (Ithaca, N.Y.: Snow Lion Publications, 2003).

31 This book has been translated into English by David Templeman as *The Seven Instruction Lineages*, but its present edition suffers from singularly poor design and layout, which makes its content difficult to ingest.

32 This is according to Gyalsé Tulku, who heard the story from his teacher, a *khenpo* (professor) at Minling Monastery.

33 Here and elsewhere in this book, names of lineages of meditation teachings appear in English, such as Ancient Instruction Lineage and Buddha's Word as Instruction Lineage, whereas names of Tibet's Buddhist institutions (monastic, educational, or meditative) appear in Tibetan, such as Nyingma and Kadampa. This is far from an ideal proposal, yet not to introduce a distinction between a Tibetan container (the institution) and its Indian content (a lineage of meditation practice, for example) seems to me very risky.

34 Dungkar Lozang Trinlé considers the end of this period to be 1231, the year the Yuan dynasty was founded in China. See *The Collected Works of Lozang Trinlé*, p. 528.

35 Assigning a single set of dates for Kyungpo Naljor seems impossible. *The Great Tibetan-Chinese Dictionary* (p. 302) and *The Compendium of Names of Himalayan Scholars and Adepts* (p. 218) give them as 978–1127; *The Collection of Shangpa Masters' Biographies* (p. 1) gives them as 990–1140. These three sources are works of modern Tibetan historians. Gö Zhonnu Pal (1392–1481), author of *The Blue Annals*, situates Kyungpo Naljor's birth in 1086 and remarks at the end of the account of his life, "His statement that he had lived for 150 years recalls that of Dampa Sangyé who, when asked on his coming to Dingri by the Lord Khri-pa: 'How old are you?' replied: 'My age is 99990!' Such symbolic utterances by saintly men should not be considered as lies." (p. 733)

36 It is easy to see why the Shangpa Kagyus are confused for yet-another-Kagyu lineage—there were so many of them! The year 1158 saw the foundation of the Pakdrub Kagyu; 1160, the Babrom Kagyu; 1167, the Marwa Kagyu; 1171, the Yelpuk Kagyu; 1171 again, the Tropu Kagyu; 1175, the Tsalpa Kagyu; 1179, the Drigung Kagyu; 1180, the Taklung Kagyu; 1181, Shukseb Kagyu; 1189, the Karma Kagyu; 1193, the Drukpa Kagyu; and 1206, the Yazang Kagyu. The "four great schools"—Dakpo, Pakdrub, Babrom, and Karma—were founded by Gampopa or by his students; the "lesser eight," by students of Gampopa's disciple, Pakmo Drupa. The lesser eight are those listed here, with the exception of the Tsalpa Kagyu, founded by Zhang Tsöndru Drakpa, a student of Gampopa's disciple, Dakgom Tsultrim Nyingpo.

37 Langri Tangpa (1054–1123) founded Langtang Monastery in 1093. He is mentioned in Patrul Rinpoché's *The Words of My Perfect Teacher* (p. 99) as an exemplary meditator who never forgot others' sufferings.

38 These figures for Kyungpo Naljor's teachers are often repeated. Some have taken the "four root spiritual masters" and the "two wisdom dakinis" to refer to a total of six main teachers and have then struggled to name the six. It should be clear from Kyungpo Naljor's own words, quoted above under the heading of Sukasiddhi's life, that the two dakinis number among the four.

39 Among these ten men, five were from central Tibet: Lumé Tsultrim Shérab, Dring Yeshé Yönten, Ba Tsultrim Lodrö, Rakshi Tsultrim Jungné, and Sumpa Yeshé Lodrö. Five came from western Tibet: Lotön Dorjé Wangchuk, Shérab Sengé, two brothers Ogyé, and Upa Dékar-wa. According to Trinlé, it is possible that they took vows not from Lachen Gongpa Rabsal, but from his student, Drum Yeshé Gyaltsen. See *The Collected Works of Dungkar Lozang Trinlé*, pp. 532-533.

40 This seems to be a longevity meditation no longer extant within the Shangpa tradition.

41 See for example, *The Collection of Shangpa Masters' Biographies*, p. 2; and *The Compendium of Names of Himalayan Scholars and Adepts*, pp. 1191 and 1320.

42 See *The Collected Works of Dungkar Lozang Trinlé*, p. 553. He reports that the basic unit of calculation was called a tem-du (*them dud*), which included persons, land, and

livestock. The Shang district held 1,400 such units, which Trinlé estimates included six persons per unit.

43 The thirteen are the following, written in Tibetan phonetics: gsol dpon, gzims dpon, mchod dpon, mgron dpon, drung yig, phyag mdzod, ma chen, sgar dpon, gdan gnyer, khang gnyer, chibs dpon, 'gag pa, and ah drung. (*Ibid.,* p. 555)

44 Bokar Rinpoché thinks Sangyé Tönpa wrote this book.

45 There remains some question of Tangtong Gyalpo's dates. *The Compendium of Names of Himalayan Scholars and Adepts*, pp. 787-788, prefers the 1361–1485 lifespan, as does Kongtrul, but the authors of the compendium signal at the end of their article on Tangtong Gyalpo that some scholars prefer 1385–1464.

46 *The Compendium of Names of Himalayan Scholars and Adepts*, p. 788, states that he constructed fifty iron-link bridges and sixty wooden bridges throughout all areas of Tibet.

47 I have heard that this preserved body of Tangtong Gyalpo was destroyed during the Cultural Revolution.

48 A short account of Kyentsé Wangchuk's life is found in Jamgon Kongtrul's *History of the Sources of the Profound Treasures and the Treasure Revealers*, pp. 567-570.

49 In his *Catalog of Shangpa Texts: The Beryl Key*, Jamgon Kongtrul reports: "Further, the transmission for many excellent works, such as… *The Cycle of Niguma's Guidance in Meditation* by Jamyang Kyentsé, have dissolved into the realm of quiescence." (p. 21a)

50 This refers to Ra Lotsawa Dorjé Drakpa.

51 I have not seen this written in any history; this account comes to me directly from Kalu Rinpoché.

52 In 1987, on a visit to the Norbu Ling-ka, the Dalai Lama's summer residence on the outskirts of Lhasa, I was able by chance to view his private library, which was closed to the public. It was a quick, furtive visit, but I couldn't resist looking at just one text label, for curiosity's sake. To my surprise, the single text I had chosen was a volume of *Taranata's Collected Works*. Since that time, I have often wondered how that collection made its way into the Dalai Lama's personal library and at what period it was added.

53 These figures and some specific details of individual monasteries' populations are given in *The Collected Works of Dungkar Lozang Trinlé*, pp. 588-591.

54 There seemed to be a little of Taranata in many outstanding lamas' mind streams. The Fourteenth Karmapa recognized Kongtrul as Taranata's rebirth; Kongtrul wrote that Kyentsé and Tai Situpa were also his reincarnations.

55 Both the painting and a woodblock print of this vision have appeared in Western publications, but to my regret I cannot recall where.

56 The four kinds of magnificence refer to material and worldly splendor in four domains—spiritual instruction, wealth, pleasure, and freedom. The words "four *kinds*

and ten *virtues*" are a play on words to suggest the name of the region Dergé, *sde dge*—kinds, virtues—in Tibetan.

57 The five sublime visions commonly refer to Buddha Shakyamuni's choices of circumstances for his birth.

58 Disciples please their master in three ways: making offerings, performing service, and putting the teaching into practice.

59 The Six Lineages are buddhas' mind lineage, awareness holders' sign lineage, great masters' oral lineage, dakinis' entrusted lineage, lineage of empowered aspiration, and yellow parchment lineage.

60 The modern edition of *The Five Treasuries*, published under the auspices of Dilgo Kyentsé Rinpoché, extends to over a hundred volumes. In addition, some of Kongtrul's large treatises are not included in that edition.

61 Gyurmé Dorjé, also known as Orgyen Terdak Lingpa (1646–1714), founded Minling Monastery.

62 According to Bokar Rinpoché, the three concerns are to eat, defecate, and sleep.

63 It seems important to repeat the words of E. Gene Smith, whose understanding of the term *Kagyu* corresponds exactly to Kalu Rinpoché's: "The term Bka' brgyud [Kagyu] pa simply applies to any line of transmission of an esoteric teaching from teacher to disciple. We can properly speak of a Jo nang Bka' brgyud pa or Dge ldan [Genden] Bka' brgyud pa for the Jo nang pa and Dge lugs [Gélug] pa sects. The adherents of the sects that practice the teachings centering around the Phyag rgya chen po [Great Seal] and the Na ro chos drug [Six Doctrines of Naropa] are properly referred to as the Dwaks po [Dakpo] Bka' brgyud pa because these teachings were all transmitted through Sgam po pa [Gampopa]. Similar teachings and practices centered around Ni gu chos drug [Six Doctrines of Niguma] are distinctive of the Shangs pa Bka' brgyud pa. These two traditions with their offshoots are often incorrectly referred to simply as Bka' brgyud pa." (*Among Tibetan Texts*, p. 40), square brackets added.

64 Translated from the French by Ngawang Zangpo.

INDEX